William Thomas Arnold

The Roman System of Provincial Administration

To the Accession of Constantine the Great...

William Thomas Arnold

The Roman System of Provincial Administration
To the Accession of Constantine the Great...

ISBN/EAN: 9783744772914

Printed in Europe, USA, Canada, Australia, Japan

Cover: Foto ©Suzi / pixelio.de

More available books at **www.hansebooks.com**

THE ROMAN SYSTEM

OF

PROVINCIAL ADMINISTRATION

TO THE

ACCESSION OF CONSTANTINE THE GREAT.

Being the Arnold Prize Essay for 1879.

BY

W. T. ARNOLD, B.A.

FORMERLY SCHOLAR OF UNIVERSITY COLLEGE, OXFORD.

'Urbem fecisti quod prius orbis erat.'—*Rutilius.*
'Perceperunt mercedem suam.'—*Augustin. De Civitate Dei.*

London:

MACMILLAN AND CO.

1879.

PREFACE.

I HAVE given a list of my chief authorities below. But I should more especially acknowledge my obligations to Marquardt and Preuss. The extent to which I have used Marquardt in the chapter on Taxation, and Preuss in the chapter on the Later Empire, has been very considerable. In the other parts of the Essay I have relied to a larger extent on my own independent reading; but I have felt throughout the disadvantage of an imperfect knowledge of the modern literature on the subject. In England I know of no comprehensive book devoted to it, but in France and Germany it has long aroused the energies of a host of enthusiastic workers. In this field the French have names which command as great respect as the most learned among the Germans. If, in particular, I have not been able to use the great work of M. Waddington, *Les Fastes des Provinces Asiatiques*, it is not owing to want of will, but to the limitations of time which the conditions under which this Essay must be written impose[1].

In printing this Essay, I have not been able to make alterations of much moment. I have, however, revised it throughout, and hope that no errors of consequence have escaped me. How inadequate the treatment of such a subject is I am only too painfully conscious; but if I had once begun to make large alterations I should not have been able to stop

---

[1] The above was written as a preface to the Essay when sent in for competition.

short of rewriting the Essay in great part, and I preferred to follow the usual, and on the whole probably commendable, custom of printing a prize essay substantially in the form in which it was written. I subjoin a list of my chief authorities so as to be able to refer to them by the author's name without giving the full title of the book as well. I naturally do not include in the list the ordinary classical authors.

Ackner and Müller. Die Römischen inschriften in Dacien. (Vienna, 1865.)
Ancyanum Monumentum (under Mommsen).
Arnold. Later Roman Commonwealth. 2 vols. (London.)
Boissier. L'Empire Romain en Orient. (Rev. des deux Mondes, July, 1874.)
Boissière. Esquisse d'une histoire de l'Afrique Romaine. (Paris, 1878.)
Brambach. Corpus Inscriptionum Rhenanarum. (Elberfeld, 1867.)
Bruns. Fontes Juris Antiqui Romani. (Tubingen, 1876.)
Corpus Inscriptionum Latinarum. Vols. i–vii. (Berlin.)
De la Berge. Essai sur le règne de Trajan. (Paris, 1877.)
E. Desjardins. Géographie de la Gaule Romaine. 2 vols. (Paris, 1876.)
——————— Les Antonins d'après l'epigraphie. (Rev. des deux Mondes, Dec., 1874.)
Dietrich. Beiträge zur Kenntniss des Romischen Staatspachtersystems. (Leipsic, 1877.)
Duruy. Histoire des Romains. 5 vols. (Paris, 1874.)
Egger. Examen critique des historiens anciens de la vie et du règne d'Auguste. (Paris, 1844.)
Ephemeris Epigraphica (supplement to the Corpus). (Berlin, 1872.)
Finlay. History of Greece. Vol. i. (Oxford, 1877.)
Flach. La table de bronze d'Aljustrel. (Paris, 1879.)
Henzen. Inscriptiones (supplementary volume to Orelli). (1856.)
Historiae Augustae Scriptores. ed. Joran and Eyssenhardt. (Berlin, 1864.)
Hudemann. Geschichte des Römischen Postwesens während der Kaiserzeit. (Berlin, 1878.)

Kandler. Inscrizioni dei tempi Romani rinvenute nell' Istria. (Trieste, 1855.)
Klein. Die Verwaltungsbeamten des Rom. Reichs bis auf Diocletian. (Bonn, 1878.)
Lentheric. Les villes mortes du golfe de Lyon. (Paris, 1877.)
Marquardt. Romische Staatsverwaltung. 2 vols. (Leipsic, 1873.)
———— De conciliis. in Eph. Epig.
Merivale. History of the Romans under the Empire. 8 vols. (London, 1865.)
Mommsen. History of Rome, English translation. 4 vols. (London, 1863.)
———— Monumentum Ancyanum. (Berlin, 1865.)
———— Schweiz in Römischer Zeit. (Mittheilungen der antiquar Gesellschaft in Zurich, 1854.)
Orelli. Inscriptiones. 2 vols. (Turin, 1828.)
G. Perrot. De Galatia provincia Romana. (Paris, 1867.)
———— Mémoire sur quelques inscriptions inédites des côtes de la mer Noire. (Rev. Archeol. 1874.)
———— Inscriptions inédites d'Asie Mineure. (Rev. Archeol. 1875.)
Preuss. Kaiser Diocletian und Seine Zeit. (Leipsic, 1869.)
Renier. Mélanges d'Epigraphie. (Paris, 1854.)
Savigny. Essay on Coloni (translated in Philological Museum, ii. 117.)
Stephan. Das Verkehrsleben in Alterthum (in Raumer's Historisches Taschenbuch. 4th series. vol. ix. pp. 1–136.)
Troyon. Monuments de l'Antiquité dans l'Europe barbare. (Lausanne, 1868.)
Watson. Cicero's Select Letters. (Oxford, 1874.)
Zell. Opuscula. (Friburg, 1857.)
Zumpt (C. T.) Decretum Tergestinum. (Berlin, 1847.)
Zumpt (A. W.) Studia Romana. (Berlin, 1859.)
———— Commentationes Epigraphicae. 2 vols. (Berlin, 1850.)

CONTENTS.

	PAGE
INTRODUCTORY	1

CHAPTER I.

What a province was. How acquired. Use of 'client princes.' How secured and organised. Moral aspect of the Roman rule 7

CHAPTER II.

The Period of the Republic 40

CHAPTER III.

The Period of the Early Empire 89

CHAPTER IV.

The Period of the Later Empire 154

CHAPTER V.

The System of Taxation 179

CHAPTER VI.

Towns in the Provinces 201

CONCLUSION 239

INTRODUCTORY.

TAKING the terms in their widest extent, the Roman provincial administration may be said to have lasted for some 700 years, from the final settlement of Sicily after the Second Punic War to the apparent destruction of the system by the barbarians. And as the fall of the Western Empire is a convenient external mark of the success of those barbarians and of the passing away of the old order of things, the date of that event, A.D. 476, might be taken as the limit in time between which and B.C. 210, the limit on the other side, that administration existed. But within this larger whole there are smaller wholes, each of which forms in itself a unity. And indeed if we press the terms Roman Provincial Administration closely, the limit might be put earlier, with the accession of Constantine. For then that administration ceased to be in any sense distinctively Roman. It has been said[1] that with Constantine modern history begins; and there are many reasons which make the date of his accession a better division—where all such divisions are necessarily arbitrary—between the old world and the new than the date which marks the fall of the Empire of the West. The tendencies which came to their full growth in the reign of Constantine had existed many of them for centuries, all of them at least since Diocletian. But coming to their completion as they did with him, Constantine seems to gather up and concentrate in his reign the forces which were a legacy from the past and were to form the future. Constantine adopted a new religion and created a new capital. The one act marks the final adoption of the religion which is that of the Western world, and the other brought into existence the Byzantine Empire, Europe's 'bulwark

---

[1] Freeman, Essays, 2nd Series, p. 310.

'gainst the Ottoman.' The monarchy which he constituted, with its hierarchy of counts and its brilliant court, was the model which later princes copied; and by his abandonment of Rome the Pope was made possible[1]. But Constantine's reign, if it looks towards the future, can be only understood in the light of the past from which it grew. The division of the Empire into the four great prefectures was the thought of Diocletian, and the principle at its base had long before been anticipated by the subdivision of the governments of Gaul and Syria[2]. So the fatal change in the municipal towns, which shows itself so clearly in this reign, was the result of the slow canker of centuries. The division instituted between civil and military functions was mainly the work of Diocletian, but had been anticipated under the early Empire in the governments of Africa[3] and Egypt[4]. The counts (comites) of Constantine grew out of the retinue which accompanied the Emperor on a provincial progress; and occur at least as early as the reign of M. Aurelius[5]. The centrifugal tendencies which had subsisted in the Empire along with its great and at one time prevailing tendencies to unity, had been already marked by Diocletian's practical abandonment of Rome; and indeed the division between East and West had always and necessarily existed, and could be made use of by Mark Antony as well as by Vespasian. Similarly Christianity was of course no new growth of the reign of Constantine, but then won the fruit of centuries of enduring effort.

If then Constantine's reign, as consummating the past and as heralding the future, is a good limit to this great subject, we

---

[1] Freeman, Essays, 2nd Series, p. 310.
[2] For the dread felt by the emperors of all the resources of Gaul or Syria being in one man's hands, see a discussion by Zumpt, Comm. Epig. ii. 133; Tac. Ann. xiii. 53, xiv. 57.
[3] Boissière, L'Afrique Romaine, p. 246.
[4] Arnold's Later Roman Commonwealth, ii. 375.
[5] See two inscriptions in Renier, Melanges d'Epigraphie, p. 80 and p. 76, where among a man's titles occurs—' comiti divi Veri per Orientem,' and ' comiti ejusdem in Oriente.'

are still left with a period of 500 years, for which it is very necessary to find subdivisions. Fortunately this is not difficult. The immense and far-reaching changes which the Empire introduced into the administration of the provinces mark off in the clearest way, and yet without any absolute breach of continuity, the Republican period from the period of the early Empire. It may be questioned whether we should make this latter period begin with Thapsus or with Actium, with Caesar or with Augustus. But the short eighteen months which Caesar had of supreme power in Rome were too little for him to do anything but sketch out the lines of a system which Augustus developed and realised, and we shall do better to fix the beginning of the Empire, as does Dean Merivale[1], on the day of the fight in the bay of Actium. It is more open to dispute as to where the next break should come. The Julian Emperors in a sense, as being of the same blood and claiming the same divine origin, form a whole by themselves; and the terrible year of civil war which followed the last of them may be regarded as a cataclysm which marks the end of one period and the beginning of another. But for our purpose it is not so. The Flavian emperors who followed do not introduce new principles of administration; though their origin in the will of the army marks so far a new departure. Nor will the fact that Suetonius makes his collection end with Domitian induce us to regard the 'Twelve Caesars' as vitally distinguished from the rest. A happier era is inaugurated when the choice of the Senate becomes the origin of imperial authority in the person of Nerva; but otherwise the emperors from Nerva to Marcus Aurelius, the Antonines as they are sometimes loosely called, may be regarded as continuing the best traditions of the Flavian emperors. With Marcus Aurelius comes a real break. He is the first emperor of the frontiers. From his time onwards the Empire has to maintain a long struggle with the barbarians; and the emperors that succeed one another in such breathless haste are the mere nominees of the soldiers. More important

---

[1] History of the Romans, iii. 328.

for our purpose are the changes in the administration, some of which had been operating silently for some time, but which now come prominently forward. The taxation for instance became felt as an intolerable burden, and its amount is henceforth continually rising. The municipia were more and more perverted from their original constitution; and the municipal offices became an instrument of oppression. The gain of the provinces upon Italy, which had been going on for centuries, completed itself with the edict of Caracalla. The progress towards administrative uniformity is shown by the perpetual provincial edict of M. Aurelius. Above all, the reforms of Diocletian were the most important changes that had taken place in the administration since Augustus[1]. I propose therefore to make the second division of the subject at the death of M. Aurelius, not absolutely binding myself to a definite date, but taking that to be approximately the period at which the changes which distinguish the Early from the Later Empire most clearly manifested themselves. But I cannot hope to include all I have to say in three sections on the Republic, the Early Empire, and the Later Empire. The financial arrangements, for instance, are too important not to be discussed by themselves; and the same applies to the administration of justice[2]. Above all it is essential to form some idea of the constitution of the towns within a Roman province. The towns were the basis of the Roman administration; through them the taxes were collected, and in them justice was administered. But, more than this, a large share of local liberty was left to them. Even Rome would have found herself unequal to the burden of governing her heterogeneous empire if she had not left a good deal to the municipal administrations. Discoveries of the highest interest and importance in the course

---

[1] 'Nous ne craignons pas d'être démentis par les juges competents en affirmant que la revolution qui a substitué sous Auguste la forme impériale à la forme républicaine, a été moins radicale que celle qu'ont operée les reformes de Diocletien et de Constantin.' Desjardins, i. 12.

[2] I have not been able, at present, to devote a separate chapter to the administration of justice.

of the last twenty years have thrown a flood of light on the internal constitution of a provincial town. The active prosperous life of these innumerable towns is the fairest feature of Roman rule; and the question of how much was left to the magistrates, and how much had to be referred to the governor at different periods, is perhaps the most interesting as it is the most difficult inquiry connected with our subject.

So much for the way in which I propose to divide the subject. But there are one or two general remarks still to make. It is exceedingly difficult in discussing the provinces of Rome not to talk of them as a whole, and as a fixed whole. But in truth the Roman world is a world continually growing, developing, changing, always tending to a uniformity but never fully reaching it. The difference between East and West is never obliterated, and at last victoriously asserts itself. The Romans showed greater power of assimilation than has been shown by any other conquerors; but even they could not assimilate a civilisation like that of Greece, which was in some respects superior to their own. So the Greek East was never organised, after the strict type of the Roman province, into colonies and municipia. If we want to see typical examples of the Roman rule we must look to the West, not to the East; to the 'savage and barbarous tribes,' as Cicero[1] calls them, of Africa, Gaul, or Spain, rather than to the polished Greeks of Achaia and Asia Minor. It is to the West also that we must look for instances of another important distinction, that between forward and backward provinces. By forward provinces I mean those which took kindly to Roman rule and flourished under it, for instance Spain and Gaul; by backward provinces those which either from having a different and equally advanced civilisation of their own, as Greece proper, or from a dead weight of barbarism, as Rhaetia, were unable to move in the ordinary Roman lines. On the whole, those provinces gained

---

[1] Ad Qu. Fr. I. i. 9: 'Afris aut Hispanis aut Gallis . . . immanibus ac barbaris nationibus.' With these he contrasts the Greeks of Asia Minor—'quod est ex hominum omni genere humanissimum.' See § 1 of the same letter.

most where there was least to lose. Rome was extraordinarily successful in civilising barbarians, not perhaps so successful in dealing with races already of a high type. It is also to be borne in mind that there is a great difference between different parts of the same country; between Northern and Southern Gaul[1] and between Northern and Southern Spain[2]. So it is easy to understand the reason of these countries having been split up into several provinces, and the difference made between the different parts of Spain when the provinces were divided between the Senate and the Emperor. Or take the modern country of Switzerland, the western part of which was in Gaul and immensely rich and prosperous, full of important towns and possessing an extensive commerce, the eastern part in Rhaetia wholly uncivilised. Perhaps the modern division of languages in Switzerland is due to the way in which Roman civilisation had sunk into the western parts, so that the Allemanni could not wholly displace it, while in the eastern parts the tongue of the conquerors easily prevailed[3].

These remarks illustrate the danger of general statements on the provinces as a whole. I shall therefore endeavour always to state to what particular province or provinces any such statements I may make specially refer. At the same time it would be absurd to ignore the large and increasing element of unity. The administration was everywhere of much the same type; a good governor in Cilicia was very similar to a good governor in Spain; and a Verres in Asia was much the same as a Verres in Sicily. The towns beginning with the greatest possible varieties of constitution tended more and more to the one municipal type; and by the time of the Later Empire the rights of individuals were the same over the Roman world. It is not therefore necessary to avoid generalisations altogether in speaking of the provinces; but it is necessary to be cautious in their employment.

---

[1] Mommsen, Schweiz in Römischer Zeit, p. 17.
[2] Arnold, Later Roman Commonwealth, ii. 366.
[3] Mommsen, Schweiz in Römischer Zeit, p. 17.

CHAPTER I.

What a province was. How acquired. Use of 'client-princes.' How secured; and organised. Moral aspect of the Roman rule.

WHATEVER may be the derivation of the word 'Provincia[1],' it is at any rate indisputable that it was not always used in the special sense which became attached to it under the later Republic. '*Provincia*,' says Mommsen[2], 'as is well known, denoted in the older language not what we now call *province*, a definite space assigned as a district to a standing chief magistrate, but simply the functions prescribed for the particular magistrate by law, decree of the senate, or agreement.' The word is of course frequently used in the early books of Livy long before there was any question of provinces in the later sense; and even under the Empire instances of a similar use occur[3]. When the first transmarine provinces were formed their government was assigned to the existing magistrates, as the business which they had to discharge during their year of office[4]. Very soon and very naturally the word came to be applied to the district itself in which that government was exercised. The

The word 'Provincia.'

---

[1] Mr. Capes, in his recent edition of Livy, xxi and xxii, p. 174, adheres to Festus' derivation of the word from *pro-vincere*, and refuses to have anything to say to the current explanation of it as a contraction of *providentia*. He says that the word is 'strictly used only in connexion with the imperium of a Roman magistrate, that is, with military and judicial functions.' But (apart from linguistic difficulties) it is hard to see the fitness of the derivation, if the word can be applied, as of course it can and is (cf. Cic. in Verr. vi. 15), to judicial functions. And, moreover, the word is certainly used of the authority of the questor, who had *potestas* but not *imperium*. See § lxvii of the Lex Repetundarum, C. I. L. i. p. 62; Cic. pro Murena, 8; Suet. Claud. 24.

[2] ii. 71, note.   [3] Zumpt, Comm. Epig. ii. 100.   [4] Mommsen, ii. 67.

word 'Conventus' has had a precisely similar history. Originally applied to the assembly of Roman citizens as a provincial town to meet the governor and act with him in trying law-suits on definite occasions, it came to be applied to 'territory from which the people assembled, and to the place in which the assembly was held[1].'

Origin and intention of Rome's foreign conquests.

It does not come within the range of this essay to narrate the history of Rome's foreign conquests. They may be said to have had their origin in the Second Punic War. That war had shown her the necessity of the possession of the 'suburban Sicily,' as Cicero calls it, if only for her own safety; and the same imperative reasons applied to Sardinia. The war had brought Roman armies into Spain, and once planted there, they remained, severe and unpopular though the service there was for many years. Philip of Macedonia's half-hearted assistance of Hannibal (together with his aggressive foreign policy[2]) secured him the active enmity of Rome; and it had all along been obvious that in the struggle between Rome and Carthage Greece would necessarily be the prize of the conqueror. One may believe this without at all condemning the philhellenism of the better class of Romans as hypocritical and disingenuous. Having once decisively asserted herself in the world across the sea[3], it was inevitable that in that chaos of factions and intrigues Rome should be called upon to play a more and more decisive part. There is evidence enough to warrant Mommsen[4] in his view that Rome's foreign conquests were not at first intentional and deliberate, but that her immediate aim was to make herself secure and all-powerful in Italy. But wars sprang up which she could not avoid, or which she had not expected[5]; her clients and allies made demands upon her which it was im-

---

[1] See Mr. Long's note to Caes. B. G. i. 54; p. 100 of his edition.

[2] Mommsen, ii. 226, 229.

[3] '*Provinciae quae mari dividuntur*' is Tacitus' name for the Greek East; Ann. ii. 43.

[4] ii. 312. Cf. Freeman, Essays, 2nd Series, p. 253.

[5] Cic. pro Fonteio, 19: 'cum tot bella aut a nobis necessario suscipiantur, aut subito atque improvisa nascantur.'

possible to refuse, and the Senate saw itself committed to the conquest and administration of half the known world, before having clearly made up its mind whether such conquests were advisable or the reverse. But in any case it was not long before the sweets of conquest made themselves felt. The remission of the tribute paid by Roman citizens in the year 167 marks an epoch. That remission was the direct consequence of foreign conquest. The sums poured by Paullus into the treasury were so immense and unprecedented as to make it unnecessary to demand the money of Romans for the purposes of the state[1]. When C. Gracchus added the taxation of Asia to the treasury[2], and fed the people by doles of foreign corn, the new system of things stands plainly revealed. The Romans are to rule and enjoy, their subjects to serve and pay. Along with these positive material advantages went an increase of the mere military spirit, of the love of conquest for its own sake, and of pride in the increasing extent of the subject world, till we find under the Empire, even so moderate and sensible a man as Agricola seriously meditating the barren conquest of Ireland, so that the Roman arms might be carried everywhere, and no country might be tempted from its allegiance by the spectacle of another's freedom[3].

Along with all this must be reckoned, in one case at all events, the necessity Rome lay under of securing herself against barbarian invasion. This was one of the reasons which led her on to the conquest of all Gaul. Caesar[4] himself hints at the danger of the Germans being allowed to settle in that country, and there prepare themselves for a march southwards; and the facts seem to show that without Roman aid the Gauls could have made no effectual resistance to their invaders. The more rhetorical Cicero[5] in two well-known passages reminds his hearers of Rome's previous dangers from the 'savage natures and vast multitudes' of the Gauls, and congratulates them that

---

[1] Mommsen, ii. 329.   [2] Ib. iii. 115, 121.   [3] Tac. Agr. 24.
[4] Caes. B. G. i. 33.   [5] Cic. de prov. Cons. 13, in Pis. 33.

the barrier of the Alps is no longer needed for the protection of Italy. The same reasons made it necessary for Rome in a later period to possess herself of the Danubian provinces. But conquest, whether deliberate or unintentional, was not the only means by which the Roman dominion spread. Pergamum, Bithynia, Cyrene, Egypt were bequeathed to Rome by will; and Rome did not refuse the splendid gifts. That it was not really independent and powerful monarchs who so acted is, however, obvious; and a more particular account of these 'client-princes,' as Mommsen has called them, will make Rome's final success in administering and assimilating her provinces easier to understand.

'Client-princes.' This system (for a system it was) lasted far into the times of the Empire; but the period when it was most extensively used, and was least beneficial, was from the commencement of Roman conquest in the East up to the definite settlement of Macedonia[1]. Till then the Roman Senate hardly seems to have made up its mind as to whether definitely to take over the countries it had conquered or not. So we find the petty kings of Asia Minor, the Seleucidae of Syria, and the Ptolemies of Egypt left in possession of their dominions subject to the hegemony, which was rather practically understood than positively defined, of Rome. So, as Mommsen[2] has pointed out, they had neither freedom nor order. They were not free, because Roman senatorial commissions were continually regulating their affairs; and their constant quarrels with one another could neither come to a definite issue, nor be controlled by a sovereign authority. No wonder then that both the Romans and the princes themselves became tired of so unsatisfactory an arrangement. The latter did not care to leave to their children the empty shadow of power[3] with which there was neither honour nor profit; and the Romans by their definite annexation of Macedonia showed that they had at last made

---

[1] Mommsen, iii. 142.   [2] Ib., iii. 42, 67, and the whole chapter.
[3] 'Umbra regis' is the expression of Tacitus, Ann. xv. 6, for one of these princes.

up their minds to a more decided policy. But this is not the last of a system which we find in full force under Claudius; and we may be sure that it would not have lasted so long if it had not possessed, in the eyes of the Romans, some positive advantages. Tacitus[1] speaks of it as 'the ancient and long-recognised practice of the Roman people, which seeks to secure among the instruments of dominion even kings themselves.' It was especially the system of Augustus, who describes his application of it in these words: 'Greater Armenia, when, after the murder of its king Artaxias, I could have made it a province, I preferred, according to the example of our ancestors, to entrust that kingdom to Tigranes, son of king Artavasdes, grandson of king Tigranes, through the agency of Tib. Nero, who was then my stepson. And the same nation, when it afterwards revolted, on its subjugation by my son Gaius, I entrusted for government to king Ariobarzanes, son of Artabanus king of the Medes, and after his death to his son Artavasdes; and when he too was slain, I sent Tigranes, who was sprung from the royal stock of Armenia, into that kingdom[2].' But Cilicia is a better instance of the system than Armenia. Augustus made it his policy to encourage the petty kings in this quarter: thus we find a dynasty of Olbe, and a dynasty of Mount Amanus[3]. In this way we find the province cut short more and more till it meant only the plain country of Cilicia. This distinction between *Cilicia Campestris* and *Cilicia Aspera* is the key to the extensive use of the system in this country. No difficulty was found in thoroughly administering and Romanising the level country from an early date. Tarsus[4] was a very considerable city long before St. Paul mentions it. But it was otherwise with the fierce hillmen whom the Romans had so often hunted down in their fastnesses, and with so little permanent effect. The description which Cicero[5] gives us of a siege

---

[1] Tac. Agr. 14.
[2] Mon. Ancyr. § 27. I translate literally, imitating the formality of the original. Cf. Suet. Aug. 48.   [3] Marquardt, i. 227.
[4] See, for instance, Hirtius, Bell. Alex. 66.   [5] Ad Att. v. 20.

of one of these hill-forts in Mount Amanus reads like a description of a raid upon the hillmen of Burmah or Afghanistan. The difference between the men of the plains and of the hills is strikingly illustrated by a passage where Tacitus[1] seems to purposely contrast the Clitae on their 'rocky mountains' with the peaceful 'farmers,' 'townsfolk,' 'merchants,' shipowners' whom they harried in the plain beneath. Rome could not have brought these districts and such as these directly under her rule without a large military force, and great expense with very little profit. And yet it was impossible for her to leave them altogether uncontrolled. So she interfered with their affairs so far as to appoint princes who would rule in her interest, and whose task it was to tame and civilise their subjects till they were fit to come directly under Roman rule. Factions within the tribe itself, or quarrels between different members of the ruling house, would give her frequent occasion for such interference; indeed we find that on more than one occasion kings are requested from her by nations beyond the frontier[2]. As it was to be expected that such princes should frequently have to control their subjects' disaffection, it was a common practice to support the Roman nominee by a small detachment of Roman troops. So when the Tigranes whom Nero had appointed to the government of Armenia arrived in his province, 'he was supported with a force of a thousand legionaries, three allied cohorts, and two squadrons of cavalry, that he might the more easily secure his new kingdom[3].' Two other passages of Tacitus[4] prove

---

[1] Tac. Ann. xii. 55.

[2] Parthia is of course the principal instance. See Tac. Ann. xii. 10, 11, xiii. 9, and the summary of Roman relations with Parthia under the first emperors by Messrs. Church and Brodribb, p. 396. But the same thing occurs in the case of the Suevi, Ann. xii. 29, 30; Cherusci, Ann. xi. 16; see also Tac. Germ. 42; Bructeri, Plin. Ep. ii. 7. Arrian, *Periplus* (Geog. Graeci Minores, ed. Müller), writing to the emperor an account of his voyage round the coasts of the Black Sea, says, § 15: 'Next to the Apsitae come the Abasci; their king is Rhesmagas; he holds his kingdom of you.' § 27 he says the same of the king of the Zilchi.

[3] Tac. Ann. xiv. 26. [4] Ib. xii. 15, 45.

that these troops were permanently stationed in the country and garrisoned strong places in it. A few cohorts and a Roman knight protected the prince of the Bosporus; and such troops though insignificant in numbers would act as a nucleus for the native army[1] and form a model which princes like Deiotarus[2], ambitious of having troops trained after the Roman fashion, would imitate. Even if there were not troops stationed actually within the kingdom, the governor of the neighbouring province would send them in case of need. For instance, when the Clitae revolted against the process of Romanisation which their king was applying to them, the revolt was put down by troops sent by the governor of Syria[3]. The particular grievance against which the Clitae revolted is an illustration of how these 'subject princes[4]' of Rome broke in their unruly subjects to the most unpleasant necessities of the Roman rule. 'They were compelled in Roman fashion to render an account of their revenue, and submit to tribute,' says Tacitus[5]. We find the same thing in Cappadocia, where king Ariobarzanes is instructed by Cicero's predecessor, Appius, to levy a tribute upon his subjects[6]. This was advised by Appius, apparently that Ariobarzanes might be enabled to pay his debts; and if other such princes were as heavily indebted to aristocratic Roman usurers as was this unfortunate monarch, the tribute must have been instituted everywhere. It should be added that some, at all events, of these kingdoms paid a tribute directly to Rome[7].

It is obvious of what service such a system as this could be to Rome. If these princes were, as Tacitus[8] says, protected by the greatness of Rome against external Empires, it is also true that they acted as a barrier between Rome and such Empires[9], to defer or altogether prevent the otherwise inevitable collisions. Without saddling herself with absolute responsibility

---

[1] Tac. Ann. xii. 16.
[2] Hirtius, Bell. Alex. 34; Cic. Phil. xi. 13.
[3] Tac. Ann. vi. 41.
[4] 'Inservientum regum;' Tac. Hist. ii. 81.
[5] Tac. Ann. vi. 41.
[6] Cic. ad Att. vi. 1. § 3.
[7] e.g. Herod; Merivale, iii. 386.
[8] Tac. Ann. iv. 5.
[9] Hirtius, Bell. Alex. 78.

or binding herself to interfere when it was inconvenient, Rome had her work done for her in the way in which she would have it. These princes were thoroughly subservient and responsible to their masters[1]; were often themselves brought up at Rome[2]; and quite understood what work Rome expected of them. A passage from Strabo[3] shows the nature of that work in a few words. He is describing the settlement of Africa after the destruction of Carthage. 'The Romans paid particular attention to Masanasses on account of his great abilities and friendship for them. For he it was who formed the nomads to civil life, and directed their attention to husbandry.' If an inscription of Britain is correctly read, it seems to mention Cogidubni Regis (also known from Tac. Agr. 14) *legati Augusti in Britannia;* and Hübner supposes this client-prince to have actually discharged the functions of imperial legate in this country[4]. Add to this that in the coins struck by such provinces the Emperor's head appears on one side, and that of the prince on the other[5]; and the part played by such princes as representing Rome to their subjects, and preparing them for the rule of Rome, will be fully understood[6].

Means of securing a province.

Where Rome did not make use of this system she secured her hold upon a country by a mixture of policy and force. To win over one tribe at all events, or to play one prince against another were easy devices, which hardly ever failed of success. The want of unity in uncivilised races made conquest easy[7]; and traitors were never wanting, when there was none of that

---

[1] Cf. Tac. Ann. xi. 8.

[2] The case of Juba, king of Mauretania under Augustus, is a remarkable one. He was a thorough Roman, and a trained man of letters; Plut. Jul. 55. 'Euseben et Philoromeum' are the noticeable epithets with which Cicero describes Ariobarzanes; Ad Fam. xv. 2. § 4.

[3] Strabo, xvii. 3. § 15; Mommsen, ii. 206.

[4] C. I. L. vii. p. 18; and Hübner's note.

[5] Church and Brodribb, Annals, p. 402; Marquardt, i. 150.

[6] See Strabo, iv. 5. § 3; Marquardt, i. 343; Boissière, L'Afrique Romaine, p. 415, for a discussion of the rationale of the system.

[7] Cf. Tac. Agr. 12.

national unity which would make treason seem a crime. Thus the Moschi were won over in Asia Minor[1]; Galgacus complains of the number of his fellow-countrymen who served against him in Britain[2]; and Caesar availed himself of the friendship of the Remi and Ædui in Gaul[3]. Similarly the mutual jealousies of the petty princes of an invaded country were dexterously made available for Roman ends. So we find the Romans in Britain upholding a wife against her husband, and sending troops to support her when in difficulties[4]. But these were merely temporary expedients; and once thoroughly established in a country, Rome secured herself there by very different measures. Wherever, owing to the natural difficulties of the country, or the exceptional spirit of the people, repression was necessary, there was a chain of 'fortresses with military garrisons[5].' We find Forts. these for instance among the Silures in Britain[6], and Tacitus commends the promptitude with which they were established in newly-conquered districts of the same province by Agricola[7]. There was of course also a line of these along every frontier; for example (not to mention more important but more familiar instances) on the northern border of the Narbonensis in the time of Caesar[8]. Colonies again, when planted in a newly- Colonies. conquered country, were really nothing but such fortified outposts on a larger scale. This is the account which Cicero[9] gives of Narbo Martius (Narbonne) in Southern Gaul; and Tacitus[10] says much the same in his brief and pointed manner of the colony of Camulodunum (Maldon?) in Britain. The natives themselves regarded them quite in this light, and hated

---

[1] Tac. Ann. xiii. 37.   [2] Tac. Agr. 32.   [3] Caes. B G. v. 54, vii. 54.
[4] Tac. Ann. xii. 40; Hist. iii. 45.   [5] Tac. Ann. xiv. 33.   [6] Ibid.
[7] Tac. Agr. 20, 22.   [8] Caes. B. G. vii. 8.
[9] Cic. pro Fonteio, v. § 13: 'Est in eadem provincia Narbo Martius, colonia nostrorum civium, specula populi Romani ac propugnaculum istis ipsis nationibus oppositum et objectum.' The same metaphor occurs Cic. de Leg. Agr. ii. 27.
[10] Ann. xii. 32: 'Colonia Camulodunum valida veteranorum manu deducitur in agros captivos, subsidium adversus rebelles, et imbuendis sociis ad officia legum.'

Roads. them as the 'headquarters of tyranny[1];' and that their hatred was sometimes not without good cause appears from the detestable oppressions practised by these same colonists of Camulodunum[2]. More important perhaps than any of these measures were the great military roads which it was the first object of Rome to drive across a conquered country. These magnificent causeways, raised considerably above the level of the ground, and with a deep ditch on each side of them from which the earth that formed them had been dug, were in themselves eminently defensible, and enabled troops to be massed on any given point with security and despatch. The great Egnatian way, running from Dyrrhachium to Thessalonica, 'that military road of ours,' as Cicero[3] calls it, 'which extends through Macedonia to the Hellespont,' was completed very shortly after Rome had possessed herself of Macedonia, and is still the main avenue of communication in those countries[4]. Besides these definite and tangible measures Rome secured her position by the attractions of commerce and a higher material civilisation. The Roman trader was ubiquitous. He even preceded the Roman arms; thus we find him crossing the Great St. Bernard and paying toll to the barbarians before either end of the pass was secured by Roman troops[5]; and wherever the Roman arms were carried, the merchants followed in crowds[6]. The immense and permanent diffusion of Roman citizens over the world which Rome had conquered was one of the chief agencies at work in levelling differences and establishing a sort of unity between its heterogeneous parts. So again the higher civilisation of Rome exercised an immense attraction upon backward races[7]. The Romans quite understood this; and an interesting and characteristic passage of Tacitus[8] shows

---

[1] Tac. Agr. 16.   [2] Ann. xiv. 51; cf. Ann. i. 59.
[3] De Prov. Cons. 2.   [4] Mommsen, iii. 43.   [5] Caes. B. G. iii. 1.
[6] Mommsen, iii. 40; Finlay, i. 47; Diod. Sic. v. 26; Duruy, iii. 257, note.

[7] This is illustrated by the case of the Ubii; see Tac. Hist. iv. 28.

[8] Tac. Agr. 21.

us Agricola of set purpose introducing the Britons to the pleasant luxuries of their conquerors. 'All this in their ignorance they called civilisation, when it was but a part of their servitude.'

If a Roman province was conquered and secured in some such way as this, how was it organised after conquest? One of the first objects of the Romans was to put an end to all leagues and combinations which might prove dangerous to their rule. In this they only followed that rule of *divide et impera* which had proved so successful in Italy. Such powerful leagues as that of Achaia at once came to an end; and if the Romans still permitted the 'community of Sicily[1]' and the 'confederacy of Lycia[2]' to exist, it was because they were quite devoid of any political significance. To break up a province as far as possible into a number of isolated units was the key-note of their policy. It is only under the Empire that we find anything of the nature of a provincial parliament; and even then it is easy to exaggerate the significance of those shadowy assemblies. Even before Rome had fully taken over a country and submitted it to her rule we find her at work destroying any national unity it might possess, and subdividing it and isolating its different parts. Thus Macedonia was broken up into four confederacies without right of intermarriage, and no one was allowed to hold landed property in more than one of the confederacies[3]. Illyria was treated in much the same fashion[4]. The later divisions introduced by Rome for purposes of jurisdiction, the *conventus* or circuits, tended, whether intentionally or not, to the same result. These divisions were quite apart from race distinctions, and must have contributed not a little to confuse and even obliterate those distinctions. Thus Strabo[5] writes: 'The places situated next to these towards the south and extending to Mount Taurus, are so

_{First organisation of a province.}

_{'Divide et impera.'}

---

[1] Cic. in Verrem, iii. 63.
[2] σύστημα Λυκίας. See Marquardt, i. 219. The Amphictyonic Council held meetings in the time of Pausanias; Paus. Phoc. viii. 3; Finlay, i. 67.
[3] Mommsen, ii. 302.   [4] Ibid. 303. .   [5] Strabo, xiii. 4. § 12.

intermixed, that parts of Phrygia, Lydia, Caria, and Mysia running into one another are difficult to be distinguished. The Romans have contributed not a little to produce this confusion, by not dividing the people according to tribes, but following another principle have arranged them according to jurisdictions, in which they have appointed days for holding courts and administering justice.' The same ends were secured by the immense variety of rights and privileges that existed over the area of a single province. The towns might be either free towns or allied towns, or Roman colonies, or municipia with Roman or Latin right, or simply ordinary provincial towns without either special privilege or special disqualification. These differences of right would depend largely upon the conduct they had severally shown while the Romans were engaged in military operations in the country. The differences of land tenure followed from the same cause. Some states had their lands taken from them for good[1]; to others they were, as the phrase went, 'restored.' 'What could be more humane than the conduct of our ancestors,' exclaims Cicero[2], who very frequently restored their property even to foreign enemies whom they had conquered?'

The Lex Agraria of 111 which regulated the tenure of the land and the payment of the taxes in the province of Africa is extremely puzzling from the number of tenures it establishes. The three main divisions are into *ager privatus ex jure Quiritium*[3], that is, land assigned to Roman colonies or to Roman citizens individually; *ager privatus ex jure peregrino*, that is, the land of free or allied towns, paying no taxes; and *ager publicus populi Romani*[4], that is, the land of conquered communities like

---

[1] Cic. pro Fonteio, 1 ; cf. Pro Balbo, 18.

[2] De leg. Agr. i. 6: 'Quid enim illis clementius qui etiam externis hostibus victis sua saepissime reddiderunt?' Cf. in Verrem, iii. 21, 37, v. 54.

[3] This land would be that of the colonies (C. Gracchus had powers for more than merely one ; see Sall. Jug. 42) founded by C. Gracchus.

[4] This land would be that of the seven free cities, Utica, Thapsus, &c., which assisted Rome against Carthage. See this important law (commonly

Carthage, which became the absolute property of Rome. But this was not all. Some towns which had started with the same rights as others, gained for this or that reason privileges to which the others were strangers. Immunity from taxation would be the chief of these, and adventurers like Antony[1] or goodnatured emperors like Claudius[2] were far from unready to make a bargain or a present of such privileges. It is obvious from all this how absolutely isolated and independent would become the interests of each single town within a Roman province. From Rome a town might get everything, but from its neighbours nothing. The citizens of one town were not as a rule allowed to hold land within the territory of another[3]; and when we find a number of provincial towns cooperating for any purpose of common advantage, as, for instance, the Spanish municipia that combined their subscriptions to build a bridge over the Tagus[4], the case is exceptional enough to excite attention. Such an instance of close intercourse again as that of the *hospitium* between different tribes in the north of Spain, of which there is epigraphic evidence[5], is almost without a parallel. *Hospitium* with Romans,—that was another matter; between Rome and the provinces the communication was easy and incessant; but between province and province, or between different parts of the same province, it was never, even under the Empire which could afford to be more liberal in those respects than the Republic, more than tolerated.

But though in these respects Rome was inflexible enough, the great merit of her administration of the provinces is, on the whole, the pliancy and adaptability of it. 'Everywhere where the Roman conquest had found a good municipal and financial organisation, it had remained content with it[6].' The Romans

Adaptability of the Roman Administration.

---

but erroneously called the Lex Thoria) in C. I. L. i. 90, and Mommsen's full discussion of it, ib. i. 96.

[1] For the traffic in such matters, of which Cicero accuses Antony, see Phil. i. 10, ii. 14, 17, 36, 38.

[2] Tac. Ann. xii. 58, 60; Suet. Claud. 25.   [3] Mommsen, ii. 68.

[4] C. I. L. ii. 760.   [5] Orelli, 156.   [6] Egger, Examen critique, p. 44.

C 2

were not cursed with the passion for uniformity; and as Tacitus[1] said of them, 'value the reality of the Empire, and disregard its empty show.' The extent to which they left the pre-existing arrangements unaltered in Egypt is an extraordinary proof of their wise conservatism. In the first place, they left the religion of the people quite untouched, and Roman governors were not above associating themselves with their ceremonies, and devoutly listening to the miraculous statue of Memnon[2]. The arrangements of the Ptolemies remained the groundwork of the government; the Roman governor stepped into their throne, was in the eyes of the Egyptians a vice-king, and had none of the ordinary insignia of a Roman magistrate. The great peculiarity of Egypt was the subdivision of the land, and here, from the absolute necessity of definite and permanent arrangements in a country whose soil was annually submerged, the Romans were more than usually conservative. The main division was into three Epistrategiæ, which were in fact Upper, Middle, and Lower Egypt. Each of these was divided into nomes; the nomes were again divided into toparchies, and the toparchies into κῶμαι and τόποι. Each of the three great divisions was under an ἐπιστρατηγός, to whom the minor magistrates were responsible. Originally there were thirty-six nomes; later on forty-seven can be pointed out, and there were perhaps more. Each nome had a town for its capital, but the town was only a part of the nome, and by no means the source of authority in it, as would have been the case in Greece, or indeed in any other Roman province. The magistrate of the nome was called νομάρχης, and by the Romans στρατηγός. These officers were native Greeks or Egyptians, appointed for three years, and were no doubt the channel through which the government reached the peasants. They received copies of the decrees issued by the prefect in Alexandria, and it was their duty to make these known to the inhabitants of their district. The

Illustrated by the case of Egypt.

---

[1] Tac. Ann xv. 31.
[2] Cf. Boissier, L'Empire Romain en Orient, p. 114; and for the protection extended by Rome to foreign religions generally, Cic. in Verrem, v. 51.

copy of the decree issued by the prefect Tiberius Alexander, found in the Grand Oasis in 1820[1], is prefaced by the following notice from the strategus: 'I, Julius Demetrius, strategus of the Oasis of the Thebais, have published the copy of the decree sent me by the prefect, Tiberius Julius Alexander, in order that you may know and enjoy its beneficent provisions.' There were also minor officials, known as κωμογραμματεῖς, whose main business it was to look after the boundaries which the Nile was continually unsettling, but who also had duties connected with the taxation of their nome[2]. The genuine Greek towns stood wholly outside the nome arrangements, and governed themselves on the usual Greek model. Alexandria however, the second city of the Empire, had too unruly a population to be allowed self-government, and was under a *juridicus Alexandriae* who was named directly by the emperor. Its population consisted of three distinct races; firstly, Greeks with administrative and judicial magistrates of their own (ἐξηγητής and ἀρχιδικαστής); secondly, Jews, with an Ethnarch, and a council of elders; thirdly, Egyptians as resident aliens or μέτοικοι[3].

It is unnecessary to point out the peculiarities of this administration. The general difference in the administration of

The Greek East.

---

[1] This decree, along with a shorter one of a previous governor, Cn. Vergilius Capito, was found by Calliaud. Letronne published it in the Journal des Savans for 1822. They have been published by Elphinstone, *Journey to the Oases*, and Hyde, *Class. Journ.* xxiii. 156, the former of whom gave a very incorrect English version of the Greek. The decrees are also printed in the C. I. Gr., and (in part) by Bruns.

[2] See the decree of Cn. Virgilius Capito. 'Let the imperial scribes, and the κωμογραμματεῖς and τοπογραμματεῖς in each nome, keep account of what is paid by the nome, in case any illegal exactions have been made, or anything else of the kind. And if they do not, let them pay 60 (denarii?) over and above the sum they have thus failed to keep account of.'

[3] This account of the administration of Egypt is in the main summarised from Marquardt, i. 279-296, where the authorities are given. The two decrees, of which I have also made some use, are of great interest and importance, particularly with regard to the fiscal arrangements. I hope to return to them later.

East and West illustrates the same marvellous readiness of Rome to adapt herself to existing circumstances. The incompatibility of Roman and Greek was a fact she early recognised; it could not be stated more strongly than it is in the Pro Flacco of Cicero; and the policy of Rome was to leave the Greek cities very much to themselves, though no doubt always favouring the aristocratic element in them, as Sparta had done before her, at the expense of the democratic element. The Romans could not deal with Greek ecclesiae[1], and the contemptuous tone in which Cicero[2] speaks of the democratic assemblies of Asia is a faithful echo of the ordinary Roman feeling. But on the whole these towns remained wonderfully unchanged, and even under the Empire, as far as inscriptions go, a town like Tomi on the Black Sea might have appeared wholly independent and outside of Roman rule, if it were not for the occasional mention of the 'sacred rescripts' (ἱεραὶ ἀντιγραφαί) of the emperor[3]. This conservatism was of course very natural. The Romans would have given themselves an immensity of trouble, if they had insisted upon a uniform administration everywhere, without any proportionate advantage. In the Greek cities of Asia Minor a municipal census had been regularly taken[4], and it was natural that the Romans when they conquered the country should make use of it. In Egypt the immemorial survey of the country was the basis of their administration. They were indeed only too glad to be saved the enormous labours of the survey in at all events one country, and in the decree of Tiberius Alexander which has been preserved to us we find the governor assuring the Egyptians that no changes in that survey were meditated[5]. It is worth adding

---

[1] A remark of Mommsen, ii. 69.
[2] 'Graeculae contionis;' Pro Flacco, 10. § 23; also 7, 8, 24 of the same oration.
[3] Perrot, *Mem. sur quelques inscriptions inedites des côtes de la mer Noire*, Revue Archeol. 1874, p. 27.
[4] Appian, B. C. v. 4. For Sicily, cf. Cic. in Verrem, ii. 53-56.
[5] Towards the end of the decree.

that the peculiar Egyptian foot-measure was maintained under their rule; just as in Gaul the *leugae* were not totally dispossessed by the Roman system of measuring by miles [1].

But the most marked instance of their conduct with regard to the existing arrangements of a province occurs in the case of Sicily. Here the Lex Hieronica, the judicial and financial arrangements established by the king who had been Rome's faithful ally, were maintained in their entirety. In particular the tithes which he had established were maintained as the regular tax; and the arrangements by which the dealings between the farmers and the middle men were controlled were carefully observed. These laws, though framed with the utmost care and even severity, were yet just, and, if they were observed, it was, according to Cicero, impossible for the farmer of the tithes to exact from the cultivator more than his due [2]. The Romans, when they made Sicily a province, took care that not only the king's laws should be maintained, but also that they should preserve his name [3]; and till the disastrous governorship of Verres, no praetor had violated its provisions [4]. Even the senatorial commission appointed during Verres' years of office to inquire into the taxation of his province, though they had at first intended to introduce reforms, ended by maintaining the law of Hiero in its integrity [5].

Sicily.

But whether the Romans were assisted by such pre-existing conditions or not, they in all cases made it their business to establish a norm of administration in any country of which they determined to make a province. A country was not thought to be really conquered till it had been bound down by Roman laws as well as overthrown by Roman arms. Cicero argues for the prorogation of Caesar's command in Gaul on the ground that the Gallic peoples had indeed been subdued, but not yet attached to Rome by laws, by a fixed code of rights, by a certain peace [6]. If this policy was thus necessary for security,

Lex Provinciae.

---

[1] Marquardt, ii. 216. [2] In Verrem, iv. 8. [3] Ib. iv. 6.
[4] Ib. iii. 60. [5] Ib. iv. 7.
[6] Cic. de Prov. Cons. 8; cf. chap. 12 and 14.

it was of course indispensable for the future government of the province. Directly after the conquest of a country, the Senate dispatched a commission of ten senators, whose business it was, in combination with the general, to settle its future government. Thus Plutarch [1] relates that Lucullus, after his campaign against Mithridates, had written a sanguine letter to the Senate. Whereupon just when he is in the midst of the dangers and difficulties which shortly afterwards beset him, 'the legates arrived for the settlement of Pontus, as if now entirely reduced.' They must have been unwelcome visitors, but notwithstanding, it appears that Lucullus with their assistance and advice did make arrangements which Pompey afterwards annulled [2]. It is not possible to say exactly how much power the legates and the general respectively had, but it is easy to understand that a successful and powerful general would settle matters pretty much at his discretion. That the Senate however gave their commissioners definite instructions as to the line of conduct they were to follow, appears from Livy's [3] account of the commission sent to assist Paulus in regulating the affairs of Macedonia. On the other hand, Caesar [4] seems to have settled the affairs of Gaul without any such interference on the part of the Senate; and there is no mention of a commission to control the arrangements of Pompey in Asia Minor. The norm of administration thus established was called, in general terms, the 'law of the province' (lex provinciae); but as applied to any particular province it would be named after its original author. Thus we find the Lex Pompeia in Pontus and Bithynia, the Lex Mummia in Achaia, the Lex Rupilia in Sicily. Such arrangements were called 'lex' on the principle of delegated authority, which was inherent in the Roman constitution; if the Senate and people gave a man authority to make such arrangements, they were law just as much as if they had been passed in the assembly and approved by the Senate [5]. The Lex Rupilia, however, is

---

[1] Plut. Lucull. 35.   [2] Ib. 36.   [3] Livy, xlv. 18.   [4] Cf. Mommsen, iv. 313.
[5] Cf. Bruns, p. 105, note; Mommsen, Stadtrechte von Salpensa und Malaga, p. 409, note.

loosely so called; for in this case there was no vote of the people to authorise Rupilius, but only a senatorial decree[1]. This law, however, happens to be the best known to us of all such constitutions, owing to the fact of Cicero having had occasion to mention it in his indictment of Verres. If we ask ourselves what sort of points such laws would be needed to settle, it is obvious, a priori, that the financial and judicial arrangements would above all require to be determined. It was impossible to leave the property and persons of the subjects absolutely to the caprice of the different proconsuls. The uncertainty and arbitrariness which was the great evil of the provincial administration under the Republic, would in this case have been aggravated a thousandfold. There does not appear, it is true, to have been an absolute obligation on the part of the governor to obey the lex provinciae; for Verres disregarded it[2]; but Cicero's language makes it plain that such conduct was unprecedented and outrageous. As the law of Hiero had already settled the financial administration, the Lex Rupilia seems to have chiefly concerned itself with the administration of justice, and laid down minute regulations as to the courts in which actions between Sicilians and Romans, between Sicilians of the same town, and between a Sicilian of one town and a Sicilian of another, were to be tried[3]. Sulla's arrangements in Asia Minor, on the other hand, seem to have been chiefly financial, and referred to the apportionment of the tribute among the different cities of the province. These arrangements were of the character of a 'lex provinciae,' inasmuch as they remained the model for succeeding governors, and were for instance copied by Pompey and Flaccus[4]. Under the Empire the financial arrangements came before everything; and the first thing that was done with a new province was to take a census in it[5]. In the Republican period the Romans had not learnt to be so systematic, and the general

---

[1] Cic. in Verrem, iii. 13.   [2] Ib. iii. 16.   [3] Ib. iii. 13.
[4] Cic. pro Flacco, 14.   [5] Marquardt, ii. 206.

plan was to maintain the taxes, which the country had previously paid, or, in some cases, to make a parade of generosity by diminishing them[1]. Such arrangements would make part of the 'lex provinciae.' In any case one innovation was always carried out, namely, the division of the country into taxation-districts, each with a town for its capital, whose magistrates were bound to pay over the amount of taxation due from the district[2]. This would imply little change in the cities of Greece and Asia Minor, but it would mean a great deal in countries like Spain and Gaul; and it helps to explain the immense attention paid by the Romans to the building and enlarging of towns in such provinces.

Essentials of the Roman rule.

We are now in a position to see what the rule of the Romans meant at first to the natives of the countries they had subdued. The essentials of that rule were, broadly, three;—the tribute, the conscription, and Roman laws. In antiquity conquest meant essentially the power to impose a tribute upon the conquered. To get your taxes paid for you was the sufficient reason for the previous expenditure of blood and treasure. Caesar's account of pre-Roman Gaul makes it very clear that the stronger tribes exacted tribute from the weaker[3]; and it is put forward as the object of the migration of the Helvetii that they intended to make the states they conquered tributary. Athens had previously yielded to the fascinations of this advantage of the stronger; and the Romans perhaps consciously put it before themselves as the end of conquest. A native regarded them, above all, as plunderers[4]; and they in their language currently and without arrière pensée spoke of

---

[1] This was done for instance in Macedonia; cf. Livy, xlv. 29. For Asia, cf. Cic. ad Qu. Fr. I. I. 11. For Numidia, in later times, cf. Merivale, ii. 367. See G. C. Lewis, Government of Dependencies, p. 123.

[2] Marquardt, ii. 190.

[3] Caes. B. G. i. 36, 44, v. 27.

[4] Tacitus probably does not mistake in the speeches he puts into the mouths of Arminius, Galgacus, Caractacus. Cf. esp. Agric. 30, 31; Ann. xii. 34.

the provincials as *stipendiarii*[1]. If we find Cicero in Cilicia The tribute. begging the Senate for reinforcements, it is that he may secure the provinces 'in which are comprised the revenues of the Roman people[2];' and if he advocates the appointment of Pompey to the charge of the Mithridatic war, it is because that war is 'formidable and dangerous to our tax-payers and allies,' and because 'the surest and largest revenues of the Roman people are at stake[3].' In his famous letter to his brother Quintus, Cicero defends the taxes imposed on Asia on the ground of their necessity for the expenses of the administration; and later, under the Empire, the large standing army obviously necessitated a large tribute. 'There can be no peace without troops, no troops without pay, no pay without tribute,' says Cerialis in that curious speech in which he, or rather Tacitus[4] through his mouth, seeks to justify the Roman rule in Gaul.

But there were some peoples so poor and backward as to be The levy. unable to pay tribute; and on these the blood-tax only was imposed[5]. These levies of troops in the provinces existed of course under the Republic; Caesar mentions them for instance as taken by him in Gaul, and the main strength of Cicero's army in Cilicia was its non-Roman element[6]; but, in the main, the practice of using provincial troops almost to the exclusion of Italian did not establish itself before the Empire. Warlike nations like the Batavi would be well content to serve under the conquering eagles, but by other peoples it was felt as a grievous

---

[1] Tac. Ann. iv. 20, xv. 25; Vell. Pat. ii. 97.

[2] Cic. ad Fam. xv. 1.

[3] Cic. pro. Leg. Manil. 2. For the way the *payers* regarded those revenues, pro Flacco, 8.

[4] Hist. iv. 74. Cf. Caes. B. G. v. 22; Strabo, iv. 6. § 3; Tac. Agric. 13, 15, 31; Ann. xv. 6. The passage from Cicero's letter to his brother, referred to, runs as follows: 'Id autem imperium quum retineri sine vectigalibus nullo modo possit, acquo animo parte aliqua suorum fructuum pacem sibi sempiternam redimant et otium.' Ad Qu. Fr. i. 1. 11.

[5] Tac. Hist. iv. 12, 17.

[6] Cic. ad Att. vi. 5. A levy in Macedonia is mentioned; Cic. Phil. x. 6. These however would be auxiliaries, not legionary troops.

burden. What do you expect of your submission, Civilis asks the Treviri, beyond a hateful service, everlasting tribute, the rod, the axe, and the passions of a ruling race[1]? The recruiting officers were sometimes not above acting as did Falstaff in a like position, and picking out rich and elderly men for service, who would redeem themselves by a heavy bribe[2]. This was bad enough, but if their conduct was often as detestable as it is described to us in the same chapter of Tacitus, it was no wonder that the levy was, to some at all events of the subject races, more odious even than the tribute[3].

Roman laws and polity. Another result of conquest was the introduction of the Roman law and polity. In a case which Tacitus describes, their immediate application to a quite barbarous people has an almost grotesque effect. 'The Frisians ... gave hostages, and settled down on territories marked out by Corbulo, who at the same time gave them a senate, magistrates, and a constitution[4]'. It was the Roman policy to introduce an aristocratic, or rather timocratic constitution everywhere[5], modelled on that of old Republican Rome[6]; and of course wherever the Romans went, they took their law with them. At first some latitude was allowed. The free and allied towns for instance were permitted, with more or less restriction, 'to use,' as the phrase went, 'their own laws;' but such classes of towns are continually diminishing, and passing into Roman municipia, or are allowed the title of Roman colonies; and, as the franchise becomes more and more widely extended, the Roman law comes to be the only law over the whole Empire. From the first, to all provincials but the specially privileged, the decisions of the Roman governor and his subordinates constituted the law; and it is well known that the governor commonly incorporated into his edict the law as

---

[1] Tac. Hist. iv. 32; see also Caes. B. G. vii. 77; Tac. Agr. 13, 15.
[2] Tac. Hist. iv. 14.   [3] cf. Ib. iv. 71.   [4] Tac. Ann. xi. 19.
[5] This point will be fully discussed later.
[6] There is a strong archaising tendency in the municipal arrangements. See this point discussed in a later section.

laid down by the urban praetors at Rome. The part which Roman law, constitutional and civil, played in civilising and organising the subject races, was fully understood by the ancients; and the mark which it has left on later history is uneffaced, and perhaps ineffaceable.

The question as to the right or wrong of the Roman rule is not one to be settled off-hand. Modern opinion, on the whole, condemns a policy of conquest and annexation, but it must be remembered that war was the normal state of things between two peoples in antiquity, unless there was a special agreement to the contrary, and that conquerors were, it might be, hated, but not, in popular opinion, condemned as wicked[1]. Moreover, as has been already remarked, the conquests of the Romans were, at first at all events, not deliberate, but were partly forced on her, and partly arose naturally out of the circumstances. Our own experience in India shows how difficult it is to stop the process of conquest once begun; and moral indignation is out of place if it condemns all conquest merely as such. The practical question of course is, as to whether the conquered country had a free, national, prosperous life before its conquest, and whether or not that conquest has given it a life more worth having than the old one. We justify our rule in India, where we are certainly aliens and interlopers to a greater degree than the Romans were in any of their provinces, by pointing to the peace and security we have given it, by dwelling on the endless petty wars and detestable tyrannies of its innumerable princes before our rule existed. In fact we say that the previous state of things was so bad that our rule is a desirable substitute. The Romans would have said, and did say, pretty much the same about their own rule; and it is quite impossible to give a fair judgment of that rule unless we have some clear idea of the state of things which it replaced. In attempting to give some account of the

Moral aspect of the Roman rule.

Necessity of an examination of the pre-Roman condition of the provinces.

---

[1] 'In ancient times it was necessary to be either anvil or hammer;' Mommsen, iii. 193; cf. 313.

pre-Roman conditions in the different provinces, I by no means profess to be exhaustive, but only to put together the most necessary materials.

Pre-Roman Gaul.

The country with which, from this point of view, we are best acquainted is Gaul. Caesar supplies us with a good deal of information, which can be eked out with occasional notices from Strabo. The point which comes out most clearly is that till the Romans conquered the country it was never free from petty wars[1]. The contest between the Arverni and Aedui in particular had been so obstinate and prolonged, that at last the Arverni sought to crush their rivals by calling in German mercenaries from across the Rhine. This had led to the settlement of 120,000 Germans on Gallic soil[2]; and it had not even benefited the Arverni and their allies; for the German king Ariovistus had established himself among the Sequani[3]. 'In a few years all the Gauls will be driven from their country, and all the Germans will have crossed the Rhine,' is the substance of Divitiacus' appeal to Caesar[4]. Ariovistus had imposed a tribute upon the Aedui[5]; and if Caesar can be trusted, that people had been reduced to a humiliating and miserable vassalage[6]. Besides having to pay a tribute, they were robbed of their lands and compelled to give hostages with every circumstance of indignity. That these 'hostages' so often mentioned were in fact prisoners, or rather slaves who were treated with great harshness, might be conjectured, and is proved by another passage of the same writer[7]. Once begun, the stream of Germans across the Rhine was incessant. Sometimes they came in small detachments; sometimes whole nations at once. Caesar puts the number of the Usipetes and Tenchtheri at 430,000[8]; and if we merely consider the fact of his having destroyed and repelled these invaders, as he had done pre-

---

[1] Caes. B. G. vi. 15: 'Hi, cum est usus atque aliquod bellum incidit (quod fere ante Caesaris adventum quotannis accidere solebat) . . .' Cf. Strabo, iv. 1, § 2; Tac. Hist. iv. 73.
[2] Caes. B. G. i. 31.   [3] Ibid.   [4] Ibid.   [5] Ibid. i. 36.
[6] Ibid. vii. 54.   [7] Ibid. v. 27.   [8] Ibid. iv. 15.

viously to the still more numerous Helvetii[1], the obligations of Gaul to Rome will appear considerable. The Gauls could not have resisted their invaders by their own strength, owing to their lack of national unity. Caesar could never have conquered Gaul if it had all resolutely united against him; but the powerful combination that was formed against him by the genius of Vercingetorix did not last; and it was an easy task for him to beat his enemies in detail. Tacitus' description of the revolt of Civilis, a century later, gives an idea of the jarring jealousies and discords that were still rife among the Gauls, and ready to burst out directly Rome's heavy hand was removed[2]. And these tribal hatreds were not all. There were two factions, according to Caesar, in every city and every tribe. The nobles were as powerful as the feudal barons of a thousand years later, and the common people were little better than slaves[3]. What with debt, the burden of taxation, and the violence of the nobles, they did indeed in many cases voluntarily resign their freedom, and attach themselves as slaves to some powerful master[4]. Along with all this went a low development of material and moral civilisation. There were no roads worth mentioning till the Romans made them; and if it had not been for the immense facilities provided by the unrivalled river-system of the country[5] there could have been but little trade. The country was so little opened out that the mountaineers regularly exacted toll from the merchants who crossed their passes. It was impossible, for instance, to cross the Great St. Bernard[6] (and the same probably applies to all the Alpine passes, as it applies to the Pyrenees[7]) without paying a heavy black-mail to the natives; and the Veneti of Northwestern Gaul laid similar burdens upon the commerce of the Channel[8]. The so-called 'towns' (oppida) of Gaul were as a

---

[1] Caes. B. G. i, passim.   [2] Tac. Hist. iv. 69.
[3] Caes. B. G. vi. 13: 'Plebs paene servorum habetur loco.'
[4] Ibid.
[5] Strabo, iv. 1. § 14, iv. 3. § 3; Merivale, i. 198, 242.
[6] Caes. B. G. iii. 1.   [7] Plut. Sert. 6.   [8] Caes. B. G. iii. 8.

rule nothing but wretched villages, as were also the 'towns' of Spain[1]. Vienna (Vienne) for example, afterwards the metropolis of the Allobroges and one of the chief cities of Gaul, had been, so Strabo tells us, nothing but a village, and owed all its magnificence to the Roman rule[2]. The general barbarism of the Gallic peoples outside the 'old province' is strongly asserted by Cicero[3], and seems confirmed by the practice of human sacrifices, which Caesar[4] and Strabo[5] mention. Strabo adds that 'the Romans put a stop to these customs;' just as we in India have put a stop to Suttee and Juggernaut.

Pre-Roman Spain.

We are not equally familiar with pre-Roman Spain; but some of the same points come clearly out. Just as in Gaul, the different tribes were continually at war; and the necessity of constant preparation for self-defence made agriculture impossible, and neutralised the natural fertility of the country[6]. Another great evil was the brigandage which the physical features of the country made so easy, that not even the Romans could wholly root it out, though they did an immense deal in that direction[7]. How wholly savage some of the races of the peninsula were appears from Plutarch's story of the miserable cave-dwellers on whom Sertorius played so clever a trick[8]. But the chief source of weakness in the country was, again, the absence of anything like national unity. 'The settlement of the Grecians amongst these barbarous nations may be regarded as the result of the division of these latter into small tribes and sovereignties, having on account of their moroseness no union amongst themselves, and therefore powerless against attacks from without. This moroseness is remarkably prevalent amongst the Iberians, who are besides crafty in their manner, devoid of sincerity, insidious, and predatory in their mode of life; they are bold in little adventures, but never undertake anything of magnitude,

---

[1] Strabo, iii. 4. § 13.   [2] Ib. iv. 1. § 11.   [3] Cic. de Prov. Cons. 12.
[4] Caes. B. G. vi. 16.   [5] Strabo, iv. 4. § 5.
[6] Ib. iii. 3. § 5. Contrast this passage with Caes. B. C. i. 85; Tac. Hist. ii. 67.
[7] Strabo, iii. 4. § 13; Mommsen, iii. 19.   [8] Plut. Sert. 17.

inasmuch as they have never formed any extended power or confederacy. If they had had but the will to assist each other, neither could the Carthaginians by making an incursion have so easily deprived them of the greater part of their country, nor before them the Tyrians, then the Kelts, now called the Keltiberians and Berones, nor after these the brigand Viriathus, and Sertorius, nor any others who desired power. On this account the Romans, having carried the war into Iberia, lost much time by reason of the number of different sovereignties, having to conquer first one, then another; in fact it occupied nearly two centuries, or even longer, before they had subdued the whole [1].' Of the great number of different races in the country none showed the capacity of developing a high type of civilisation by itself. The 'unmitigated barbarism' which Dean Merivale [2] ascribes to them is perhaps too sweeping an expression if we remember what Strabo tells us of the Turdetani [3]; but it certainly seems that the stimulus of Phenician or Greek or Roman civilisation was needed to enable them to make great and permanent progress. Under Roman rule Spain was exceptionally fortunate. The country was as a rule well governed [4]; it enjoyed profound peace [5]; and it assimilated the Roman civilisation perhaps more readily than any other province [6]. South-eastern Spain was wonderfully rich and prosperous, and studded with cities which enjoyed an intense and vigorous municipal life [7].

It is not worth while to go through the other provinces in equal detail. But it may be pointed out that Britain, like Gaul and Spain, was racked by incessant wars [8]; that there was no national feeling in the country wherewith to inspire courage

Pre-Roman condition of other provinces.

---

[1] Strabo, iii. 4. § 5; Falconer's translation.
[2] Merivale, ii. 157.
[3] Strabo, iii. 1. § 6; cf. Mommsen, ii. 207.
[4] Mommsen, iii. 20.
[5] Caes. B. C. i. 85; Tac. Hist. ii. 67.
[6] Cf. Merivale, ii. 157.
[7] It is curious that so much of our evidence as to the municipal arrangements within a Roman province comes from Spain. I refer of course particularly to the Lex Salpensana and Malacitana, and the Lex Ursonitana.
[8] Caes. B. G. v. 11.

D

and union against Rome, and that the standard of civilisation was a very low one[1]. Illyria was rendered insecure by brigandage[2] till the Romans put a stop to it, and had been a perfect nest of pirates[3]. Numidia had been exposed to the predatory excursions of the Moors[4]; just as Egypt had been apparently to those of the Ethiopians[5]. To Egypt the Roman rule was a relief. She exchanged a master who was both incompetent and despotic for a master who was despotic but competent. In either case the rule was that of foreigners; and it would be absurd to suppose that the mass of the Egyptians entertained any sentimental feelings with regard to the few last vicious and feeble representatives of the line of the Ptolemies. Greece, exhausted by internal dissensions, viewed the Roman conquest with satisfaction[6]. 'If we had not been quickly ruined we should not have been saved' was the current saying, which Polybios has preserved to us[7]. Asia Minor, protected against the pirates and the barbarians, would have been well off under Roman rule if it had not been for the tax-gatherers and the usurers. 'Let Asia consider this,' says Cicero, 'that no calamity of foreign war or intestine discord would have been wanting to her if she were not protected by this Empire[8].' Rome put an end to riots in the towns[9], and to brigandage in the country[10]. She exacted a tribute it is true, but then, says Cicero, the Asiatics paid tribute before, and some of them more than they do now[11]. It was no loss to the country that it should be rid of its petty kings; Roman rule at its worst was better than that of a Pharnaces[12]. 'In the whole peninsula of Asia Minor the Roman conquest had nowhere suppressed a

---

[1] Strabo, iv. 5. § 2.   [2] Hirtius, Bell. Alex. 42.   [3] Mommsen, ii. 73.
[4] Auct. Bell. Afr. 97.   [5] Strabo, xvii. 1. §§ 12 and 53.
[6] Mommsen, ii. 292, iii. 51; Finlay, i. 18.
[7] Polybius, xl. 5. § 12; quoted by Finlay, i. 20.
[8] Cic. ad Qu. Fr. i. 1. 11.
[9] Cic. ad Qu. Fr. i. 1. 8: 'Nullas esse in oppidis seditiones.'
[10] Ibid.: 'Sublata Mysiae latrocinia.'
[11] Cic. ad Qu. Fr. i. 1. 11; cf. Mommsen, ii. 274; Finlay, i. 39, note.
[12] Hirtius, Bell. Alex. 41.

truly independent, rich and powerful political life, because nowhere had it met with such a life¹.' Where such a life did in some measure exist in this country, it was not national but municipal, and Rome interfered to a very slight extent with the internal affairs of the towns.

We are now in a better position to discuss some of the charges brought against the Roman rule. 'From Mummius to Augustus the Roman city stands as the living mistress of the dead world, and from Augustus to Theodoric the mistress becomes as lifeless as her subjects².' 'The extension of equal rights to all the subjects of a common master was after all a very poor substitute for national independence or for full federal or municipal freedom³.' By a 'dead world' I understand a world without any active political life, without self-government, and without ambition; a world which had peace and material prosperity perhaps, but no freedom and no self-respect. The second passage implies an answer to an objection. Does not, it might be urged, the extension of the franchise through the period of the Republic and the early Empire constitute an object of ambition, and a means of securing independence? Maybe, we are answered, but that is 'a very poor substitute for national independence, or for full federal and municipal freedom.' Let us consider this last point first. Ideally no doubt it would be a very poor substitute; but practically and as a matter of fact was it a substitute for anything of the sort? Where was the national independence which Rome destroyed? In Macedonia, perhaps, alone of all her conquests. There was no nation, we have seen, in Spain, none in Gaul, none in Britain, none in Asia Minor. It is impossible not to lament the extinction of Macedonia⁴, but it must at the same time be remembered

---

¹ Perrot, Quelques inscriptions des côtes de la mer Noire, p. 30; Mommsen, ii. 216, 219.
² Freeman, Essays, 2nd Series, p. 336.
³ Ibid. p. 321. This passage refers of course directly to the Empire; but it opens up several large questions which apply to the Roman rule as a whole. ⁴ Mommsen, ii. 203.

that Rome had not provoked the struggle, and it may be questioned whether the Macedonian government had enough vitality left, if quite exempt from Roman interference, to defend its subjects from the perpetual encroachments of the barbarians, as Rome defended them [1]. If then the Roman rule did not in the great majority of cases destroy national independence—there being none to destroy—still less did it destroy 'municipal freedom.' It is plain matter of fact that where they found municipal arrangements existing, the Romans let them alone and even encouraged them; and where they did not exist they made it their first object to introduce them [2]. The amount of independence enjoyed by these towns was considerable, and all the evidence goes to prove that the life that went on in them was a busy and active one; that their elections aroused a genuine political interest; and that their magistrates were conversant with affairs, and trained by the experience of public life. The municipal arrangements, though terribly perverted by Constantine and his successors, were on the whole both successful and permanent; and when, after the cloud of barbarism was passing away, the 'free towns' begin to appear in Europe, we may regard them as no new growth, but as derived more or less directly from the provincial municipia of the Empire.

These municipal arrangements form one element in the answer to the question, Were the provinces dead and stagnant, or on the contrary alive and vigorous in their life? But it may be said that after all municipal life is very different and very inferior to national life; and that if the provinces had the one, they in no sense possessed the other. Now national life in the strict sense they had not. Those ties of like blood, like speech, like interests, like traditions, which go to build up a modern nation, hardly existed under Rome. But those feelings which

---

[1] Cic. pro Font. 20. The foreign policy of Macedonia was in this period execrable. Such crimes as the sack of Cios and Abydos do much to alienate our sympathies; see Mommsen, ii. 226, 232.

[2] See Marquardt's 1st vol. passim. It is needless to give references here. The municipal arrangements will be discussed later.

are the precious part of national unity, the self-respect which springs from the consciousness of being part of a great and powerful whole, the loyalty and the patriotism it evokes, can exist apart from unity of place or even of blood. 'I indeed think that both her and all municipal citizens have two fatherlands, the one of their birth and the other of their citizenship,' says Cicero[1]. The liberal policy of Rome gradually extended the privileges of her citizenship till it included all her subjects; and along with the *Jus suffragii* went of course the *Jus honorum*. Even under Augustus we find a Spaniard consul at Rome[2]; and under Galba an Egyptian is governor of Egypt[3]. It is not long before even the emperor himself is supplied by the provinces[4]. It is easy to comprehend therefore how the provincials forgot the fatherland of their birth for the fatherland of their citizenship. Once win the franchise, and to great capacity was opened a great career. The Roman Empire came to be a homogeneous mass of privileged persons, largely using the same language[5], aiming at the same type of civilisation, equal among themselves, but all alike conscious of their superiority to the surrounding barbarians. The Gauls of Provence and the Spaniards of Boetica were more Roman even than the Romans themselves. If we are to be so indignant with the Roman rule, we ought to be still more indignant with our rule in India. Political freedom and self-government is no more possessed by the Hindoos than it was by the provincials; and the Hindoos are worse off in that there is no prospect open to them of rising to high office, or to the vice-royalty, while corresponding prospects were open to the subjects of Rome. If then there was, speaking broadly, no conscious inferiority to make the

---

[1] Cic. de Legg. ii. 2. Cf. the remarks which Dio puts into the mouth of Maecenas; Dio Cassius, lii. 19.

[2] Cornelius Balbus.   [3] Tiberius Alexander; Tac. Hist. i. 11.

[4] Nerva was a Spaniard.

[5] Claudius took away the franchise from a Greek who could not speak Latin (Suet. Claud. 16). For other instances to illustrate this point see Duruy, iii. 384, note.

provincials regret the past, but every reason to make them
aspire to the future, it would be a great mistake to regard them
as so many mean-spirited slaves who had not the courage to
resist their masters. They did not feel themselves to be slaves;
and what with their share of local independence and their hopes
of the Roman franchise, they were not slaves. Moreover, though
it is possible to make too much, it is also possible to make too
little of the peace and material prosperity they enjoyed under
Rome. It was the first duty of a Roman governor to protect
his province from inroads from without. Caesar, though so busy
with his conquests in further Gaul, yet found time to protect the
frontier of Illyricum from the Pirustae[1]; and it is one of the
heaviest charges which Cicero brings against Piso that he had
not protected his province against the Thracians[2]. The chaos
into which the administration fell in the later years of the Republic caused neglect in this as in other matters; but with the
Empire we see the custody of the frontiers made a point of the
first importance. All such impediments to trade, as those in
Gaul and Spain already mentioned, were done away; and with
the clearance of the Mediterranean from pirates came an immense development of commerce[3]. The Roman occupation
of Egypt gave a great impulse to the trade with India. 'I was
with Gallus,' says Strabo, 'at the time he was prefect of Egypt,
and accompanied him as far as Syene and the frontiers of
Ethiopia, and found that about 120 ships sail from Myos-
hormos to India, although in the time of the Ptolemies scarcely
any one would venture on this voyage and the commerce with
the Indies[4].' So the district of Batanea (Haouran), now almost
impassable for European travellers, was covered with posts, and
rendered perfectly secure under the rule of Rome[5]. Every-

---

[1] Caes. B. G. v. 1.   [2] Cic. in Pis. 40.

[3] Strabo, iii. 2. § 5. 'Pacatum volitant per mare navitae,' says Horace, Od. iv. 5.

[4] Strabo, ii. 5. § 12; cf. xvii. 1. § 13.

[5] Boissier, L'Empire Roman en Orient, p. 119. His chief authority is M. Waddington, who has traversed the district.

where within the charmed circle of the Roman dominion was peace; sometimes it is true secured by stern measures, as in parts of Britain [1] and in the valley of Aosta [2]; but as a rule the sternness was reserved for the barbarians without, and the peace was only a blessing to the provincials. No progress was possible to countries distracted by petty wars which could never lead to a decisive issue. Agriculture becomes impossible, and all the arts. Outposts of civilisation, like the Greek cities on the Black Sea, must have welcomed the Roman rule as that of friends and deliverers. Ovid shows us how miserable had been the condition of Tomi before the Empire asserted itself against the barbarians in that region; and its ruins and inscriptions show us its prosperity half a century later [3]. The material condition of the provinces, partly no doubt for selfish reasons, was well looked after. Parts of Algeria now wholly barren were fertile and populous, owing to their unsurpassed system of irrigation [4]; and their roads and bridges are still the most durable memorials of their Empire.

But it must be allowed that these praises apply in strictness only to one period of the Roman rule, a period of about 200 years from Actium. The next section will show how far these duties were performed by Rome under the Republican government, and will seek to show the main causes of the maladministration in the provinces, which made that government equally mischievous and impossible.

---

[1] 'Solitudinem faciunt, pacem appellant;' Tac. Agr. 30.

[2] The Salassi were exterminated by Augustus; Strabo, iv. 6. § 7. The severity seems to have been beyond what was needful (cf. Finlay, i. 53), though Augustus, as if foreseeing possible blame for his action in this matter, expressly declares that no people was attacked wrongfully. (Mon. Anc. § 26: 'Nulli bello per injuriam inlato.')

[3] Perrot, op. cit. p. 21.   [4] Boissière, L'Afrique Romaine, p. 73.

CHAPTER II.

The Period of the Republic.

SECTION I. *Historical Outline*[1].

THE great struggle against Hannibal left the Senate the all but undisputed government of Rome. Originally a mere consulting board, assessors of the king or consul, the Senate had become the supreme executive body. That the government solely by the comitia and the magistrates should by experience be found wanting was as inevitable at Rome as at Athens. Rome was more fortunate than Athens in that she could develop a new organism to meet the need. The growth of the power of the Senate was all the more natural and legitimate the less it possessed strict legal standing-ground. But the fatal dualism thus introduced into the constitution—the Assembly governing *de jure*, and the Senate governing *de facto*—made all government after a time impossible. The position of the Senate being, strictly speaking, an unconstitutional one, it was open to any demagogue to bring matters of foreign policy or administration before an Assembly which was without continuity, without special knowledge, and in which there was no debate. Now, if the Senate governed badly, the Assembly 'could not govern at all[2];' and there could be, in the long run, but one

---

[1] In this sketch I have attempted to give an account of the different modes of appointment to provincial governorships; of the duration of the governorships; and of the authority of the Senate. The power and duties of the governor, and his subordinates; the amount of control exercised over the governor; the misery of the provinces, and its causes, require a separate treatment.   [2] Mommsen, ii. 359.

end to the constant struggle between the two sources of authority.

In the epitome of Livy, between a mention of the subjection of Illyria (B.C. 229) and of the war against the Cisalpine Gauls (B.C. 225) occurs the brief statement: 'The number of praetors was increased to four[1].' Now we know that a revolt against the new Roman authority took place in Sardinia in the year B.C. 226. We are therefore enabled with tolerable certainty to put the commencement of regular provincial government in the year B.C. 227. Whether before this date Sicily and Sardinia were governed by quaestors under the superintendence of the consuls, as Mommsen[2] supposes, cannot be proved, but is not improbable, as Rome had a more or less permanent hold on parts at all events of the two islands for some years past. The names of these two provincial praetors are known. They are—C. Flaminius, the same man who afterwards fell at Thrasymene, for Sicily; and M. Valerius, a man not otherwise known, for Sardinia. The same authority which tells us this tells us also that these two praetors cast lots for their provinces[3]. Each had one or more quaestors given him (in Sicily at all events later on there were two quaestors), who were charged with the management of the income and expenditure. The praetorships were annual, for no better reason than that the city praetorships were annual; and of course the quaestors were changed along with their superiors. The next provincial governments were Hither and Further Spain, which were established in the year B.C. 179. Experience had taught the Romans the mistake of annual governorships in such a country as Spain, and a special law had assigned two years of office to the praetors sent to that country[4]; but the com-

The first provinces.

---
[1] Epitome, lib. xx; Klein, Die Verwaltungsbeamten, &c., pp. 11, 199.
[2] Mommsen, ii. 67.
[3] Solin, 5. 1: 'Utraque insula in Romanum arbitratum redacta iisdem temporibus facta provincia, cum eodem anno Sardiniam M. Valerius, alteram C. Haminius praetores sortiti sunt.' Klein, loc. cit.
[4] The *Lex Baebia*; Mommsen, ii. 212.

petition for command in the provinces was too great for the law to be maintained, and the principle of annually changing the governors grew into a constitutional maxim. With these two new provinces went two new praetors, and the total number was now, therefore, six. Here for the present stops the election of new praetors; and it becomes therefore necessary to inquire how the new functions[1] established in the period between the settlement of Spain and the reforms of Sulla were discharged. The matter was managed by prorogation. After the urban praetors and the consuls had held their year of office in Italy, they were sent for a year to a province. Thus every year, besides the two consuls and the six praetors, there would be two ex-consuls and ex-praetors available for foreign service. As there was in law no difference between a magistracy in Italy and one in the provinces, there was nothing to prevent this arrangement; and as the Senate could prolong a man's term of office in a province for a year, or could refuse to do so, it practically had a very large control over the provincial appointments[2].

Lex Sempronia.

These arrangements were a natural enough growth, and in no way an affair of legislation; but there was one very important law passed during this period, which remained in force for the following century. This was the *Lex Sempronia* of C. Gracchus so often mentioned by Cicero[3]. It was to the effect that the Senate should each year decide before the election of the consuls what provinces they were to govern. It did not deprive the senators of their power to decide what the provinces for the consuls of the current year should be, but by obliging them to decide this point *before the elections* it sought to prevent favouritism in one case and unfairness in

---

[1] Five new provinces—Macedonia, Africa, Asia, Narbonensis, Cilicia; and the presidency of the new standing court of *Repetundae*, which had been established B.C. 149; Mommsen, iii. 366.

[2] Mommsen, ibid.

[3] Cic. de Prov. Cons. 2 and 7; Pro Balbo, 27; Ernesti's Index Legum, p. xxix.

another, and thereby to deprive them of means of influence[1]. As it turned out, the Senate had no difficulty in making use of the law for their own purposes; and when, for instance, they expected the election of Caesar, they took care to provide beforehand that he and his colleague should have the important province of the roads and forests[2].

The position of the Senate had been steadily deteriorating during this period. Even during the Second Punic War we find the comitia assuming the functions of the executive, and appointing generals against Hannibal[3]; and when the Senate wished to declare war against Philip, the comitia at first positively refused its assent[4]. As every measure to have legal force had in the last resort to come before the comitia[5], the Senate had to manœuvre in every possible way to win the comitia over to their views, to induce it for instance to sanction the prolongation of Flamininus' command in Macedonia[6]. The assembly was not long in dropping any feelings of awe or respect it may still have felt in regard to the Senate; it only needed hardihood and a certain contempt for tradition to overturn a system of tacitly usurped and tacitly acknowledged authority; and when the Gracchi, with however good motives, had set the example, inferior demagogues were quick to follow it. The worst of it was that the government of the Senate was so bad and so unequal to the ever-increasing charges of the state, that there seemed good and reasonable ground for interference. Their conduct of the Jugurthine war, for instance, was so shameful that it is hardly wonderful that the people should have angrily set its authority aside, and directly appointed Marius to the conduct of the war. But this action, though legal, was yet in the highest degree unconstitutional, and was far from being justified by any superior capacity for affairs possessed by

Position of the Senate.

---

[1] Mommsen, iii. 118.
[2] Merivale, i. 172; Mommsen, iv. 203.
[3] Mommsen, ii. 120, 128.
[4] Ib. ii. 233.
[5] Caesar, B. C. i. 6, complains: 'In reliquas provincias praetores mittuntur: neque expectant quod superioribus annis acciderat, ut de eorum imperio ad populum feratur.'
[6] Mommsen, ii. 243.

the Assembly. It however was to a certain extent practically justified by the circumstances; but when shortly afterwards the Assembly gave Marius the command in Asia, though Sulla had been already appointed, and though Marius was a private person, it is obvious that it was using its powers simply for party purposes : and to that there could be but one outcome. Such interferences however were in this period still rather the exception than the rule; the people had not yet completely banished the consciousness of their own incapacity. On the whole the Senate was left to conduct matters of foreign policy and finance, and the executive generally. The Senate still resolved on declarations of war, still settled new provinces by its commissioners, and still exercised control over its generals. The state of things typified by the Vatinian and Manilian laws did not yet exist in this period; but forces were at work of which it was the natural development.

Sulla's Laws.

The next great step in the legislation for the government of the provinces was made by Sulla. He raised the number of praetors to eight; and made a law that provinces should in future be governed not by consuls and praetors, but by proconsuls and propraetors, a particular province being assigned to a proconsul or a propraetor, according as it needed more or fewer troops[1]. This would make ten magistrates every year eligible for provincial command; and there were at this time ten provinces[2]. These governorships were made strictly annual; and there was a clause to the effect that the governor must leave his province within thirty days after the arrival of his successor[3]. Thus it became impossible for the comitia to give a man direct military

---

[1] Livy, xli. 8, says of Sardinia: 'Propter belli magnitudinem provincia consularis facta est.' In Macedonia the proconsul Piso was succeeded by the propraetor Q. Ancharius; Marquardt, i. 381, note 3.

The most obvious difference between the proconsul and propraetor was that the former had twelve, the latter only six fasces; Marquardt, i. 381.

[2] Sicily, Sardinia, the two Spains, Macedonia, Asia, Africa, Narbonensis, Cilicia, and Cisalpine Gaul; Mommsen, iii. 368.

[3] Cic. ad Fam. iii. 6 ; Mommsen, iii. 369. For other clauses of the law see Ernesti's Index Legum, p. xviii.

command; and as the prorogation to the provincial governorships still remained, strictly speaking, in the hands of the Senate, Sulla meant no doubt to make a man feel that he owed his appointment to it, and not to the Assembly. In this then, as in his other laws, it appears that Sulla's chief aim was the rehabilitation of the senatorial authority. But the Senate could not be restored to what it had been; and though Pompey's legislation ten years afterwards did not disturb these particular arrangements, the Senate yet failed to draw any particular advantage from them. In fact the Senate had already practically nullified Sulla's policy and stultified themselves, when seven years earlier they had given Pompey the command against Sertorius, though he had previously held no curule magistracy whatever[1]. In so doing they not only violated Sulla's laws but every rule of the constitution, and had no right to be surprised if the tables were before long turned upon them, and the comitia imitated their own lawlessness. It was not many years before Pompey received, this time from the comitia, the conduct of the Pirate War, and shortly afterwards of the Mithridatic War, in each case with powers which transcended the strict republican limits altogether. The Vatinian Law giving Caesar Gaul for five years, and the Trebonian Law giving Pompey Spain for five years, followed in the same track; and when Pompey further governed Spain from Rome by his legates[2] it became obvious that the foreign conquests had brought a strain to bear upon the constitution which at last destroyed it. *The extraordinary commands.*

Apart from these extraordinary commands, it had already become the custom for the great majority of governors to stay longer than the strict year in their provinces. The Senate did not send them their successors when the year was out, and so they stayed where they were, like soldiers on guard, till relieved. So we find Verres three years in Sicily[3]; Fonteius three years in Gaul[4]; Q. Cicero three years in Asia[5]. In fact, Cicero's *Provincial commands commonly prolonged.*

---

[1] Mommsen, iv. 27.   [2] Plut. Pomp. 53; Mommsen, iv. 311.
[3] Cic. Div. in Caec. 4.   [4] Cic. pro Font. 10.
[5] Ad Qu. Fr. i. 1. Murena was in Asia from 84 to 82 B.C., Lucullus from

example shows that a governor had to take a great deal of trouble not to stay longer than his year in his province; and he was able to leave it when he did, not because a successor was sent him, but by leaving one of his officers as his representative. The simple reason of this state of things was that two consuls and eight praetors were not enough for fourteen provinces[1].

Jobbery practised in regard to such appointments.
The provincial appointments had by this time to a large extent become a matter of intrigue. The legal arrangement was that the Senate should assign what the provinces were to be for a given year, and that then those eligible for such commands should divide them amongst themselves by lot, the consuls casting lots when designate, the praetors while their year of office was going on[2]. But if an ambitious man wanted a particular province, there was a much simpler way of going to work. Lucullus wanted to be appointed to the province of Cilicia. Now the influential tribune of the year was Cethegus; and the person influential with Cethegus was his mistress Praecia. So Lucullus made friends with Praecia, and induced her to use her interest with her lover. She did so; and a law was passed, giving Lucullus what he wanted[3].

Pompey's arrangement of the five years' interval.
The last important law affecting the appointments to the provinces before the *Leges Juliae* was a law of Pompey's, passed in the year 52 B.C., and arranging that provinces should only be given after five years' interval. That is, instead of a man being sent directly to his province after his year of office was over, on the first of the next January, he had to wait five years before becoming eligible[4]. This was primarily intended

---

74 to 66, Servilius Isauricus in Cilicia from 78 to 75; see Marquardt, i. 384, note 5.

[1] Marquardt, i. 385. In B.C. 50 there were five consular provinces—two Gauls, two Spains, and Syria; and nine praetorian. For a list of the latter see Watson, p. 237, note.

[2] In Verr. iv. 95: 'Quas ob res, quid agis, Hortensi? Consul es designatus: provinciam sortitus es.' Marquardt, i. 382.

[3] Plut. Lucull. 6. Cf. Suet. Jul. 11: '*Conciliato populi favore* tentavit per partem tribunorum ut sibi Aegyptus provincia plebiscito daretur.'

[4] Suet. Jul. 28; Dio Cassius, xl. 56; Watson, p. 145.

as a blow against Caesar, as it obviated the difficulty the Senate would otherwise have had in giving him a successor immediately on the expiration of his command, that is on March 1, 49 B.C.; but it also, for the next few years at all events, would enable the Senate to control the provincial appointments pretty much at its pleasure[1].

When Caesar had attained supreme power this law was done away with, though afterwards restored by Augustus[2]. Remembering how his own power had been attained[3], he took care to limit the tenure of a praetorian province to one, of a consular province to two years[4]. Other arrangements of his were to raise the number of praetors to sixteen[5] and of quaestors to forty, half of whom (both praetors and quaestors) were to be nominated by himself. He assigned all the praetorian provinces, the consular ones being still left nominally to the Senate[6]. He could also nominate honorary praetors who would be eligible for provinces; he decided which province should be assigned to whom; and he had the right of recall[7]. Above all, he was probably given proconsular power throughout the whole Empire[8]. The governors were further controlled by the new *legati legionis propraetore*, all of whom he, as imperator, directly appointed[9]. Lastly, to obviate possible opposition from the Senate, its numbers were raised from 600 to 900, the new members being all men devoted to his interests[10].

<small>Caesar's arrangements.</small>

---

[1] Mommsen, iv. 324; Watson, p. 288, *fin*.
[2] Dio Cassius, xlii. 20, liii. 14; Marquardt, i. 382.
[3] This is the way Dio Cassius, xliii. 25, puts it.
[4] Cic. Phil. i. 8, ii. 42, iv. 3, viii. 9; Merivale, i. 392.
[5] At first from 8 to 10; then to 14; afterwards to 16. Dio Cassius, xlii. 50, xliii. 47 and 51; Suet. Jul. 41; Watson, pp. 487, 489.
[6] Dio Cassius, xlii. 20; Watson, p. 488. Of course without sortition.
[7] Mommsen, iv. 480, 534.
[8] Ad Att. ix. 17. § 1; Dio Cassius, xli. 36; Watson, p. 489.
[9] A probable conjecture of Mommsen, iv. 488.
[10] Cic. ad Fam. xiii. 5. § 2; Suet. Jul. 47, 76, 80; Dio Cassius, xliii. 47; Watson, p. 488.

Section II. *The Governor.*

The governor of a Roman province united in his single person civil and military authority. He was commander-in-chief and supreme judge, and (though this was the special business of the quaestor) largely interfered in matters of finance. The special feature of the Roman system was its union in one single head and hand of functions which the modern system takes care to separate. In this way their system produced men of the most extraordinary and varied capacity. The Romans, one would think, expected more from human nature than it could give, but nevertheless they often got what they expected; on the other hand, the strain was too excessive for ordinary men, and tended to put them out of the field. The Romans could not avail themselves of the services of the majority of competent men, who may make good specialists but nothing more, so easily as we can. So a Roman governor was either a wonderful success, or a gigantic failure; and the opportunities of harm possessed by a vicious and incompetent administrator were beyond calculation.

The first business of a Roman governor was to publish his edict. Cicero wrote his at Rome[1]; and it was the custom for it to be made known in the province before the governor entered upon his office. The urban praetors exactly in the same way issued their edict on entering upon their office at Rome: the difference was that at Rome the edict was controlled and had to adapt itself to the body of civil law, of which the Twelve Tables long remained the nucleus; while in the province it was only controlled by the lex provinciae and the local codes, to neither of which unfortunately was the governor absolutely obliged to conform[2]. In theory each new governor might issue a completely new edict; but in practice it was not

---

[1] Cic. ad Fam. iii. 8. § 4.
[2] For the difference between law and edict, see Cic. in Verr. ii. 42; Mommsen, Stadtrechte von Salpensa und Malaga, p. 390 foll.

so, partly because each governor would in this way have given himself a great deal of unnecessary trouble, and partly because by any great innovations he would have been sure to have injured the web of complicated interests in his province, and so have made enemies, and courted an accusation. Great part of the edict was traditional, and passed on from praetor to praetor without change; '*edictum tralaticium*' Cicero calls it[1]; and in this way a regular code of law was built up in the provinces, just as the urban praetors built it up at Rome. The regulations of the lex provinciae would be largely copied into the annual edicts. The Lex Rupilia for instance had allowed each city to use its own laws, at all events in certain cases; and this provision had been regularly copied into edict after edict, and was even, in form, maintained by Verres[2]. In the same way we know from Cicero that it had been one of Aquillius' arrangements that no slave in Sicily should be allowed the use of weapons; and this too was copied in all successive edicts[3]. Moreover these provincial edicts were, as regarded many points of civil law, largely modelled upon the edicts of the urban praetors. As regards the law of inheritance, Cicero informs us that not only previous praetors of Sicily, but even Verres himself, had transferred word for word into their edicts the regulations accustomed to be issued at Rome[4]; and in that famous passage which is the chief source of our knowledge for this subject he says that all points which his edict does not definitely mention, he will settle according to the 'urban edicts[5].' The edict of a particularly good or famous governor would become a model for his successors; we find Cicero for instance largely copying from that of the incorruptible Scaevola[6]. A governor would give some idea of what his government was going to be by the nature of the edict he issued; all edicts for instance would deal largely with the treatment of the publicani, and if the edict unduly and

The governor's edict.

---

[1] Cic. ad Att. v. 21. § 11; ad Fam. iii. 8. § 4.
[2] Cic. in Verrem, iii. 27.   [3] Ib. vi. 3.   [4] Ib. ii. 46.
[5] Cic. ad Att. vi. 1. § 15.   [6] Ib.

E

scandalously favoured them, as did that of Verres[1], the unfortunate provincials would know what to expect. The edict, again, dealt with the whole question of usury and debt; Cicero fixed the rate of interest recoverable under his jurisdiction[2]; and its provisions would therefore largely concern not only the Roman bankers (negotiatores) in the province, but the different towns and states, all of which were as a rule deep in debt to these extortioners. A good governor would insert a clause in his edict to prevent the cities ruining themselves by extravagant expenditure on the complimentary deputations sent to Rome in honour of his predecessor[3]; and above all, nothing would so clearly distinguish a good and liberal governor from one of the opposite character as the amount of independence he left to the cities of his province[4]. Cicero seems to have allowed them an unusual amount of autonomy, while Verres overrode them in every particular[5].

Relation between incoming and outgoing governor. Directly the governor arrived in his province, the former governor, even though still in the country, became by right a private person. He had no authority to do any official act, and Appius' conduct in holding a court of justice after Cicero's arrival was so unusual as to have the character of a slight, which Cicero takes credit to himself for not resenting[6]. The new governor could absolutely change and abolish the old one's acts. Thus Appius complained of the changes introduced by Cicero[7], and Pompey annulled the arrangements of Lucullus[8]. It was a very unheard-of thing for a governor to reverse a judicial decision of his predecessor, but there was nothing positively to prevent it, and Verres in fact did it[9]. The want of continuity thus inherent in the administration was a great evil. That one governor should undo the arrangements of another was satisfactory enough if it was a Cicero undoing the

---

[1] Cic. in Verr. iv. 10; cf. ad Fam. iii. 8. § 4.
[2] Cic. ad Att. vi. 1. § 15.
[3] Cic. ad Fam. iii. 8. § 4.
[4] Cic. ad Att. vi. 1. § 15, v. 21. § 11.
[5] Cic. in Verr. iii. 13.
[6] Cic. ad Att. v. 17; ad Fam. iii. 6 and 8.
[7] Cic. ad Att. vi. 1.
[8] Plut. Lucull. 36.
[9] Cic. in Verr. iii. 28.

arrangements of an Appius; but it was not so satisfactory when the case was reversed; and in any case the uncertainty introduced into life must have been, to the provincials, hateful and mischievous.

The duties of a governor were, as has been already said, partly military and partly civil. It is possible to make out from Cicero's letters how a governor who stayed only the strict year in his province spent his time. Cicero entered his province at Laodicea on July 31, B.C. 51. After spending a few days in hearing complaints and redressing grievances, he proceeded to Iconium, which he reached Aug. 24. There he reviewed the army, and set out at its head southwards, reaching Tarsus Oct. 5. He then immediately set out to chastise the hostile tribes of Mount Amanus, bringing the campaign to a successful conclusion by Dec. 17. After spending the few remaining days of the year at Tarsus he returned to Laodicea on Jan. 5, and administered justice there till May 7. On that day he set out again for Cilicia proper (his province extended far beyond Cilicia), reached Tarsus on June 5, and remained there administering justice and winding up his affairs till July 17. On Aug. 3, B.C. 50, he embarked at Sida in Pamphylia[1].

Distribution of a governor's time.

Whatever may have been the exact parts of the year employed upon the discharge of the different civil and military functions[2], there was, in provinces needing an army, always this double work for the governor to discharge. Caesar in the midst of his dangers and conquests found time to hurry off to Hither Gaul to hold the circuits after each campaign[3]; and his civil appears to have been as successful as his military administration. The weight and authority which the possession of military force in

---

[1] Watson, pp. 147, 151, and his references.

[2] In Sicily the praetors went round their circuits administering justice in the summer, as then the harvest was being got in, all the labourers were at work, and the tax-payers could not conceal their real property (In Verr. vi. 12 and 31). But in less peaceful provinces the summer would commonly be taken up with military operations, and the winter devoted to the administration of justice.

[3] Caes. B. G. i. 54, vi. 44, viii. 4 and 46.

his own person must have given a civil administrator is obvious enough, but that was a doubtful advantage, for the fault of the Roman system was not that the governors had too little authority, but too much.

Military duties.

As commander-in-chief, besides directing the levies[1] and calling out, in case of need, any Roman veterans that might be living in the province[2], the governor had an immense source of influence and could inflict a great deal of misery by the power he possessed of quartering his troops for the winter in any town of the province he pleased. This was what the provincials dreaded more than any other oppression, and they were willing to bribe the governor with a round sum to be exempt from such formidable visitors.

Jurisdiction.

But it was in his capacity as supreme judge that the proconsul must have impressed himself most strongly upon the minds of the provincials. Under the Empire the provinces were regularly divided into *conventus* or districts for judicial purposes, corresponding to our 'circuits.' Thus there were four circuits in Baetica, three in Lusitania. In the republican period the word is hardly yet used in this technical sense, but from the first a certain number of towns were set apart as convenient centres, 'where the praetor was accustomed to make a stay, and hold a court[3].' To these centres the Roman citizens dwelling in the neighbourhood resorted at fixed intervals, so as to form a ready-made body of jurymen, from whom the praetor might appoint fit persons to try the several cases brought before him. It was one of the complaints brought by Cicero against Verres that he repeatedly passed over these capable and respectable persons[4], and appointed judges from his own good-for-nothing retinue. To these centres the cases that had

---

[1] Hirtius, Bell. Alex. 50.   [2] Cic. ad Att. v. 18.
[3] In Verr. vi. 11. § 28 : 'Ex iis oppidis in quibus consistere praetores et conventum agere soleant.' The phrase 'forum agere' is also used in the same sense, Cic. ad Att. v. 16 and 21. § 9, vi. 2.
[4] Cic. in Verr. iii. 13 : 'Selecti e conventu aut praepositi ex negotiatoribus nulli.'

JURISDICTION OF THE GOVERNOR.

arisen in a large surrounding district were brought. Cicero did most of his judicial work at Laodicea, assigning one month to the cases of the district of Cibyra and Apamea, and two months to the cases of Synnada, Pamphylia, Lycaonia, and Isauria[1].

In all cases the praetor presided, except where he delegated his authority to his subordinates, but he was assisted, and no doubt to a certain extent controlled, by his assessors,—always apparently Romans settled in the province[2],—whom he appointed to try the case along with him[3]. There was however nothing to prevent a governor deciding a case simply on his own authority, but it would be an unusual and excessively unpopular proceeding, and even Verres hesitated before he made up his mind to incur the odium of such an act[4]. On this occasion the Roman knight who was counsel for the defendant refused to conduct the case before Verres alone, and indignantly left the court[5].

It must not be supposed that all cases arising in the province came before the praetor. The free and allied towns had their own laws, and lay, by right, wholly outside his jurisdiction. Thus a charge of sacrilege was brought by a Samian against a Chian, and tried by Chians. The number of cases that came before the praetor as compared with those that came before the

---

[1] Cic. ad Att. v. 21. § 9.

[2] In the S. C. giving freedom and immunity to Asclepiades for his services in the war against the pirates, one clause specially privileges him either to be tried by the laws of his own country, or if he preferred it, 'before Roman magistrates, with Italians for judges.' The Latin 'apud magistratus nostros Italicis judicibus' is in part a supplement, but can be taken for certain, as the Greek exists in full :— ἢ ἐπὶ τῶν ἡμετερῶν ἀρχόντων ἐπὶ Ἰταλικῶν κριτῶν. C. I. L. i. p. 110.

[3] A passage of Cicero, ad Att. ii. 16. § 4, looks as if the governor was assisted in his judicial decisions by a body of legal advisers, just as in military matters he commonly asked the advice of his officers. The 'consilium' mentioned in this passage may perhaps be a similar body to that mentioned Pro Balbo, 8 and 17, whose authority was necessary to legalise a general's bestowals of the franchise; see Watson's note to ad Att. ii. 16. § 4. p. 75.

[4] Cic. in Verr. vi. 9.   [5] Ib.

Jurisdiction.

local courts would depend upon the arrangements of the *lex provinciae;* upon the amount of liberty claimed by the towns; and last, but not least, upon the inclination of the governor to respect those liberties. So the people of the little town of Bidis in Sicily had apparently a right to settle legacy cases by their own municipal law, but Verres ignored the right[1]. Another right granted to the Sicilians was that no man should be forced to give security to appear in any court (forum) but that of his own district. It would of course have been ruin to a poor man to have to leave his business, and make a journey, and appear in a court held at the other end of the island. This right too Verres disregarded[2]. In those provinces in which there were numbers of Roman colonies and municipia, the jurisdiction of the governors and of the towns existed side by side, each keeping no doubt within its accurately defined limits. The *lex Rubria,* by which Caesar organised the municipia of Cisalpine Gaul, empowered the municipal magistrates to decide all civil cases where the money involved did not exceed 15,000 sesterces[3]. The *lex Julia Municipalis* contained a similar provision[4], and not improbably allowed the duumviri *criminal* jurisdiction over slaves[5]. This *lex Julia* was probably the norm for the municipal charters of Roman and Latin towns in the provinces; and in the law of Malaga published under Domitian we find the following clause: 'In the case of money demanded in the name of the municipium from any citizen[6] or settler[7], if the sum is not less than 1000 sesterces, and not so great as to [come within the jurisdiction of the proconsul, let the duumvir or prefect decide about it[8]].' It appears then that the more important civil cases and the great mass of the

---

[1] Cic. in Verr. iii. 22, 24, 25.   [2] Ib. iv. 15, 40.
[3] The existing fragments of the *Lex Rubria* are printed; C. I. L. i. p. 115.
[4] This can be made out from § 116 of the law; C. I. L. i. p. 119.
[5] This is a conjecture of Mommsen, but is supported by the analogy of the Pro Cluentio, 64–66.
[6] 'Municeps.'   [7] 'Incola.'
[8] § 69 of the *Lex Malacitana*; C. I. L. i. p. 260. The words in brackets are the certain supplement of Mommsen.

criminal cases would regularly come before the Roman governor, and the minor civil cases, the ordinary law business of daily life, before the duumvirs of the towns of Roman constitution, or the other local magistrates of non-Roman towns; while the difficulties of having two different codes of law existing side by side gradually disappeared, as the provincial towns adopted the Roman law in preference to their own [1], and so paved the way for the bestowal upon them of the regular municipal constitution.

In the performance of his judicial functions the governor was armed with absolute powers. In theory, though no doubt this was much mitigated in practice, the provinces were perpetually under martial law. The governor was, in the first place and before all, commander-in-chief, and the rods and axes which had to be laid down on his return to Rome attended him everywhere throughout his province. So he could punish with imprisonment or death; and no one, unless he were a Roman citizen, would in strictness have a right of appeal. This was perhaps the chief advantage of being a Roman citizen in the provinces, and the one most coveted by the provincials. In civil cases, however, it appears that sometimes a second trial was allowed by a new governor, on security for double the amount at issue being deposited by the appellant [2].

The governor had also large powers in the matter of finance. Finance. It was the quaestor who kept the accounts; but it depended mainly upon the governor whether the sums transmitted to Rome were large or small [3]; and it was in his power to remit [4] and probably to impose taxation. Above all, his dealings with the farmers of the taxes were most important for the welfare or misery of his province. In Cicero's opinion the right manage-

---

[1] Cic pro Balbo, 8; Ortolan's Roman Law, Part I. § 187.
[2] Cic. pro Flacco, 21.
[3] In Sicily, for instance, this would depend upon how the tithes were sold; and the whole of the Verrines shows the influence the governor had in this respect. [4] Cic. in Verr. v. 9; ad Fam. iii. 7.

ment of these gentry was the prime difficulty of a governor. It was dangerous and troublesome to quarrel with them; and on the other hand, if left to their own devices, there was no hope for the provincials[1]. There are indications that Cicero himself was not resolute enough to control them as he should have done[2]; just as he was certainly too indulgent to those other harpies of the provinces, the Roman bankers.

Absolute nature of the governor's authority. The authority possessed by the governor was then, in its reference to the provincials at all events, essentially absolute. It was recognised to be such by the Romans themselves[3]; and the restrictions which they sought to put upon his action shows this in a clear light. It was apparently illegal, or at all events invidious, for a governor to buy anything in his province; and to obviate the necessity of his doing so, he was provided with everything that he could be supposed to want at the public expense[4]. Why was this? 'Because they thought it a theft, not a purchase, when the seller could not sell at his own price. And they knew very well that if a provincial governor wanted to purchase something that was in another man's possession, and was allowed to do so, that it would come to this, that he would get whatever he pleased, whether it was for sale or not,

---

[1] Ad Qu. Fr. i. 1. 13.

[2] Cic. ad Att. vi. 1. § 16; vi. 2 and 3. Such phrases as 'cumulate publicanis satisfactum,' 'publicanis in oculis sumus,' 'publicanos habeo in deliciis' are significant.

[3] Cic. in Verr. iv. 17; ad Qu. Fr. i. 1. 8.

[4] It is commonly said that the governors were not salaried in this period, and in the strict sense they were not. In theory the provincial as the urban magistrates were sufficiently compensated for their labours by the glory of being allowed to serve their country. But besides that they had no expenses of maintenance or travel (Dio Cassius, lii. 15; Cic. in Verr. v. 5, vi. 18 and 32; Mommsen, ii. 338), the sums allowed them for the expenses of the administration were on so lavish a scale that it was easy to save largely out of them, and probably few governors acted like Cicero in refusing to keep what thus remained over, either for himself or his retinue (Cic. ad Att. vii. 1. § 6). The *vasarium* or outfit of Piso, governor of Macedonia, was 18 million sesterces. Cic. in Pis. 35: 'Nonne sestertium centies et octogies, quod, quasi vasarii nomine, in venditione mei capitis ascripseras, ex aerario tibi attributum, Romae in quaestu reliquisti?'

at whatever price he chose to give for it[1].' The same thing is illustrated by the story Cicero tells of the conduct of Lucius Piso, when praetor of Further Spain[2]. He had lost his gold ring; so he sent for a goldsmith, while seated on his tribunal at Corduba, and weighed him out the necessary amount of gold. He then ordered the man to set up his bench in the forum, and there and then make the ring in the presence of every one. This was affectation no doubt, but affectation is not often so significant. The fact is that in his province the governor was a king; the praetor of Sicily indeed lived in Hiero's palace[3]. Cicero takes credit to himself that he did not, like other governors, make difficulties about admitting any one to audience, and employed no chamberlain whose intervention it was first necessary to secure[4]. He speaks exactly as a Louis XIV might have spoken. A formidable and impressive figure must a governor, even a good one, have been to the provincials, holding as he did in his hands the issues of life and death, and all powerful for worldly weal and worldly woe. They familiarised themselves with that austere figure later on, when better protected against its will. They even came close enough to it to discover that if the sword was steel the rest of the figure was sometimes of clay; but they never quite lost the spell, in this period so strong, of the

> Heart-shaking sound of consul Romanus.

SECTION III. *The Governor's Subordinates.*

1. The provincial quaestors were perhaps originally instituted with the idea of lessening the power of the governor by subducting from it all financial functions[5]. In Sicily there were two quaestors, and one in every other province. We do not

---

[1] Cic. in Verr. v. 5. [2] Ib. v. 25. [3] Ib. vi. 12.
[4] Cic ad Att. vi. 2. § 5; cf. ad Qu. Fr. i. 1. 8. § 25.
[5] This is Mommsen's view, ii. 67.

The quaestor.

certainly know their full number before Sulla[1]; but only that he raised it to twenty; and Caesar after him to forty. When the quaestor left Rome he took with him the chest containing the money which was to supply all the expenses of the administration, and into which the taxes of the province were paid: of all these at the end of his term of office he had to render account[2]. He had his own jurisdiction, corresponding to that of the aediles at Rome[3]; or the governor could if he pleased delegate to him his judicial authority. Thus we find young Caesar sent round Baetica by his praetor for the administration of justice[4]. The quaestor also had military duties, partly connected with the levying and equipment of troops[5], and partly with the direct leadership of men, at all events in times of emergency[6]. Cicero left his quaestor as governor of the province, in the interval between his own departure and the arrival of his successor[7]; and under the Empire we find a quaestor governing a province for ten years continuously[8]. The quaestors were not directly appointed by the governors, but assigned to the different provinces by lot[9]. Caesar and Pompey were guilty of a considerable irregularity when they directly appointed their quaestors without the previous observance of this form[10]. Though their appointment was of this fortuitous character, the Romans laid great stress upon the almost paternal relationship which existed or should exist between the quaestor and his superior[11]. This was natural enough, considering that the quaestors were always quite young men at the outset of their career; but it had important practical consequences. It was, for instance, an impossible impiety for a quaestor to give evidence against the consul or praetor under whom he had

---

[1] Mommsen, iii. 360, note, 369, note. Tac., Ann. xi. 22, gives a sort of history of the quaestorship
[2] Cic. in Verr. ii. 14.   [3] Gaius, i. 6; Marquardt, i. 390.
[4] Suet. Jul. 7; Cic. Div. in Caec. 17.   [5] Plut. Sert. 4.
[6] Cic. Phil. x. 6.   [7] Cic. ad Att. vi. 6. § 3.   [8] Suet. Otho, 3.
[9] Marquardt, i. 388, and his authorities.   [10] Cic. ad Att. vi. 6. § 4.
[11] Add to Marquardt's references, Pliny, Epist. iv. 15.

served in a province[1]. At the same time it was expected of him that he should exercise some sort of control upon a tyrannical superior[2]; and the governor was accustomed to take his advice in important matters[3]. On the other hand, his superior could quash a legal decision of his[4], and could even (though this would be an extreme course), if he chose, dismiss him[5].

2. There were, as a rule, three legates in a consular, one in a praetorian province. Their appointment was an indefeasible privilege of the Senate, which could vary their number at pleasure, and in special cases increased it to ten, and even fifteen. The governor would however let the Senate know whom he wished appointed, and as a rule no doubt his request would be complied with. The governor generally proposed relatives or friends for the office; they were his subordinates and he was responsible for them. If they proved incompetent he dropped them; if the contrary, they received a district to look after, with the fasces but without the axe, possessing jurisdiction in civil cases but not in criminal. If a legate won a victory it was the governor who received the credit of it, as the legate could not take his own 'auspices[6].' The harm an ill-disposed legate could do was very considerable; Verres was nearly as mischievous when legate, as he was when praetor[7]; and if the provincials complained, the governor refused to decide the matter himself, as not within his jurisdiction, but referred them to Rome[8].

<small>The legati.</small>

3. The comites were something like our attachés or secretaries of legation, young Romans of birth who were taken into the provinces to learn the business of administration. So Cicero took with him his son, his nephew, and a relation of Atticus. Catullus was a *comes* of C. Memmius in Bithynia. The comites were chosen by the governor, who was responsible for their good behaviour. They were supported at the public

<small>The comites.</small>

---

[1] Cic. Div. in Caec. 18, 19. [2] Ib. 10. [3] Cic. in Verr. vi. 44.
[4] Cic. Div. in Caec. 17. [5] Cic. in Verr. iv. 58.
[6] Summarised from Marquardt, i. 387, and his authorities.
[7] Cic. in Verr. i. 4, ii. 16. [8] Ib. ii. 19.

charge, and their number could be controlled by the Senate[1]. A position as comes gave a man a good opportunity of looking after any property he might possess in the province[2]; or was accepted with the undisguised motive of making a little money. Catullus' object in expatriating himself to Bithynia seems to have been nothing more respectable[3], and Cicero apparently transgressed use and wont when he refused to divide the £8000 saved from the allowance made for administration, among his subordinates[4]. Their influence in the province may be gathered from the epithets applied to them by Horace[5]; and on the other hand from the remark of Cicero, that Verres' retinue did Sicily more harm than would have been done by a hundred troops of fugitive slaves[6].

The prefects.

4. Besides other minor officials, the dragomans, interpreters, bailifs, lictors, architects[7] (meaning rather what we should call engineers), there were also the prefects. Strictly speaking, these were three in number, and all of a military character[8]; but the prefecture, for which Scaptius asked Cicero, and which Cicero refused to give to any Roman negotiator, seems to have had judicial duties connected with it. The L. Volusius whom Cicero sent to Cyprus to administer justice[9] was not a legate, for we know the names of Cicero's four legates from another passage[10], but probably a praefectus, and it was for the post which he held that Scaptius asked. Roman money-lenders asked for these appointments for the sake of the small military force that went with them, and which enabled them to put

---

[1] Marquardt, i. 391, and his authorities.   [2] Cic. pro Caelio, 30.
[3] Catullus, ix. 9. 13, xxviii. 6. 9; Ellis' Commentary, p. l.
[4] Cic. ad Att. vii. 1. 6.
[5] 'Stellasque salubres Appellat comites;' Horace, Sat. i. 7. 24.
[6] Cic. in Verr. iii. 10.
[7] Marquardt, i. 393: also among the attendants of a colonial commission; ibid. 429; see Cic. de Leg. Agr. ii. 12 and 13. Under the Empire, at all events, local talent is used; see Pliny, Epist. x. 49.
[8] Sociorum, castrorum, fabrorum, is Watson's note to Cic. ad Fam. vii. 5. p. 188.
[9] Cic. ad Att. v. 21. § 6.   [10] Cic. ad Fam. xv. 4. § 8.

the screw on procrastinating debtors¹. And no doubt most governors were laxer in giving them than was Cicero.

SECTION IV. *The control of the Governor by the Senate.*

Besides the fact that in the great majority of cases a governor owed his appointment to the Senate, there were a number of ways in which the Senate could control and influence his action. The Senate supplied him with the money for his troops², and it was their decision which settled how large a force his was to be. Cicero, for instance, complained to the Senate of the insufficient number of troops provided him³. A governor was expected to keep up a regular correspondence with the Senate⁴, and was liable to have his policy altered or overridden at their decree⁵. A governor setting out for his province received their definite instructions, especially with regard to the conduct he was to follow with allied states or princes⁶; and on his return had to give in his accounts to the Senate⁷, besides leaving one or more copies in the province⁸. The Senate could also bestow or refuse the coveted honours of the triumph or *supplicatio*⁹; and a governor's arrangements needed their confirmation to be valid¹⁰. Any extraordinary illegality on the part of a governor could be met by their special decree¹¹; and it was not apparently in the power of a governor to make requisitions of ships or money without their consent¹².

Here are the elements of an efficient control; yet in practice

---

¹ Cic. ad Att. v. 21. § 10. Such *praefecti* are of course quite different from the prefects of islands, and other small appointments to which it was not worth while to send a regular governor. These latter were directly appointed by the Senate with full powers. There was, for instance, a praefect of the Balearic Islands; see Mommsen, ii. 74.
² Plut. Pomp. 20.   ³ Cic. ad Fam. xv. 2.   ⁴ Cic. in Pis. 16.
⁵ Cf. Mommsen, ii. 269.
⁶ Caes. B. G. i. 35; Cic. ad Fam. xv. 2. § 4.   ⁷ Cic. in. Pis. 25.
⁸ Cic. ad Att. vi. 7.   ⁹ Cic. de Prov. Cons. 7; in Pis. 19.
¹⁰ Mommsen, iv. 195; Pompey's case.   ¹¹ Cic. in Verrem, iii. 39.
¹² Cic. pro Flacco, 12; Mommsen, ii. 298.

Inefficiency of the senatorial control. the senatorial supervision was absurdly inadequate. The Senate was called to two tasks at once, either of which singly would perhaps have exceeded its powers,—the management namely of the provinces, and the struggle against the democracy. Just when the utmost watchfulness, concentration, and unanimity were needed for foreign affairs, the Senate was distracted and divided by the party politics of Rome. The instinct of self-preservation made her turn chiefly to what seemed most nearly to concern her own welfare; and the reins of empire began to slip from her slackened grasp. The unauthorised raid of Manlius Vulso upon Galatia shows this at an early date; later on comes Gabinius' impudent entry into forbidden Egypt [1]. The magistrates gained steadily upon the Senate. Extraordinary and prolonged commands followed one another in quick succession; and such commanders did not trouble themselves to send in reports or ask advice. Without continuous or efficient control, the administration became a chaos. Cicero complains of 'the neglect of provincial affairs [2];' and in so far as they were attended to, they were made the stalking-horse by which one political party attacked another. To administer rightly the heterogeneous mass of Roman subjects needed unwearied diligence at least, and an organisation in thorough working order. The Senate was too much interested in the other game it had to play to give itself this enormous trouble; and notwithstanding disconnected efforts here and there, the governors were, if they chose, practically exempt from its control.

SECTION V. *The control of the Governor by his Province.*

Apart from the definite protection of the law, it was a great advantage to a provincial to be under the patronage of some powerful Roman. The governor of the province would be careful of injuring persons thus protected: 'the Spanish governors felt that no one could with impunity maltreat the

---

[1] Cic in Pis. 21.   [2] Cic. pro Plancio, 26.

clients of Cato[1].' It was a common thing for whole peoples Patrons and clients.
to become the clients of the Roman generals who had first
conquered them[2]. Thus we find a Fabius patron of the Allobroges[3]; the Marcelli of Sicily[4]; and the elder Cato of Spain[5].
This patronate was often hereditary; it was so for instance in
the case of the Marcelli, the Fabii, and the Minucii[6]; and in
the inscriptions recording the clientship of towns or individuals
the relationship is often acknowledged on both sides as valid
for their posterity[7]. The duty of a patron to his clients was
recognised as clearly as in the old days when both patron and
client were Romans[8]. In particular a patron was expected to
further his client's interests, if any business, legal or other,
brought the latter to Rome. The patron of a provincial town
was anxious to secure its advantage[9]; and the tie must have
been a close and real one if Bononia was specially thanked by
Octavian for joining with the rest of Italy to take his side in the
civil war, regardless of the hereditary clientship between itself
and the Antonii[10].

But the protection of the patronate was shadowy and unsub- The Roman franchise.
stantial compared with the privileges attached to the possession
of the Roman citizenship. The martial law under which all
other provincials lay, did not apply to him who could say with

---

[1] Mommsen, ii. 339.

[2] Cic. de Off. i. 11. § 35: 'Ut ii qui civitates aut nationes devictas bello in fidem recepissent, eorum patroni essent more majorum.' Mommsen, Römische Forschungen, p. 361.

[3] Appian, B. C. ii. 4; Merivale, i. 216.

[4] Liv. xxvi. 32; Cic. in Verr. ii. 49.

[5] Cic. Div. in Caec. 20. Under the Empire we find a patron of Narbonensis, Henzen, 6954; Britain, Orelli, 366; not to mention others. Caesar had been patron of Baetica.

[6] Minucius Rufus is mentioned as patron of the Ligurians; C. I. L. i. p. 73. no 199; a position he owed to his father having conquered the country.

[7] Cic. pro Flacco, 22; in Verr. v. 41. The common form in the inscriptions is, 'eum cum liberis posterisque suis patronum cooptaverunt' ... 'liberos posterosque eorum in fidem clientelamque suam recepit.'

[8] Cic. in Verrem, iii. 47; Plin. Ep. iii. 4.

[9] Cic. ad Fam. xiii. 64.   [10] Suet. Aug. 17.

St. Paul 'I am a Roman.' At least four laws were passed to secure Roman citizens from the rods and axes of the magistrate[1]; and a lex Julia of B.C. 8 punished the magistrate guilty of putting to death, torturing, flogging or imprisoning a Roman citizen who had appealed, by outlawry, or, in other words, 'interdiction from fire and water[2].' Only a Roman citizen could appeal against a decision of the governor[3]; and the trial of Rabirius and the banishment of Cicero made it evident that not even a consul, acting with the authority of the Senate, could put a citizen to death without trial. It was a minor advantage that the harbour or octroi duties levied by a free town were not paid by Roman citizens[4]; and that they had the almost exclusive right to serve on provincial juries. The flagrant violation of all these rights by Verres is in Cicero's eyes perhaps his most atrocious crime, as it would be the one which would most surely rouse the indignation of the people of Rome. Cicero says that wars have been waged (as we waged our little war with Abyssinia) 'because Roman citizens were said to have been ill-used, or Roman vessels detained, or Roman merchants robbed[5];' and his indignation becomes scathing and terrible, as he relates how Roman citizens had been tortured, executed, even crucified by the orders of a Roman governor.

Unfortunately, though the whole of Italy gained the franchise in this period, it gained it not otherwise than at the sword's point; and this great concession was not, for a long time, followed by similar indulgences to the provincials. Individuals here and there who had done Rome notable services were rewarded with the franchise all through this period; but Caesar was the first Roman statesman who bestowed it upon whole provinces. It was generally bestowed for military services.

---

[1] A *lex Valeria* and three *leges Porciae*; C. I. L. i. p. 71: also, apparently, a Sempronian Law; Cic. in Verr. vi. 63.

[2] This was the crime of 'vis publica,' mentioned by Tac. Ann. iv. 13; see Church and Brodribb's note, p. 346.

[3] Marquardt, i. 396, and his authorities.

[4] Marquardt, ii. 263.   [5] Cic. in Verr. vi. 58.

Marius for instance, who was perhaps the first Roman general to give it without direct senatorial authority, rewarded his Gallic soldiers with it after Vercellae. Sulla seems to have been liberal in this respect[1]; and Pompey claimed the acknowledged right of a Roman general to make it the reward of loyal service. The oration delivered by Cicero for Cornelius Balbus, as also that for the poet Archias, turns upon this question of the franchise. Apparently the claim of a general to bestow it, unless he was specially authorised by a previous law[2], was in strictness invalid, and actions might be brought against the enfranchised person. But Cicero does not hesitate to assert that 'no one ever lost his action who was proved to have been presented with the franchise by any one of our generals[3].' The advantages to Rome of being able to reward distinguished military service by so coveted a prize, are too obvious to need recommendation by the eloquence of Cicero[4]; more remarkable is the fact of its being made the reward for an accuser who had secured a conviction for extortion[5]. But Julius Caesar after all was the first to give it with a liberal hand. He enfranchised the soldiers of his Alaudæ legion[6]; and, if Antony may be trusted, intended to give Sicily at all events the Latin right[7]. He also encouraged learning by enfranchising 'all professors of medicine at Rome, and all teachers of liberal knowledge[8].' If this policy had been begun earlier, and carried out boldly by a succession of statesmen, some of the worst miseries under which the provincials in this period laboured would probably have been averted.

The provincial deputations so frequently mentioned in Cicero do not seem to have been of much consequence, unless they came for the express purpose of setting the law in motion against a governor. In one case we find it mentioned that a

Provincial deputations.

---

[1] Cic. pro Scauro, *passim*; in Verr. v. 17. [2] Cic. pro Balbo, 8.
[3] Ibid. 23. [4] Ibid. 9, 13, and 21.
[5] Ibid. 13 and 22. This was a provision of the severe Lex Servilia.
[6] Suet. Jul. 24.
[7] Cic. ad Att. xiv. 12; Phil. i. 10; Merivale, ii. 394. [8] Suet. Jul. 42.

provincial deputation, sent for a quite different purpose, had attended to the courts and there supported by their presence a former quaestor of the province who was undergoing trial[1]. But such cases must have been rare; and in any case it does not appear that such demonstrations, even if permitted, could have been of practical assistance. Equally futile but more humiliating were the *encomia* which a province was wont to send after its governor, on his leaving the province. These were most eagerly sought for, perhaps most punctiliously exacted by the worst governors. Appius had his from the Cilicia which he had 'plundered and all but ruined[2];' and even Verres received one from Syracuse. The Senate knew very well what these forced praises were worth, and, Cicero hints, paid very little attention to the deputies who brought them[3].

<small>Leges Repetundarum.</small>

But if the laws had only been carried out, there would have been little need of anything else to protect the provinces. From an early date there had been laws passed against extortion, and in these there was no lack of severity. The first of them was the Calpurnian Law passed in the year B.C. 149. 'Lucius Piso, tribune of the plebs, was the first to pass a law about extortion,' is Cicero's account[4]. 'The avarice of the magistrates gave birth to the Calpurnian laws,' says Tacitus[5]. The *Lex Junia*, which followed, passed between B.C. 149 and 124, is only known by its being mentioned in the *Lex Acilia*. This latter law, passed probably in the year B.C. 125, is more than once noticed by Cicero as having been exceptionally severe, and is probably the law of which considerable fragments still remain to us. Next followed the *Lex Servilia* of B.C. 111. Under this law were the two infamous accusations of Scaurus and Rutilius, the knights being then in possession of the juries. One of its provisions was that curious one already mentioned, that an accuser who secured a conviction should be rewarded with the Roman franchise. Sulla B.C. 79 passed a law dealing

---

[1] Cic. pro Plancio, 11.   [2] Cic. ad Att. v. 15.   [3] Cic. ad Fam. iii. 8.
[4] Cic. Brutus, 27.   [5] Tac. Ann. xv. 20.

with the secases, but nothing is known of its contents except what may be indirectly gathered from the notices we possess of the later Julian law. This *Lex Julia* clearly laid down what requisitions a governor might make upon his province. He could claim wood, salt and hay, besides shelter, when travelling, but was required to pay for everything else [1]. It also followed the Servilian and Cornelian laws in ordaining that if the accused could not upon condemnation restore what he had extorted, those who had received any part of the proceeds from him might be prosecuted for it [2]. It also expressly forbade provincial governors to leave their province to enter a neighbouring kingdom, unless specially authorised by the home government; doubtless with a view of preventing such excursions as that of Gabinius into Egypt [3]. It seems to have been full of excellent provisions, and still stricter than any of the previous laws on the same class of offences [4].

But it is possible to go more into detail than this. We possess a good part of the *Lex Acilia*, from which at all events the following points can be made out:—

The persons liable to accusation are these—dictator, consul, praetor, master of the horse, censor, aedile, tribune of the plebs, quaestor, *triumvir capitalis*, *triumvir agris dandis assignandis*, tribune of the soldiers [5]. None of these could be accused while their term of office lasted. An accuser could ask the praetor for a lawyer to plead his case, and could refuse the lawyer offered. The necessary 650 jurymen were to be chosen by the *praetor peregrinus* within ten days after the passing of the law. They had to be of not less census than 400,000 sesterces. No one who was or had been tribune of the plebs, quaestor, *triumvir capitalis*, tribune of the soldiers, to be chosen;

---

[1] Cic. ad Att. v. 16; Watson, p. 225.   [2] Cic. pro Rabirio Postumo, 4.
[3] Cic. in Pis. 21.
[4] Cic. pro Rab. Post. 4. A list of these laws in chronological order is given by Mommsen, C. I. L. i. p. 54.
[5] Equites therefore were not liable; cf. Cic. pro Rab. Post. 5.

no present or past senator[1]; no gladiator, actor or convict; no one under thirty or over sixty years of age; no one living more than a mile outside Rome; no father, brother, or son of one of the above-named magistrates, or of a senator. Twenty days after the accuser had given in the name to the praetor, one hundred were to be chosen by the praetor out of the 650 jurymen. No relation of the accused was allowed to be on the bench; and the praetor had to swear that he had chosen no man with any sinister motive. Then the praetor was to tell the accused that he might pick fifty out of the hundred jurymen; and if the accused did not avail himself of this privilege the accuser might do so. The jury were to be told to estimate the damages; which went on the principle of restoring the same amount as had been extorted, if extorted *before* this law; but if *after* this law, a double amount. The money was to be got out of the man's goods or his bail, and lodged by the quaestor in the treasury, and then if claimed, paid over to the persons injured[2]. If not claimed within five years, the money was to remain in the treasury. The accuser, or that one of the accusers who was considered by the jury to have done most to secure the condemnation, was to be made a Roman citizen, he and his sons, and lineal posterity; and to be incorporated in the tribe to which the condemned man had belonged. If such an accuser did not care to accept the franchise, still the right of appeal was to be given him, just as if he had been a citizen.

---

[1] 'Quive in senatu siet fueritve.'

[2] The essence of these suits, as their name (*de repetundis*) denotes, lay in the restitution of wrongfully acquired property. In the trial of Verres the damages were laid at one hundred million sesterces (Cic. div. in Caec. 5); in that of C. Cato at only 18,000 sesterces (in Verr. v. 10); in that of Dolabella at three million sesterces (Cic. in Verr. ii. 3 and 38). Even when quadruple of the original exaction was paid, Zumpt—de legibus judiciisque repetundarum, Berlin, 1847—thinks, and it is probable enough, that the whole sum was paid over to the provincials to make up for the great expenses of a prosecution; cf. Tac. Ann. iv. 20; Plin. Ep. iii. 9; Cic. in Verr. ii. 3, v. 8.

Exceptional difficulties might no doubt now and then be put in the way of provincials desirous to avail themselves of these laws[1]; and it is possible that none but very bad cases of extortion were tried under them; but it cannot be said that on the whole the task of the accuser was rendered unduly difficult. On the contrary, any possible trouble or danger of the provincials were lightened if not removed by the practice which Cicero[2], Tacitus[3] and Plutarch[4] notice of young Romans making their début in public life by one of these accusations. When Cicero is defending a provincial governor thus accused, he hints pretty openly that the accuser's motive was often nothing better than mere notoriety; and if the zeal shown in such cases was often as excessive as that which he ascribes to the accuser of Flaccus[5], the suggestion was probably a well-grounded one. If an accuser wished to secure conviction, he visited the province in person, and went about from town to town collecting evidence[6]. He was armed apparently with special powers, could subpœna any one to attend at the trial and give evidence, and if difficulties were made about the production of any municipal document could positively insist upon its being shown to him[7].

Facilities allowed to an accuser.

But though the laws were good enough, and though there was superabundant machinery to keep them effective, they yet in fact accomplished little or nothing. The reason of this was that the struggle of parties going on all during this period was fought out in the domain of the law-courts; the *judicia* were coveted as an instrument of political power. The original arrangement was that the Senate supplied the judges for the courts, and that therefore a senator on his return from his province was, if accused, brought to trial before fellow-senators most of whom would in their turn some day command a province, and would then perhaps need for themselves the

Political importance of the judicia.

---

[1] Cic. in Verrem, iii. 4, 27.
[2] Cic. pro Caelio, 30.
[3] Tac. de Orat. 43, fin.
[4] Plut. Lucull. 3.
[5] Cic. pro Flacco, 5, 8, 15.
[6] Ibid.
[7] Cic. in Verr. v. 66.

indulgence which their friend expected of them. Caius Gracchus, casting about for a weapon against the Senate, saw that he could wound them most effectually through the law-courts. He therefore passed a law to transfer the *judicia* from the Senate to the Knights. In the fifty years between Gracchus' legislation and that of Sulla several attempts were made to admit the Senate at all events to an equal share of these privileges, but without effect[1]. Sulla summarily deprived the equites of all judicial authority whatever, and transferred it wholly to the Senate (B.C. 81). This only lasted a decade; and then Pompey had the *Lex Aurelia* (B.C. 70) passed, which divided the whole body of jurymen between senators, knights, and *tribuni aerarii*. Lastly, Caesar (B.C. 46) excluded this third class, and divided the appointments equally between the Senate and the Knights [2].

The Senators and equites as judges compared.

It is obvious that in these changes the interest of the provincials was not the main object in view. It is difficult to say whether they suffered most when the Knights were judges alone or when the senators alone. Cicero claims a decided superiority for the decisions of the Knights, and contrasts their incorruptibility with the shameless venality of the Senate[3]. It is very possible that they were less accessible to bribes; but that did not of necessity make their hold of the courts an advantage to the provincials. These latter only exchanged the whips of the governor for the scorpions of the publicani. *Publicanus* and *eques* are in fact identical terms; and as long as the governor let the farmers of the taxes do exactly what they wanted, there was no fear of his being condemned on his return. On the other hand, if a governor endeavoured to

---

[1] A *Lex Servilia* of this period divided them between both orders, but was either not passed, or soon abrogated; Mommsen, iii. 135. Drusus contemplated a law to the same effect.

[2] Augustus restored the trib. aerarii, and added a fourth decury; Caligula added a fifth.

[3] Pseudo-Ascon. in Caec. Divin. 8 says the Knights were better than the Senators; Appian, B. C. i. 22, says they were not; see Merivale, i. 63.

protect the unfortunate provincials against their oppressors, he exposed himself to great danger. One of the best governors the province of Asia ever had, Rutilius Rufus, was condemned and banished *for extortion;* and Lucullus lost his command through similar endeavours to control them.

Perhaps however the ten years' exclusive possession of the courts by the Senate after Sulla's and before Pompey's legislation were the black-letter years of the provinces. In these ten years fall the trials of Cn. Dolabella, C. Antonius, and Verres. The trial of the latter was perhaps one of the immediate causes which brought about the *Lex Aurelia*[1]; and it is possible that Cicero, when he published the five orations against Verres which he had *not spoken*, had this result in view[2].

Section VI. *The condition of the Provinces.*

'All the provinces are mourning, all the free peoples are complaining; all kingdoms remonstrate with us for our covetousness and our wrong-doing; on this side of the ocean there is no spot so distant or so remote that in these latter times the lust and wickedness of our countrymen have not penetrated to it. The Roman people can no longer withstand, I do not say the violence, the arms, the warfare of all nations, but their complaints, their lamentations, and their tears.' Such is the picture given by a Roman of one period of the Roman rule[3]. But they are the words of a great rhetorician on a great occasion, and it may be doubted how far they represent the literal truth. Unhappily there is too much definite evidence to leave any doubt, and other strong passages of the same author, where there can be no question of deliberate rhetoric, point in the same direction. When Cicero says that the 'mildness and self-denial' which he showed in Cilicia seemed 'incredible' to

---

[1] Watson, p. 5. [2] Cf. Cic. in Verr. i. 13. 15.
[3] Cic. in Verr. iv. 87; cf. pro lege Manilia, 22: 'Difficile est dictu, Quirites, quanto in odio simus apud exteras nationes propter eorum, quos ad eas per hos annos cum imperio misimus, injurias ac libibines.'

the provincials¹, he indirectly passes the worst condemnation on the Roman rule. In the same spirit is that passage of his letter to his brother Quintus in which he speaks of the cities receiving in him 'a guardian, not a tyrant,' the households 'a guest and not a pillager².' Even in writing a formal letter to the Senate, where, if anywhere, one might suppose unpleasant truths would be kept out of sight, Cicero speaks casually and by the way of the 'harshness and injustice of our rule³.'

Deterioration of the Roman rule.

There was, if Cicero may be trusted, a regular deterioration visible in this rule. It was much better in the earlier years of foreign dominion than it was in his own generation⁴. The praises which Polybios gives to the incorruptibility of the first Roman governors of Greece confirm his view⁵; and it was very natural that the Romans should take some little time to be wholly corrupted by the seductive influences of absolute power and easily-acquired riches⁶. But from the first, if we except perhaps the philhellene tendencies which made educated Romans look tenderly upon Greece, there was little or no idea that Rome had duties to the provincials as well as rights. If a governor spared them, it was more often from his self-respect and feeling of what was due to his own dignity and character

Roman theory of their rule.

than from humanity. The theory of the Romans as to the provinces was that they were the 'estates of the Roman people⁷.' Their importance for the State lay wholly in the revenues derived from them. So the well-being of the inhabitants, except so far as it affected their tax-paying power, was not of much consequence; but the well-being of the land was

---

¹ Cic. ad Att. v. 18: 'Quibus incredibilis videtur et nostra mansuetudo et abstinentia.'

² Cic. ad Qu. Fr. i. 1. 2: 'Quum urbs custodem non tyrannum, domus hospitem non expilatorem recepisse videatur.'

³ Cic. ad Fam. xv. 1: 'Acerbitatem atque injurias imperii nostri.'

⁴ Cic. in Verr. ii. 22.

⁵ Polybios, vi. 56. 13; Finlay, i. 24; Mommsen, ii. 298, 330.

⁶ Tac., Ann. ii. 54, states with force the view as to the corruption of the Roman character by foreign conquest.

⁷ 'Praedia populi Romani;' Cic. in Verr. iii. 3.

of the greatest. To this was in part due the special attention paid by the Romans to tillage, to the building and maintenance of roads, and to the establishment of commercial centres. To pretend, as Cicero[1] does, that the motive of the Romans was humanity was nonsense; but if the former motive, however selfish[2], had been kept steadily in view, the provinces would have been well off[3]. It would be a great mistake to suppose that the misgovernment of the provinces was regarded with toleration either by public opinion or by the law. Unfortunately the men whose collective opinion was so meritorious, were not equally sound as individuals. The temptations were too strong and the control too imperfect for the average man not to yield to the one and to take advantage of the other.

The governor as possessing the most power with the least responsibility had it in his power to inflict the greatest amount of misery. The jobbery connected with the appointments told severely in the last resort upon the provinces. If a man paid heavily to get his province, he expected to recoup himself during his administration of it. But then he could not do that without exposing himself to a trial for extortion. The judges however on such trials were not above a liberal bribe: all that was necessary therefore was to make enough out of the province to have something to offer to them. Verres ruled Sicily for three years; and according to Cicero he boasted that the gains of the first year would be enough for himself, those of the second year for his friends and patrons, those of the third year, which was the most productive of all, for the judges[4]. So these trials were turned from a defence of the provincials into their worst scourge; and Cicero says that he expects deputations to the Senate to beg for their abolition[5]. In any case it

Miseries inflicted by the governor.

---

[1] Cic. div. in Caec. 5; in Verr. vi. 44.
[2] Passages which illustrate the selfishness of the motive are—Cic. in Verr. iv. 50 and 55; Pro lege Manilia, 6; De Leg. Agr. ii. 30, where Cicero shows that the tribute always ceased with war or other disturbance.
[3] See Marquardt, i. 398.
[4] Cic. in Verr. i. 14; cf. iv. 19, sub fin. [5] Cic. in Verr. i. 14.

was well understood that a man did not expatriate himself from the pleasures of Rome for nothing[1]: to get a province was the recognised means of setting a bankrupt on his legs again[2]. So regular were the extortions of the governor, that when Cicero was eccentric enough to abstain from them, the grateful people of Salamis told him that they had been able to pay their debts with 'the praetor's fund[3],' with the money, that is to say, which had hitherto been yearly laid aside to conciliate their master's good-will. And even if the governor was himself well-intentioned, it was very difficult for him to resist the importunities of his dependents and acquaintances. The comites for instance came to the province to make money, and would regard any unusual rectitude or honesty in the governor as an eccentricity mischievous to their interests. Besides this he was continually being pestered by the letters of influential Romans, begging him to get in a debt for them, or to send them wild beasts for the shows[4], or to exempt some lands of theirs in the country from the municipal taxes[5]. It seemed as if a governor was sent to a province not in the interests of the State, but to carry out the wishes of a pack of spendthrifts and usurers.

Progresses. If we wish to go more into details, the varieties of ill-usage endured by the provincials are so numerous as to be embarrassing. Even when on his way to his province, and before he had yet actually reached it, a Roman governor might be if he chose a burden to the cities through which he passed. Some of Verres' worst enormities were perpetrated in Achaia[6], though he was merely passing through that country on his way to Cilicia: and the immense credit which Cicero takes to himself for demanding little or nothing from the places through which he passed on his way to his province would be

---

[1] Apparently the Romans regarded a provincial command as a great nuisance. 'Hujus molestiae' is the phrase used by Cicero in writing to his brother (ad Qu. Fr., i. 1. 1); and when Cicero was himself in Cilicia, he was always longing to be back in Rome again.
[2] Cic. in Pis. 6. [3] Cic. ad Att. v. 21: 'In vectigali praetorio.'
[4] Cic. ad Fam. viii. 4, 6. [5] Ib. viii. 9. [6] Cic. in Verr. ii. 17.

by itself a proof that other governors did not observe a similar moderation [1].

But it was not only the governor and his staff who had the right to claim lodging and entertainment without paying for it. If a senator could get a *legatio libera* granted him by his fellow-senators, he could travel in the provinces in this way, armed with the authority of a regular legate, though without either duties or responsibilities, and for as long a time as suited his convenience. Money-lending, and in fact all business, being of a personal character, and almost always managed directly by the principals, it was a common thing for a senator to get one of these lieutenancies given him in order to hunt up a debtor [2] or a legacy [3] in some distant province. That these persons abused their authority, and were burdensome and almost intolerable to the provincials, is expressly told us by Cicero [4]. Cicero himself did his best to put an end to so disgraceful an anomaly, and would have had a *senatus consultum* passed for their total abolition, if a tribune had not interposed his veto. So he contented himself with limiting their duration to one year [5], a period which Caesar afterwards extended to five [6]. It was one of the benefits of the Empire that it got rid of these vexatious and harassing appointments [7].

<small>Legationes Liberae.</small>

Somewhat analogous but far worse mischiefs were caused by the billeting of troops in this or that city of a province for winter quarters. In his speech for the Manilian law Cicero doubts whether more cities of the enemy have in late years been destroyed by arms, than friendly states by this system of

<small>Quartering of troops.</small>

---

[1] Cic. ad Att. v. 10, 16, 21. For the billeting of the governor, &c. on a journey within his province, see Cic. in Verr. ii. 24, 25.

[2] Cic. pro Flacco, 34.   [3] Cic. de Lege Agr. i. 3. § 8.

[4] De Lege Agr. i. 3: 'Hereditatum obeundarum causâ, quibus vos legationes dedistis, qui et privati et ad privatum negotium exierunt, non maximis opibus neque summâ auctoritate praediti, tamen auditis profecto quam graves eorum adventus sociis vestris esse soleant.' Cf. de Lege Agr. ii. 17.

[5] Cic. de Legg. iii. 8.   [6] Cic. ad Att. xv. 11.

[7] See also Mommsen, iv. 158; Marquardt, i. 418.

quartering¹. It is one of the special praises which Plutarch gives Lucullus, that he never once quartered his troops upon a friendly Greek city²; whereof, he adds, the soldiers much complained. Sertorius won the hearts of the Spaniards by not quartering his troops upon them³; and when Caesar did so, he did it avowedly to punish a town⁴ or to bribe his men⁵. It can easily be imagined what misery and shame might be inflicted by the excesses of a rough soldiery, bent upon making up for the fatigues of the campaign by a winter of idleness and debauch. In a law giving freedom to the people of Thermessus in Pisidia, one of the provisions is that no Roman governor shall be allowed to quarter troops upon them except by special authority of the Senate⁶; and rich towns in the province of Cilicia (and no doubt also in other provinces) regularly paid the governor large sums to be excused this terrible visitation. The people of Cyprus, for instance, paid 200 Attic talents (nearly £50,000)⁷.

Other petty oppressions. The petty oppressions of different kinds which the governor had it in his power to inflict were innumerable. It was apparently the practice in certain provinces to make requisitions of wild beasts for the Roman shows; and the natives could be set to a compulsory hunt after them⁸. Still worse was the

---

¹ Cic. pro Lege Manilia, 13. ² Plut. Lucull. 33.
³ Plut. Sert. 6; and for the insolence of the soldiers quartered at Castulo, ib. 3.
⁴ Caesar, Bell. Civ. ii. 18. ⁵ Ibid. 31.
⁶ C. I. L. i. p. 114. No. 204: 'Nei quis magistratus prove magistratu legatus neive quis alius milites in oppidum Thermessum majorum Pisidarum agrum Thermensium majorum Pisidarum hiemandi causa introducito, neive facito quo quis eo milites introducat quove ibi milites hiement, nisei senatus nominatim utei Thermessum majorum Pisidarum in hibernacula milites deducantur decreverit.'
⁷ Cic. ad Att. v. 21. § 7. Plutarch, Sert. 24, speaks of Asia as βαρυνομένην δὲ ταῖς πλεονεξίαις καὶ ὑπερηφανίαις τῶν ἐπισκηνῶν.
⁸ Cic. ad Att. vi. 1. § 20; ad Fam. viii. 9. In the long run the beasts were almost exterminated, and districts rendered habitable which would otherwise have been too dangerous; cf. Strabo, xvii. 3. § 15; Mon. Anc. § 22. Augustus accounted for 3500 African wild beasts; Titus showed 5000 beasts in one day; Suet. Tit. 7; cf. Spartian, Hadr. 7 and 19.

common exaction of money from the cities under pretence of its being a voluntary contribution towards the expenses of the aedile at Rome. This is probably the purpose for which Caelius begs Cicero to get him a sum of money out of the cities of his province[1]. These contributions were so regular a thing that they had a technical name (*aurum aedilicium*). Cicero speaks of them as a 'severe and iniquitous tax[2];' and if we may argue from one known case, as much as 200,000 sesterces was got out of the cities of a single province as their contribution to the pleasures of the sovereign people[3]. Perhaps still more vexatious were the expenses incurred by the cities on temples, statues, commemoratory festivals in honour perhaps of an infamous scoundrel who had fattened upon their miseries[4]. The deputations to Rome to sing the praises of such a governor were another source of expense which an honest man like Cicero would either abolish or greatly curtail, even at the risk of offending his predecessor[5]. Then there were the 'compliments,' in reality compulsory presents, to the governor on the occasion of the valuing of the corn which a province had to supply[6]; and the numberless opportunities of extortion which a governor possessed in virtue of his supreme authority over the taxation.

But the collectors of the taxes were more formidable even than the governor. The system of middle-men which the Romans had adopted saved trouble in the administration no doubt, but at a terrible expense to the provincials. In some provinces, for instance Spain, fixed payments had been introduced immediately upon conquest; and for these therefore no middle-men were necessary. But in others, such as Sicily, Sardinia, and Asia, the chief tax was not a fixed one, but consisted in a tithe of the annual produce. So there were, of

The Publicani.

---

[1] Cic. ad Att. vi. 1. § 20.
[2] 'Gravi et iniquo aediliciorum vectigali;' Cic. ad Qu. Fr. i. 1. 9. § 26.
[3] Cic. ibid.; cf. Mommsen, ii. 338.
[4] There was a festival called *Verrea* in Sicily; Cic. in Verr. iii. 63.
[5] Cic. ad Fam. iii. 8. § 2.   [6] Cic. in Verr. iv. 38, 42; in Pis. 35.

course, variations in its amount; and it seemed simpler and more convenient that the administration should be assured of a definite sum beforehand without being dependent upon the goodness or badness of the harvests. So it was the practice to let out such taxes to a society of rich men, perhaps invariably Roman knights, for a period of five years. Such a society then paid over the lump sum at which the taxes had been let out to it, and sent some of its members to the province to act the part of tax-gatherers. If the harvests were good during the period they would gain largely on their original payments; if they were bad they would nominally lose. Such contracts were therefore of a speculative character; and indeed Mommsen regards the publicani as corresponding to the stock-brokers (*Börsenspeculanten*) of a modern capital. But as a matter of fact they secured themselves with tolerable certainty against losses, at the expense of the tax-payers. Their power in the provinces was so great that even Cicero hints to his brother Quintus to advise the provincials not to insist too rigorously upon their legal rights against them, lest worse should befall them[1]. It is only too probable that they habitually and as a matter of course exacted more than their due[2]; and the control of the governor, who alone had authority over them[3], was wholly inefficient. If a governor kept them to their legal right their hatred to him knew no bounds[4]; and they could be exceedingly dangerous to him, particularly when the *Judicia* were in their hands, on his return to Rome. Lucullus owed his recall to their determined ill-will; and Rutilius his banishment. So most governors acted like Verres, and shared the plunder with them. The law expressly forbade any governor to invest money in their societies; but Verres did so[5]; and

---

[1] Cic. ad Qu. Fr. i. 1. 12.
[2] Cf. Appian, B. C. v. 4: Τῶν δὲ ταῦτα παρὰ τῆς βουλῆς μισθουμένων ἐνυβριζόντων ὑμῖν καὶ πολὺ πλείονα αἰτούντων; St. Luke iii. 13.
[3] Verres threatened to make them pay eight-fold if they exacted more than their due; In Verr. iv. 8, 10, 21, 47.
[4] Cic. pro Plancio, 13, illustrates this in the case of Scaevola.
[5] Cic. in Verr. iv. 56.

even if the law was not thus impudently broken, the vast majority of governors were shamefully subservient to them[1]. The governor could do a great deal for them by forcing the cities of his province to pay up their arrears[2]; or by supporting them with military force[3]; and in the exceptional cases in which a governor from good or bad motives was unfriendly to their interests, he could apparently do them a good deal of mischief[4]. If a debtor could not or would not pay, they had legal power to put in their claim and take temporary possession of his property[5]; and, it is hinted, the actual measures they took were often far more violent and summary than this[6]. Besides the tithes, the customs' duties were regularly farmed to these middle-men, even in countries where all the other taxes were got in by the direct system. Such dues were paid in the Italian harbours till far down in the life of Cicero, and were regularly collected by the publicani who had contracted for them. The complaints of their rapacity were great even in privileged Italy, and Cicero says he can 'imagine what is the fate of the allies in remote provinces when even in Italy I hear the complaints of Roman citizens[7].' They had the right of search[8]; and were in fact custom-house officers, the difference being that they were considerably stricter and more arbitrary than is possible for such officials now. Their interests were so much more directly involved, that this is not at all surprising.

The miseries which the publicani inflicted might be gathered from the bitter hatred which was felt for them[9]. When Cicero wishes to give his hearers a strong impression of the loyalty and

---

[1] Cic. in Verr. iv. 41.
[2] Cic. ad Fam. ii. 13; ad Att. vi. 2. § 5; pro Plancio, 26. We find even Cicero condescending to apply to provincial governors, who were friends of his, to further their interests; ad Fam xiii. 9, 65.
[3] Cicero, de Prov. Cons. 5, speaks of garrisons for their protection.
[4] Cic. in Pis. 17. One could almost forgive Piso his other sins for this!
[5] Cic. in Verr. iv. 11.   [6] Ibid.   [7] Cic. ad Qu. Fr. i. 1. 13.
[8] Cic. de Leg. Agr. ii. 23; Marquardt. ii. 262, and his authorities.
[9] If direct evidence is wanted, see Plut. Lucull. 7.

friendliness of the Sicilians, he tells them that 'they are so fond of our nation that they are the only people where neither a publican nor a money-lender is an object of detestation[1].' The Romans fully allowed that this hatred was deserved. Livy tells us that the Senate actually gave up the working of some mines in Macedonia and other lands which brought in a great revenue, 'because they could not be managed without the publicani, and wheresoever there was a publican, there either the law was a dead letter, or the allies were no better than slaves.'

The Negotiatores. The *negotiatores* or money-lenders were the complement of the publicani. They were often knights like them[2]; and held a similar, perhaps slightly inferior, social position. They could not be senators, as the law expressly forbade senators to engage in such business[3]; but were often the agents of senators who stayed at Rome and pocketed the profits of their shameful trade. That they were not looked down upon by public opinion is shown by a passage in which Cicero describes how a negotiator in Sicily was accustomed to entertain the governor and other officials of the province, apparently almost on a footing of equality[4]. They were in fact as a rule those knights or moneyed men for whom there was no room in the societies of the publicani. There was an immense deal of capital at Rome which could neither be absorbed by the only two recognised modes of employment for it in Italy—farming and money-lending—nor by investing it in a society of publicani. This surplus capital poured itself out upon the provinces in a golden stream, only to return to Rome in still larger volume before long. The men of business who settled themselves in the provinces after the soldiers had done their work were bankers, brokers, money-lenders, money-changers, anything in fact but legitimate traders. That in this period they never were, though under the Empire the word negotiator is no doubt more loosely used, and with a wider meaning[5]. The

---

[1] Cic. in Verr. iii. 3, vi. 3.   [2] Ib. v. 20.   [3] Marquardt, i. 401.
[4] This was Cn. Calidius; Cic. in Verr. v. 20.
[5] Ernesti first clearly pointed out the definite technical sense in which the

same man could not be publicanus and negotiator at the same time [1], but there was nothing whatever to prevent him being both at different periods [2]. The amount of money invested in this way was so large that when the outbreak of the Mithridatic war dislocated all business operations in Asia, credit at Rome was seriously affected [3]. There were such numbers of these bankers in Gaul that, according to Cicero, not a single payment passed from hand to hand without the intervention of one of them [4]. They were particularly numerous and influential in Africa [5]. Cato formed three hundred of them into a council for the government of Thapsus [6]; and they furnished the Pompeian generals with money [7]. As they had taken the losing side, Caesar made them pay heavily for their mistake. Their contribution was two million sesterces; five million sesterces were required from the Roman settlers of Adrumetum; and it is especially noticeable that in each case the sum paid by the Romans settled in the place was larger than that imposed on the citizens themselves [8].

These bankers had of course large dealings with private persons; but they had also to do with foreign princes, and with provincial towns. P. Sittius, afterwards the well-known *condottiere* in Africa, had dealings of this sort, in particular with the king of Mauretania [9]; and Brutus and Pompey had both lent money to the unfortunate Ariobazanes [10]. Similarly the Rabirius Postumus, whom Cicero defended, had the king of Egypt among his debtors [11]. But much more frequent and

---

word is used during this period. His views are summarised in his Clavis Ciceroniana, sub voc.

[1] 'Distinguuntur publicani a negotiatoribus,' says Ernesti, and refers to Cic. in Verr. ii. 3; pro Flac. 16; pro Lege Manil. 7; ad Att. ii. 16. He does not however add the necessary qualification of the text.

[2] Cic. pro Rab. Post. 2; Suet. Vesp. 1.   [3] Cic. pro Lege Manil. 7.

[4] Cic. pro Fonteio, i. § 11.   [5] Sall. Jug. 65; Boissière, pp. 183, 184.

[6] Plut. Cat. Min. 59; Merivale, ii. 359.   [7] Hirtius, Bell. Afr. 90.

[8] Merivale, ii. 367.   [9] Cic. pro Sulla, 20; Merivale, ii. 350.

[10] Cic. ad Att. vi. 1. § 3.

[11] Cic. pro Rab. Post. 2.

much more important were their dealings with the provincial towns. What with the legal taxation and the illegal exactions of the publicani, the towns of Asia Minor (to take the instance with which we are most familiar) were unable to pay their taxes. There were two ways of raising the money, by imposing a tribute upon their own citizens, or by borrowing[1]. Unfortunately the latter fatal course was too often adopted, and the town fell into the hands of one of the numerous negotiatores, who were ever on the watch for such an opportunity. There was no law to regulate the rate of interest in the provinces, as there was in Italy, and it often rose to 24, 36, or even 48 per cent. The latter was the rate claimed by Scaptius from the Salaminians. The hopeless and miserable indebtedness brought about by such a state of things was not viewed with entire satisfaction at Rome, and a law was passed (*Lex Gabinia*) to make such loans to towns illegal. But the law was a dead letter; it was in one case at all events evaded by special senatorial decree[2], and the unholy system was still in full force under the early Empire[3]. The sums owed were often very large. Nicaea in Bithynia owed eight million sesterces to a ward of Cicero's[4]; and it was worth the while of the people of Apollonia to bribe their governor with two hundred talents to prevent being obliged to pay what Cicero calls 'their just debts[5].' A governor could do a great deal to relieve the cities of his province of old debts and to discourage them from contracting new ones[6]; but he more often preferred to give their creditors the support of his authority, when they demanded payment. This might be done by comparatively gentle means, and ostensibly at all events by moral influence[7]; but more often, it is probable, by doing what Verres promised to do, namely by putting the lictors at the service of a creditor[8].

---

[1] Cic. pro Flacco, 9: 'In aerario nihil habent civitates, nihil in vectigalibus; duo rationes conficiendae pecuniae aut versura aut tributo.'
[2] Cic. ad Att. vi. 2. § 1. [3] Tac. Ann. iii. 40.
[4] Cic. ad Fam. xiii. 61; cf. Ib. xiii. 56.   [5] Cic. in Pis. 35.
[6] Cic. ad Qu. Fr. i. 1. 8. [7] Cic. pro Murena, 20. [8] Cic. in Verr. ii. 29.

The indebted cities were really in a state of absolute bondage to such creditors as these. A wealthy Roman negotiator in a little country town which owed him money was worse than an Eastern tyrant. To read such a story as that which Cicero tells of the ruin and shame thus brought upon the little town of Apollonides in Asia is enough to sicken the heart and fire the blood with idle though righteous indignation. Even in a well-known and prominent place like Salamis in Cyprus, five of the municipal senators were locked up and starved to death by that same Scaptius who sought to get a prefecture from Cicero, in order to enact again, if it seemed profitable, a similar tragedy. And it is right to remember that Scaptius was but the tool of no less a man than Brutus. An agent is not bound to have a conscience; and it is impossible to acquit Brutus of a heavy share of guilt in this miserable business. And yet it cannot be supposed that Brutus was worse, or even as bad, as many other money-lenders. With such facts as these in view it is no wonder that the negotiatores were detested in all the provinces, and that a revolt generally began by a massacre of them[1].

But all this was as nothing compared to the state of things caused by the Mithridatic and Civil Wars[2]. The miseries of the people of Asia are proved by the enthusiasm with which they welcomed Mithridates, and by the terrible massacre of the Roman citizens of the province[3]. But their sufferings were all the worse in the end. Their country was made a battle-ground of the contending armies; the licentious and mutinous soldiers of Fimbria were let loose upon them to work their will unchecked; and when Sulla had brought the campaign to a successful conclusion he imposed a fine of 20,000 talents upon their cities[4]. Still worse than this was their lot in the Civil Wars. Pompey and his lieutenants needed money, and

The effects of war in Asia.

---

[1] Caesar, B. G. vii. 3, 42; Tac. Hist. iv. 15.
[2] Besides the instances mentioned in the text, Illyria seems to have suffered largely from the civil dissensions; Hirtius, Bell. Alex. 42.
[3] Appian, Mith. 61; Val. Max. ix. 2.   [4] Plut. Lucull. 4.

made requisitions which had to be obeyed¹: it was fortunate that Caesar proved a milder conqueror than they had reason to expect. The treatment they received from Brutus and Cassius, and afterwards from Antony, filled up the measure of their sufferings. Brutus made them pay over ten years' tribute in one year, and when Antony visited them after Philippi, he demanded a similar sum². The unfortunate cities represented to him their absolute inability to pay it; and he with difficulty consented to its being changed into nine years' tribute payable in three yearly instalments. These incredible exactions proved too much even for the wealth of Asia³, broken and ruined as the country had been by a succession of the most terrible misfortunes; and a universal bankruptcy followed⁴, which Augustus had to meet by a remission of taxes, and even by a general cancelling of debts⁵.

Greece.

The condition of Greece was not much better. Athens in particular stood a long siege from Sulla, and when taken was treated with the most terrible severity⁶. There was such a massacre that very few of the original citizens survived. When, under Tiberius, Piso passed through the place on his way to Syria, he 'terrified the citizens of Athens in a bitter speech, with indirect reflections on Germanicus, who he said had derogated from the honour of the Roman name in having treated with excessive courtesy, not the people of Athens, who indeed had been exterminated by repeated disasters, but a miserable medley of tribes⁷.' Sulla also treated Boeotia with great severity⁸, and though the Greek cities found comparatively merciful masters in Caesar and Augustus, it was unfortunate

---

[1] Caesar, B. C. iii. 3, 31, 32.
[2] Appian, B. C. v. 4; Marquardt, ii. 197.
[3] Cicero, pro Leg. Manil. 6, illustrates that wealth.
[4] Dio Chrys. i. p. 601 R; Marquardt, i. 400, note 5.
[5] Marquardt, ii. 199. To all the other misfortunes of Asia we may add (if it is possible to argue from the cities of Cilicia—Cic. ad Att. vi. 2. § 5— to the cities of Asia) that their own municipal magistrates plundered the local revenues.
[6] Finlay, i. 26 and 54.   [7] Tac. Ann. ii. 55.   [8] Finlay, i. 54.

that the great majority of them took the losing side in the Civil Wars[1]. Greece fell rapidly into a state of decline, from which it did not recover[2]. The poor soil of the country needed a full population and all the advantages of peace and wealth to keep it cultivated; and even under the early Empire, Greece is that part of the Roman dominions on which it is least pleasant to dwell[3].

Even in the western half of the Empire the provinces were badly off, though their sufferings were not to be compared to those of Greece or Asia. Spain was alienated by a succession of bad governors[4], and so was not unwilling to throw in its lot with a rebel like Sertorius. The account of the governorship of Cassius Longinus, which we happen to possess, lets in a lurid light upon the possible misdoings of a governor even in a province generally so well treated as that of Spain. It is significant however that the citizens of Italica (Santi-ponce) made a plot against him, in which part of his own army joined, and very nearly succeeded in assassinating him. The Spaniards had still enough of their high spirit left to make it dangerous to oppress them; and this, along with their fortunate exemption from the publicani, contributed greatly no doubt to the general good treatment which they enjoyed. Sicily seems to have been tolerably treated on the whole[5]. But the three years of Verres' rule were years of unexampled misery and wrong; and Lepidus, the third member of the second triumvirate, did his best to follow in his footsteps. There is indeed no part of the Roman world

---

[1] Sparta was an exception, as it sent troops to Octavius. Brutus promised his soldiers the sack of Sparta and Thessalonica in the event of victory; Finlay, ibid.

[2] Cf. the well-known letter of Sulpicius to Cicero.

[3] The fact that the circumstances of Greece were in many respects exceptional is to be borne in mind in reading the strictures on the Early Empire in Finlay's first vol.

[4] Plut. Sert. 6.

[5] The island had brought no accusations against its governors before that against Verres.

where some infamous governor had not left his mark. 'There have been many guilty magistrates in Asia, many in Spain, in Gaul, in Sardinia, even in Sicily itself,' says Cicero[1]. A Gabinius ill-used Syria[2], a Piso or a C. Antonius Macedonia[3]. And even if such a governor was exiled for extortion, he had it in his power to make the people who received him miserable[4].

General remarks on the Republican administration. Such an administration as that which I have attempted to describe could not in the nature of things be permanent. Its machinery was bad, and its agents were worse. If a government can avail itself of men of high character and capacity, an imperfect system can be made to work tolerably well; but there can be no hope when both the system and the men are equally wanting. The system had at least three cardinal faults:—the inadequacy of the senatorial control; the thoroughly bad and unscientific system of taxation[5]; and the annual change of governor. The imperfect execution of the laws intended to control the governor is hardly a fault of the system. The laws themselves were good enough, but men could not be found who could be trusted to carry them out honestly without fear or favour. It was indispensable that the interests of the judges and of the executive should be divorced from the interests of the governors, before reform was possible. Collision was at all events better than collusion of interests.

Incapacity of the Senate. Events at Rome co-operated with the misgovernment of the provinces to put an end to the authority of the Senate. Sheer disorder and incompetence must, after a time, become intolerable to every one; and the fact that it was not possible to take a sea-voyage without danger can hardly have been viewed with much patience[6]. It was also becoming evident that the pro-

---

[1] Cic. in Verr. iii. 65; cf. vi. 48. [2] Cic. in Pis. 21.
[3] Cic. in Pis. 40; Finlay, i. 38.
[4] e. g. C. Antonius in Cephallenia; Strabo, x. 2; quoted by Finlay, i. 47.
[5] The only country in Europe which maintains the system of tithes and middle-men is Turkey, and there are signs that Turkey is giving it up. 'The Porte has resolved upon trying in one vilayet the conversion of the tithes into a land-tax;' Reuter's telegram, in *Daily News*, Oct. 10, 1878.
[6] Cic. in Verr. vi. 25, 38; ad Att. xvi. 2.

vinces could not much longer supply the taxation, unless they were better treated. We find repeated hints in Cicero of the 'existing difficulties of the treasury[1],' and those Romans who could look at all beyond the immediate present could not fail to perceive the dangers in store for them, unless their administration was in every part drawn together and strengthened and held in control. As the Senate had proved its absolute incompetence in the judgment of every one, was the Assembly to be the supreme executive body? That was still more out of the question; and what then remained except a military despotism which should at all events secure peace and good management?

The large and protracted commands, instances of which had long been frequent, pointed in this direction. Nominally the idea of each province as a separate and independent unit still existed; it was a special favour when one governor admitted another into his province[2], unless the step was dictated by military necessities[3]. But such a system would not work in practice. On special occasions we find several provinces lumped together under one command; Greece for instance with Macedonia and Illyria[4]; or Further with Hither Gaul. Military reasons would of necessity bring about this violation of the traditional mode of regarding the provinces. In so far as the Republican government discharged its paramount duty of protecting the provinces from external enemies, it did so by means of large commands which violated both the letter and the spirit of the existing constitution. Pompey's command against the pirates involved the subordination to him of all governors into whose province the war might carry him, and he was permitted to appoint legates to represent him, each of whom in virtue of such appointment acquired the imperium[5]. This surely was change enough; but when Pompey further ruled the province from Rome by means of legates, we see

The large commands.

---

[1] Cic. de Prov. Cons. 5 ; pro Balbo, 27.   [2] Cf. Cic. in Verr. ii. 29
[3] Cic. ad Att. vi. 5.   [4] Cic. Phil. x. 11.
[5] Plut. Pomp. 25; Mommsen, iv. 104.

the regular imperial system in full bloom. The commands given to Caesar, to Crassus[1], and those proposed to be given by the Agrarian Law—which Cicero combated—to a commission of Ten[2], were equally unconstitutional. The Senate saw its authority threatened by such commands, and regarded them with great jealousy[3], while the democrats supported them on that account with all the greater zeal. Their, as a rule, signal success induced even moderate men to regard them at all events as an unavoidable necessity.

Necessity of reform in the army. With the rapid extension of the Roman dominion, the need for a strong and compact military administration had become more and more pressing. At present there was no such thing as a Roman army, but only detachments of troops stationed in the different provinces, practically owing obedience only to the governor, and without organic cohesion of any kind. The necessity for re-organisation betrayed itself here perhaps more clearly than in any part of the system, and the need was both recognised and met by Augustus. But in every part of the administration the same phenomena were visible. The provinces had been governed without any definite scheme or purpose, in accordance with the pressing needs of the passing hour; and a retrospect of the past, reconsideration of the present, and anxious deliberation for the future could be no longer delayed. One of those critical points had arrived at which long-existent forces finally and overpoweringly assert themselves, and from which must date a new departure.

---

[1] Merivale, ii. 7.   [2] Cic de Leg. Agr.; Mommsen, iv. 171.
[3] Cic. pro Leg. Manil. 9. He is defending Lucullus' recall: 'Vestro jussu coactus qui imperii diuturnitati modum statuendum vetere exemplo putavistis;' cf. Cic. Phil. xi. 7, 8.

CHAPTER III.

The Period of the Early Empire.

JULIUS CAESAR had shown a capacity of rising to the needs of his time, which makes us all the more regret his untimely death. Such radical and beneficent reforms as that of the abolition of the tithes in Sicily and Asia; such comprehensive measures as his *Lex Julia Municipalis;* such practical improvements as those involved in the survey which he ordered, and in his reformation of the Calendar; all these and many more were the work of eighteen months of Empire. He had shown a wise economy in his restriction of the corn largesses, and an unexpected conservatism in his dealings with the law courts. Above all, his immense system of colonisation, along with his liberality in the bestowal of the franchise and his treatment of the Senate, shows how fully he had grasped the idea of an equally-privileged and homeogenous Empire, and how he sought on the one hand to send Rome into the provinces, and on the other hand to bring the provinces to Rome. *The policy of Julius Caesar;*

Augustus with his narrower intellect was not equally capable of taking advantage of his unexampled opportunity. He regarded it as his duty to follow out the lines of his adoptive father's policy; but he had a talent for details rather than a genius for great combinations, and he deserted his guidance just where he should most closely have followed it. An examination of the measures which the two emperors either proposed or carried out, in so far as they affected the provinces directly or indirectly, is indispensable for an understanding of the period. *of Augustus.*

Julius saw that one great cause of the misery of the provinces lay in the iniquitous system of taxation. He therefore, besides remitting for the present half of the taxation of Asia, abolished the tithes altogether; and did the same probably also in Sicily. This meant an immense deal, for besides that definite sums known beforehand were substituted for an ever-varying tithe, the publicani, except for the customs' duties and other indirect taxes of minor importance, were done away with. Augustus maintained this arrangement, and though we still hear complaints of the publicani under his successors, their opportunities for wrongdoing were greatly diminished, and a great decline sets in from the position of consideration and social dignity which, in the eyes of the Romans at all events, they had formerly enjoyed.

The Census.

Of still greater importance in respect of the taxation was the census. The great fault of the taxation of the earlier period had been its irregular and arbitrary character. This largely proceeded from the want of any definite register of property, which would make a fair apportionment possible. And if this was injurious to the provincials, it was also a fatal impediment to good government that it was impossible to calculate with any exactness the revenue beforehand. But to take a census implied immense and continued preliminary labours. The only country which had been adequately surveyed before the Romans took the work in hand was Egypt; and here the Romans were content to leave well alone. But in the other, particularly the Western provinces, the work had to be done from the beginning; and in the hurry and confusion of the last years of the Republic it could not be even considered. But with the accession of Caesar comes a momentary rest and lull; and Caesar seems at once to have put his hand to the commencement of this great work. His *Lex Julia Municipalis* settled the census arrangements for Italy[1]. It was to be taken in each municipium or colony by the chief municipal magistrates; and deputies sent with the result to Rome, fifty days before the day fixed for the conclusion of the census in the capital. If a man had houses in more than one municipium, he could have his census taken at Rome; but all other Italians must have it taken in their own municipium. It is noticeable that nothing is said

---

[1] See § 142–158 of the Law; C. I. L. i. p. 120.

here of those smaller towns, *fora* or *conciliabula*, which along with *municipia, coloniae*, and *prefecturae* make up an exhaustive classification of the political units recognised by Rome. The fact was that they had no magistrates capable of taking the census—no *quinquennales*—and so were attached for these purposes no doubt to a neighbouring municipium.

There is here no question of a survey. The *agrimensores* had indeed done their work long ago in every part of Italy; and the whole country was thoroughly mapped out. But before a census could be taken in the provinces, the first surveys had of necessity to be made. A survey of the whole Empire was ordered by Caesar[1], and carried out by Augustus.

The necessary labours commenced in the year B.C. 48, and did not end till late in the reign of Augustus. Zenodotus, entrusted with the survey of the East, terminated his labours in the year B.C. 31; Theodotus, to whom was given the North, in the year B.C. 25; Didymus, in the West, in the year B.C. 27[2]; and Polycletus, who had the South, in the second or third year of the Christian era. Simultaneously the collection of geographical materials of every kind had been actively proceeded with; and from them under Agrippa's supervision[3] had been made a map, the model of such subsequent ones as that of Peutinger or the Itinerarium. Augustus had also ordered these materials to be made into a book under the title of *Chorographia*; and this was used by Strabo and Pliny.

The Survey.

---

[1] The earliest mention of this survey is unfortunately very late, occurring as it does in an interpolated passage of the geographer Julius Honorius, whose date is certainly before 540 A.D., when he is mentioned by Cassiodorus, but probably not earlier than A.D. 450. (See Riese, p. xxi.) The passage reappears with additions in the *Cosmographia* generally known under the name of Ethicus Hister, who in other parts of his 'absurda confusio' (Riese's title for his work) borrows from Orosius. He probably lived in the latter part of the fifth century, shortly after Honorius and Orosius. (Riese, p. xxviii.) The treatises of Honorius and Ethicus are given in full in Riese's *Geographi Latini minores* (Heilbronn, 1878). Both Riese and Marquardt accept the famous passage on the survey of the Empire as of historical value.

[2] Riese, pp. 21 and 72.   [3] See Pliny, N. H. iii. 3, *fin.*

After the survey was completed, it was possible to take a census, so as to ascertain both the population and the paying power of the Empire. The main positive authority for this universal census is the Monumentum Ancyranum[1]; but it is possible to point to several occasions on which a partial or local census was taken. We know that Augustus himself held a census (B.C. 27) in the three Gauls which was afterwards taken by Drusus (B.C. 12) and Germanicus (A.D. 14); and again later on under Nero (A.D. 61) and Domitian. In the case of Judaea again, the census was taken on its being united to the province of Syria; and the same measure was carried out, notwithstanding its unpopularity, in other provinces immediately on their formation, for instance in Britain and Dacia.

The census—as already hinted—was a much easier matter in the senatorial provinces, which already had for the most part something of the kind, than in the imperial provinces, where were few towns and little civilisation. Labours of great difficulty had to be carried out in these provinces, to make a census possible, but once started it was a regular business enough, carried out by imperial officials in *all* provinces—senatorial as well as imperial. These officials fall into three classes:—

1. The district officers who made out the lists or, when this was done by the local magistrates, had a revising power. They were called *adjutor ad census—censor* or *censitor*. So we find the census of the free state of the Remi (Rheims) taken all by itself, and its censor named. The officials of the second class could not of course do the work of the whole province, and so it had to be thus parcelled out. In this way is to be explained the curious inscription which calls a man *censitor provinciae Lugdunensis, item Lugduni*—meaning that to a general supervision of the lists of the whole province, this official joined the special duty of taking the census in Lyons itself. Where the towns were not so large and important as this, one man could of course take the census in a considerable number. Thus we

---

[1] Mon. Anc. § 12. In the years B.C. 28, 8, and A.D. 14.

find one man—in this case nothing but a cavalry officer—taking the census of forty-four civitates in Africa[1]. No such officials interfered with whatever towns of Roman or Latin constitution there might be in the province. In all such, whether colonies or municipia, the *quinquennales* (so called because, though they only held office for one year, there was always a five years' interval from one census to another) took the census themselves, and sent in the results to the provincial censor[2]. It will be noticed how closely these arrangements are copied from those of the *Lex Julia Municipalis*. 2. A provincial censor in each province, who can be pointed out at all events in the three Gauls, Lower Germany, Tarraconensis, Lusitania, Gallaecia, Pannonia, Thracia, Mauretania, among imperial; and in Narbonensis and Macedonia among senatorial provinces. The lists of his province were deposited in the archives of his capital, and a copy forwarded to Rome. These officials were at first always of senatorial rank; the first Roman knight who was entrusted with the duty ('*primo umquam Eq. Rom. censibus accipiendis*' runs the inscription) is probably not much earlier than the year A.D. 200. These later equestrian censors are distinguishable by being always called *procurator*, whereas the title of the earlier provincial censor of senatorial rank was *legatus*[3]. 3. The supreme control lay with the emperor, to whom were addressed petitions about the tribute, and who increased or diminished the payments. His minister for this work was no doubt the one called *magister a censibus* or *magister a libellis*[4].

With the materials gained mainly through the surveys and the census, Augustus was able to compile that *Breviarium Imperii* which Tiberius read to the assembled Senate after the death of its author. 'This contained a description of the resources of the State, of the number of citizens and allies under arms, of the fleets, subject kingdoms, provinces, taxes

The Breviarium Imperii.

---

[1] Henzen, 6946.
[2] See Marquardt, i. 486, for the Quinquennales, but, especially, Henzen, 7075, p. 423.   [3] Henzen, 6944.
[4] See Renier, *Mélanges*, pp. 46–70; Marquardt, ii. 210 foll.

direct and indirect, necessary expenses and customary bounties[1].' A similar account is given by Suetonius[2] and Dio Cassius[3], with the addition that along with this Breviarium, and with the directions as to his funeral, went another volume containing that 'Record of his achievements' (*Index rerum gestarum*) which we know under the name of the *Monumentum Ancyranum*. In this way a regular budget came into existence which kept the government regularly informed of its probable revenues, and tended to control undue exactions. It was no longer open to a governor to send as much or as little from his province as he pleased. The regularity and method thus introduced into the administration enabled a largely increased amount of taxation to be obtained from the provinces without oppression. But it is not possible to regard with entire satisfaction the first beginnings of that perfectly organised and terribly effective machine of taxation which in the end destroyed the Empire and strangled the provincials in its iron grasp. These effects however, though they then for the first time appeared perhaps in germ, took two centuries to become formidable, and meanwhile the arrangements of Augustus secured a regular and fairly equitable system. It is in these arrangements, impressive by their enormous scale, that Augustus best understood and carried out Caesar's design.

Transmarine colonies.

The system of transmarine colonisation commenced by Julius was actively carried out by Augustus. The objects of the system were to provide for the superabundant poor population of Italy, and to hold out a prospect to the soldiers after they had served their time. Caesar settled in all 80,000 Italians across the sea[4]; and in particular Corinth and Carthage, which the Republic had destroyed, were colonised by the first emperor[5]. Augustus in the Monumentum Ancyranum records: 'About . . . thousand Roman citizens served under my standard, of whom I planted more than 30,000 in colonies[6].' Again: 'I

---

[1] Tac. Ann. i. 11. [2] Suet. Aug. 101. [3] Dio, lvi. 33.
[4] Suet. Jul. 42. [5] Dio, xliii. 50; Plut. Caes. 60. [6] Mon. Anc. § 3.

planted military colonies in Africa, Sicily, both Spains, Achaea, Asia, Syria, Gallia Narbonensis, Pisidia[1].' The numerous colonies calling themselves by the title of *Julia Augusta* are among those thus founded by Augustus[2]. In the majority of cases these new settlers were attached to existing cities, which were thereby raised to the rank of colonies, and not settled in entirely new foundations[3]. Unfortunately Augustus' arrangements seem to have been marked by a good deal of unnecessary and mischievous arbitrariness. Thus the colony of Nicopolis, founded in memory of Actium, was formed by compelling Epirots, Aetolians, and Acarnanians to desert their existing homes and settle in it whether they wished or no[4]. On the other hand, it must be put down to the credit of Augustus that he paid for all lands on which he settled his colonists, both in Italy and in the provinces. According to his own account he was the first who ever did so. 'That I did, first and alone of all men who planted military colonies in Italy or the provinces[5].'

In this way something was done to check the pauperism of Italy, to provide a future for the soldiers, and to Romanise the provinces. But it was all of little use if it did not go along with a liberal bestowal of the franchise. Otherwise the founding of these privileged colonies in the centre of an unprivileged district could only intensify the hateful feeling of legal inferiority, as mischievous to the Roman as to the provincial, which it should have been the object of a great statesman to do all in his power to eradicate. Julius had seen this clearly, and all the evidence goes to show that he had every intention of doing all that in him lay to put an end to this invidious and fatal difference between Rome and her subjects. It was by such extension of her franchise and such incorporation of new elements that Rome had become great; and every principle of statesmanship urged her to continue in the same path. Augustus, however, broke with these traditions. Partly from financial

The bestowal of the franchise.

---

[1] Mon. Anc. § 28. [2] Perrot, *de Galatia provincia Romana*, p. 144.
[3] This appears from a comparison of § 16 with § 3 of the Mon. Anc.
[4] Finlay, i. 61. [5] Mon. Anc. § 16.

causes, partly from that ultra-Roman sentiment which was both natural to him and diligently cultivated, he drew the line sharp between the conqueror and the conquered[1]. So the process was made a slow and gradual one, and only accomplished by Caracalla in the third century, when, but for the timid conservatism of Augustus, it might have been accomplished in the first. The number of citizens in the year B.C. 70 was 450,000[2], in B.C. 28 it was over 4,000,000. This shows the immensity of its extension in that period of forty-two years, and a large share of this good work is to be ascribed to Julius. The *Monumentum Ancyranum* permits us to see in great detail what was the part played by Augustus. In the year B.C. 28 was taken the first census; the number of Roman citizens was 4,063,000. A second was taken in B.C. 8; the number was 4,230,000. A third in A.D. 13; the number was 4,937,000[3]. That is to say, in forty-one years the increase was only 900,000, a number which can be explained entirely by the natural growth of population[4], and which compels us to suppose that the franchise was given very sparingly[5].

Augustus and the Senate.

The same tendencies appear in Augustus' treatment of the Senate. Julius had raised its numbers, had largely admitted provincials, and, in so far as he paid it any attention at all, appears to have aimed at making it representative of all classes of the State[6]. The same policy is shown by creating at his simple will and pleasure a number of new patrician families[7]. Augustus changed all this. He admitted no one into the Senate who did not possess at all events 1,200,000 sesterces (about £10,000); he entertained the idea of restoring it to its primitive number of 300[8]; and did at all events reduce it from the number at which it had been left by Caesar, to 600. He gave

---

[1] If the wise and liberal sentiments which Dio puts into the mouth of Maecenas were ever uttered, Augustus certainly paid no attention to them.
[2] Livy, Epit. 98; Duruy, ii. 506.   [3] Mon. Anc. § 8.
[4] At its present rate the population of England doubles in 52 years.
[5] Under Claudius the number was 5,984,072; Tac. Ann. xi. 25.
[6] Suet. Jul. 41, 80.   [7] Ib. 41.   [8] Dio, liv. 14.

it a great deal of nominal power and dignity; and put this plutocratic assembly more in the forefront of the State than ever. He appears to have regarded himself as a reformer entirely in the conservative interest; and now that the comitia had been practically reduced to a nullity, the emperor and the Senate were left confronting one another as the sovereign powers of the State. But in reality the power of the emperor rested on something very real, the arms, namely, of his soldiers; and the power and dignity of the Senate on nothing but his will. Augustus, however, handed over to the Senate a large share of the administration; and Tiberius followed in the same track. The trials for extortion, the complaints and demands of the provinces, in fact the chief judicial and executive business, came regularly before the Senate. It is not long before it also became the chief legislative chamber. The last regular law was passed in the year A.D. 97 [1], and after that date the legislation of the Empire took the shape either of senatus consulta or of imperial edicts. It is not till the reign of Septimius Severus that a senatus consultum was passed for the last time [2]. But the elaborate make-believe of Augustus could not be concealed for long; he himself had to compel the possessors of the necessary census to enter the Senate against their will [3]; and the upshot of his policy was to give the Senate an outward dignity and apparent power which not only made it sometimes misunderstand its real position, but inevitably made it an object of jealousy and suspicion to a bad emperor. Tiberius, making it a sort of religion to follow in his adoptive father's steps, imitated him in his treatment of the Senate [4], and, in form at all events, referred to it all important matters. Caligula was the first emperor to show plainly his suspicion of it and aversion from it [5]; and after him every wicked emperor regularly made a sacrifice of its best members. Claudius paid it a great

---

[1] Under Nerva; see Poste's Gaius, p. 18. Preuss however, p. 3, says under *Nero*. I have not been able to find the authority of either statement.
[2] Ortolan, Part i. § 350.   [3] Dio, liv. 26.
[4] Tac. Ann. iii. 10, iv. 15; Suet. Tib. 30.   [5] Suet. Calig. 49.

deal of respect¹, and on his accession Nero promised to observe the same policy². But before long we find him vowing that he would be rid of it³; no important matter was referred to it⁴; and its members—men like Poetus Thrasea—were sacrificed to his insane jealousy. If we regard simply the interests of the senators themselves, Augustus' attempted rehabilitation of their authority does not seem to have been an unmixed advantage to them. The utter want of dignity and self-control which Pliny describes as characterising their meetings in the time of Trajan⁵, is what we should expect of an assembly which was the victim of a bad emperor and the spoilt child of a good one.

Relation of Augustus' policy to that of Julius in other respects.

In some minor points Augustus partly imitated and partly deviated from Caesar's policy. He restored to the *tribuni aerarii* the place in the juries which Julius had taken from them; and the principle of the five years' interval between urban and provincial office again became the law⁶. Julius' brilliant idea⁷ of codifying the undigested mass of Roman law does not seem to have made any impression on Augustus; and it was left to Hadrian to commence and to Justinian to complete the work. On the other hand, he saw himself obliged, as Julius had been obliged, to maintain the ruinous and hateful system of corn largesses. Caesar had reduced the number of recipients to 150,000⁸. Augustus fixed it at 200,000⁹; and at that number it remained till the time of Alexander Severus. It would be superfluous to dwell upon the mischiefs of the system, as perpetuating and emphasising the odious position of superior privilege enjoyed by the Roman mob, as destroying the agriculture of Italy, and as establishing a heavy drain upon the corn-producing provinces. But on the other hand, it must be remembered that the strength of the tie thus established between Rome and the

---

¹ Suet. Claud. 12. ² Tac. Ann. xiii. 4. ³ Suet. Nero, 37.
⁴ Tac. Hist. iv. 9. ⁵ Plin. Ep. iii. 20, iv. 25, viii. 14.
⁶ Dio, liii. 14; Marquardt, i. 382. ⁷ Suet. Jul. 44.
⁸ Suet. Jul. 41; Mommsen, iv. 475. The number had been 320,000—figures which permit us to argue to the population of Rome. Marquardt puts it at 1,600,000. ⁹ Mon. Anc. § 15.

provinces which fed her[1], brought selfish motives into play on the side of equity and indulgence, and prevented even the worst and most careless of emperors from tolerating misconduct in the governors of the land which grew the 'sacred corn[2].'

There seems to have been no comprehensive plan left by Julius to assist Augustus in his organisation of the army. The great commander no doubt perceived the necessity of an organised defence of the frontiers, but preferred to settle for himself what these frontiers should be before defending them[3]. So the whole scheme must be taken to be the work of Augustus, assisted doubtless by the advice of Maecenas and by the practical co-operation of Agrippa[4]. A famous passage of Tacitus gives the number of the legions in each province in the reign of Tiberius[5]. There were twenty-five in all, divided tolerably equally among the frontier provinces, with the exception that the Rhine was guarded by the extraordinarily powerful force of eight legions. The number of auxiliaries was about the same as that of the legions, and we are able to argue to a total force of about 320,000 men. Besides this, there were the three fleets which guarded the eastern and western coasts of Italy and the southern coasts of Gaul[6]. Their respective stations were

Organisation of the Army.

---

[1] Tac. Ann. xii. 43. The necessity of the foreign supplies to Rome was so absolute that the shipowners were specially exempted from taxation (Tac. Ann. xiii. 51). Regular fleets, belonging to the State, the *classis Alexandrina* and *classis Africana*, brought the corn to Rome (Stephan, Das Verkehrsleben, &c. p. 41). Under the Republic this necessity obliged Octavian to come to terms with Sext. Pompey (Merivale, iii. 250). Vespasian had the idea of starving Italy into submission by holding Egypt; see Tac. Hist. iii. 8, 48, iv. 52.

[2] 'Annonae sanctae;' Orelli, 1810; Henzen, 5320, &c.; quoted by Boissière, p. 66, note 2.

[3] It is well known that Caesar entertained the widest schemes of conquest, and was preparing for a Parthian expedition when assassinated.

[4] For the value of Agrippa, see Dio. liv. 28; Duruy, iii. 285.

[5] Tac. Ann. iv. 5.

[6] Ibid.; Suet. Aug. 49. The *praefecto Juliensium* mentioned in an inscription, Henzen, 6943, was probably not a mere municipal prefect, as all his other titles are military, and as the place was of great military importance. Henzen supposes him to have been of the nature of a *curator*, assigned to

Ravenna, Misenum, and Forojulium. There were, further, the troops stationed in Italy, of which the most famous were the praetorian guards, but these do not at present concern us.

For many years the Roman forces had been tending to the condition of a standing army. The continuous campaigns in the East or in the Gauls had not admitted of the men being disbanded for many years together[1]; and with the decay of the old martial spirit it had become more and more difficult and even impossible to attract men of any means or standing to the ranks. Marius had admitted the proletariate, and since his day military service had hardened more and more into a regular profession. A civic soldiery is only possible where the campaigns are brief and tolerably decisive, and not too far distant from home. It may be doubted whether any continental nation could raise its armies by conscription if, like England, it had to send its soldiers for a term of years to India. Augustus systematised and regulated these tendencies, and we are not wrong therefore in regarding him as the author of the standing army. The passage in Maecenas' speech in which he gives his advice to Augustus about the army, is in reality a summary of what Augustus actually effected[2]; and there, as in the corresponding passage of Suetonius[3], it is clearly brought out that the great change Augustus made was to define strictly the duration and the conditions of service[4]. The time of service was probably fixed at twenty years[5], though in some cases the veterans were kept under the standards for a longer period; and

---

the place by the emperor with authority transcending that of the duoviri, and, I presume, specially responsible for the dockyards and arsenals.

[1] Merivale, iii. 45, 46, gives instances of this.
[2] Dio, lii. 27; Egger, p. 53.   [3] Suet. Aug. 49.
[4] Χρόνον τακτὸν στρατευμένους, says Dio. 'Ad certam stipendiorum praemiorumque formulam. Definitis .. temporibus militiae et commodis missionum,' says Suetonius.
[5] Twenty years in the legions, twenty-five in the auxiliary forces, twenty-six in the fleets, were the regular periods; Bruns, p. 178. Cf. Mon. Anc. § 17: 'Qui vicena plurave stipendia meruissent.' For longer periods, cf. Tac. Ann. i. 18; Suet. Tib. 48.

at its expiration a man was given his honourable discharge (*honesta missio*), received the promised bounty (3,000 sesterces), was commonly enfranchised—he and any one whom he might marry—if not already a Roman citizen[1], and was settled on land, of the quality of which there were frequent complaints, in the neighbourhood of the frontier he had helped to guard. The great expenses of these bounties, though necessary to give the commander a hold upon his soldiers and to make them content with their position, could not be met without special measures. Augustus accordingly instituted the military treasury (*aerarium militare*). 'In the consulship of M. Lepidus and L. Arruntius I paid 100,700,000 sesterces in the name of Tib. Caesar and myself into the military treasury which was established by my design to pay bounties to soldiers who had served twenty or more campaigns[2].' This was the original endowment of the fund; but it was also supported by the proceeds of two new taxes, the tax of five per cent. on all legacies, except those left to near relatives or those of less value than 100,000 sesterces, and the tax of one per cent. on all goods bought or sold in Italy. Both caused great complaints, as their practical effect was to do away with the exclusive privileges Italy had hitherto enjoyed; but Augustus insisted, and in course of time both were extended to the provinces. Augustus appears to have made a hobby of his new treasury, and besides his own contributions to it received promises of subscriptions from foreign kings and peoples[3]. Other extraordinary sources of its revenue are sometimes mentioned. For instance, when Agrippa Postumus was banished his confiscated property was devoted to it[4]. Its administration was entrusted to three men of praetorian rank, appointed by lot, and serving for a term of three years[5]. In the third century these officials were chosen directly by the emperor[6].

The aerarium militare.

---

[1] Cf. the *diplomata* printed in Bruns, p. 177. Fifty-seven such diplomata have been found in the different provinces.
[2] Mon. Anc. § 17.   [3] Dio, lv. 25.   [4] Ib. lv. 32.   [5] Ib. lv. 25.
[6] Ib. lv. 25.

Services of the troops.

In these ways, though not without difficulty [1], sufficient money was procured to discharge these payments. But as the soldiers had also to be regularly paid and fed and equipped, these sums by no means represented the one item of expenditure upon the army. But anything was worth paying for peace and security; and this the standing army secured for nearly 200 years. Nor are these the only services by which the army discharged the debit side of its account. Marius' canal in Narbon Gaul was the first of a great series of works by which the natural facilities of the provinces were improved. The soldiers were pioneers and road-makers as much as fighting men, and the spade and the sword were equally familiar to them. Drusus [2] and Corbulo [3] carried out similar works to that of Marius; and if the idea of making a canal between the Saone and the Moselle [4] had been carried out, it would have been a work of the most brilliant utility. Such works as these, or the building of amphitheatres [5], or still more frequently the making of roads and bridges [6], were ordered by the generals partly for purposes of discipline and partly with the conscious intention of improving the material condition of the province [7]. Less premeditated but not less welcome was the development of towns out of the legionary camps. The towns of Leon in Spain and Caerleon in England [8] are two instances out of the multitude that might be adduced. Posted on the frontiers during their time of service, or settled on lands near it after their dismissal, the soldiers acted in both capacities as a centre from which Roman civilisation could extend itself. The army also acted as a medium for bringing the most different races of the world into close acquaintanceship. Tacitus is perhaps too uncompromising [9] when he says that 'all that is sound in the armies is foreign [10],'

---

[1] Suet. Tib. 48.   [2] Suet. Claud. 1.   [3] Tac. Ann. xi. 20.
[4] Tac. Ann. xiii. 53.   [5] Boissière, p. 133.   [6] Tac. Ann. i. 20.
[7] To previous references add Suet. Aug. 18; Tac. Ann. xvi. 23.
[8] The first being certainly, and the termination of Caerleon probably, derived from Legio; see Renier, *Inscriptions de Troesmis*, in the Rev. Archéol. xii. p. 414, note 1.
[9] Preuss, p. 7, seems to be of this opinion.   [10] Tac. Ann. iii. 40.

and that 'it is by the blood of the provinces that the provinces are conquered[1];' but there can be no question of the immense foreign element in the army even from an early date. It was the general practice to post troops raised in one country in a far distant one. Thus we find Spaniards in Switzerland[2], Swiss (Rauraci) in Britain[3], Pannonians in Africa[4], Illyrians in Armenia[5].

It is noticeable that in all cases the troops were on the frontiers. Rome did not find it necessary to keep garrisons in the interiors of her provinces, as we are obliged to do in India. The whole of Gaul was held by a single garrison of 1200 men at Lugdunum[6]; the eight legions on the Rhine were busied solely with the defence of the frontier against the Germans. Strabo tells us the same thing of Egypt; the frontier had to be guarded against the Ethiopians, but there were hardly any troops in the interior[7] of the country. Not one of the 500 towns of Asia had a garrison[8]. Such a state of things can be fairly put down to the credit of the Roman rule. It was partly no doubt due to the tremendous severity of her conquests[9], but still more to the fact that she bestowed upon the conquered very positive advantages. She had the art of making her subjects emulate and copy her own civilisation. The peace which her arms secured put a spade in the hands of the peoples instead of a sword, and allowed the labouring millions to trade and dig and bring the waste lands under tillage, without thought for their own defence. The provincials seem to have been generally disarmed, according to the advice which Dio puts in the mouth of Maecenas[10]. We find traces of a local militia here and there; for instance, in the

No troops within the provinces.

---

[1] Tac. Hist. iv. 17.   [2] Mommsen; Mon. Anc. p. 46
[3] C. I. L. vii. No. 66; Mommsen, *Schweiz*, p. 25.   [4] Tac. Ann. iii. 9.
[5] Ib. xv. 26.   [6] Desjardins, *La Gaule Romaine*, p. 12.
[7] Strabo, xvii.   [8] Josephus, Bell. Jud. ii. 16.
[9] The cold and clear narrative of Caesar yet leaves a nightmare impression of the awful bloodshed by which his results were obtained. Cf. Merivale, ii. 74.
[10] Dio, lii. 27.

law of the colony of Ursao[1]; but the general principle was that enunciated by Maecenas, that the provincials should have all their fighting done for them by the Roman army[2]. The result of this was that the provincials lost the military spirit, and without any kind of military organisation could make but a very imperfect resistance to the barbarians, once the troops on the frontier failed them[3]. The stress of events so far proved the Roman policy a failure, but before condemning it too unconditionally it would be necessary to convince ourselves that if arms had been put in their hands, the provinces would have been secure from internecine discord.

Partition of provinces between Senate and Emperor. But perhaps the most conspicuous of Augustus' changes was the partition of the provinces between himself and the Senate[4]. The principle of division was that those provinces which enjoyed absolute peace, the older provinces, such as Sicily, Narbonensis, and Asia, should be entrusted to the Senate, while the frontier provinces, which needed military force, went naturally to the commander-in-chief. In this way Augustus pretended to relieve the Senate of the cares and dangers of Empire, while leaving it its advantages, but in fact secured himself the reality of power. The division was an eminently natural one, and had been anticipated under the Republic by the distinction made between consular and praetorian provinces. All new provinces, as requiring, at first at all events, the presence of troops, came as a matter of course under the emperor; and thus the original number of twelve imperial, as compared with ten senatorial provinces, was continually being increased. The emperor reserved to himself the right of modifying these arrangements if he thought fit. Thus Achaia

---

[1] Cf. § 103 of the law, and § 98; Bruns, p. 111. (The law was only discovered in 1870, and is not in the Corpus.)

[2] Cf. Finlay, i. 28.

[3] The gallant resistance of Autun to the usurper Tetricus seems to show that a good deal could have been done by the provincials if they had had any sort of military organisation.

[4] The authorities are Suet. Aug. 47; Strabo, xvii. 3. § 25; Dio, liii. 12.

and Macedonia were transferred by Tiberius from the senatorial to the imperial category[1]; and again restored to their old position by Claudius[2]. Moreover, the proconsular imperium possessed by the emperor over the whole Empire enabled him to interfere at will with the senatorial provinces. Thus when Vologeses invaded Asia, the governor, Avidius Cassius, was directly appointed by the emperor[3]; and if a proconsul died during his year of office the emperor could directly nominate his successor[4]. The Senate of itself requested the emperor to appoint a proconsul to a province in which there was anything like a serious war to be apprehended; Tiberius appointed the proconsul to conduct the war against Tacfarinas[5]; and in exceptional circumstances a legate could be sent to assume the governorship of a proconsular province[6].

The governors of the senatorial provinces were appointed in much the same way as they had been under the Republic. Pompey's arrangement of the five years' interval was maintained as the minimum; but after Augustus' death we find it extended to ten or even thirteen years. These provinces were assigned by lot as under the old system[7]; as a rule, after the previous grades of aedile, quaestor, and the higher urban offices had been passed through and held only for a year. The two oldest consulars cast lots for the consular, the praetors also by seniority for the praetorian provinces. Two provinces, Asia

Mode of appointment to senatorial provinces.

---

[1] Tac. Ann. i. 76.

[2] Suet. Claud. 25. Sardinia had been senatorial and became imperial; Henzen, 5419; Boissière, p. 295. Bithynia became definitely imperial under Hadrian.

[3] Zumpt, Comm. Epig. ii. 92.

[4] Orelli, 3651; an inscription of the time of Vespasian, part of which runs as follows: 'Proc. provinciae Asiae quam mandatu principis vice defuncti Procos. rexit.'

[5] Tac. Ann. iii. 32.

[6] Pliny was thus sent to Bithynia; cf. Plin. Ep. x. 12, where Pliny thanks Trajan for granting a relative the *proconsulship* of Bithynia.

[7] Suet. Aug. 47: 'Ceteras proconsulibus sortito permissit.' Tac. Ann. iii. 71. The quaestor too by lot; Suet. Vesp. 2; Tac. Agr. 6 and 42. Quaestors of course were only in senatorial provinces.

and Africa, remained consular, and the appointments to these were the most dignified and the best paid; the rest were praetorian. But whether the provinces were consular or praetorian, and whether the governors were men of consular or praetorian rank, in any case all governors of senatorial provinces were called indifferently proconsuls [1], just as all governors of imperial provinces were called by the historians indifferently, though inaccurately, propraetors [2]. In outward dignity the proconsuls were far above the imperial legates; they had ten or even twelve fasces, whereas the legate had only five [3]; but they had little of the reality of power. As they had no military authority they did not possess the power of life and death over any soldiers in their province; and as their office was merely annual they made a very different impression to the imperial legate who scarcely ever stayed less than three, and sometimes as much as eight or ten or even more years in his province. It is no wonder, therefore, that Tiberius found a difficulty in inducing capable persons to stand for such appointments [4]; and if we still find traces of the old feeling which regarded a province as a prize [5], it must have been rather for the salary connected with it than for any power or special profit to be obtained from it. An ambitious man would rather covet a post as imperial legatus, and if a man wanted to become rich the surest way of doing so would be through a procuratorship [6].

The governors of Imperial provinces. In theory the emperor was himself the governor of all his provinces; but as he could not be in twelve different places at once, he appointed in each a legate to represent him. The full title of such governors was *legatus Augusti pro praetore;* and this is the way they are invariably designated in the inscriptions.

---

[1] Cf. the passage of Suet. quoted in the above note; Perrot, *de Galatia prov. Rom.* p. 115.
[2] Tac. Ann. xv. 22, where propraetors and proconsuls is an exhaustive classification of provincial governors; Marquardt, i. 409, note 4.
[3] 'Quinquefascalis dum agerem;' Ephemeris Epig. p. 205.
[4] Tac. Ann. vi. 27.   [5] Ibid. xv. 19; Hist. iv. 39.
[6] Ibid. xvi. 17; Suet. Vesp. 16.

They might be either of consular or praetorian rank; and the provinces to which they were assigned were themselves also either consular or praetorian — an arrangement which was so far of importance that if consular legates had been sent to a province in the first instance, it was only very rarely that praetorian legates were substituted, and *vice versa*[1]. The provinces in which there were several legions, were always governed by consular legates; and it became common, and would no doubt be welcome, to address such legates simply as 'consulares[2],' thus clearly distinguishing them from the legates of praetorian rank.

These legates were appointed directly by the emperor, and for as long a time as he pleased. Dio makes Maecenas give the advice to Augustus not to let any legate of his rule a province less than three years or more than five, for so they would stay long enough to know their province thoroughly, not long enough to become dangerous[3]. And this was perhaps the generally observed rule[4]; Agricola, for instance, was three years in Aquitania[5]. But the exceptions are very numerous. Galba governed Spain for eight years[6], Sabinus was in Moesia for seven[7], and we find C. Silius legate in Gaul A.D. 14, and still in Gaul ten years afterwards[8]. Sometimes these appointments lasted even for life[9]: Tiberius in particular was famous for keeping his governors long at their posts[10]. It was a still greater innovation when a suspicious emperor like Tiberius did not allow a legate or proconsul to proceed to his province at all, and the 'farce of governing' was gone through, while the governor remained at Rome[11].

What constituted the vital difference between these legates

---

[1] Perrot, *Galatia*, p. 68.

[2] So we find that after Augustus by consular and praetorian provinces are meant imperial; by proconsular provinces are meant senatorial. Cf. Capitol. M. Aurelius, 22; Marq. i. 409, note 5.

[3] Dio, liii. 23. [4] This is Zumpt's opinion; Comm. Epig. ii. 87.

[5] Tac. Agr. 9. [6] Plut. Galba, 4. [7] Tac. Hist. iii. 75.

[8] Ann. i. 31 and iv. 18. [9] Ann. i. 80. [10] Josephus, Antiq. xviii 6.

[11] Ann. i. 80, vi. 27; Hist. ii. 65, 97; Suet. Tib. 63.

The legate and the proconsul. and the proconsuls was not merely the longer duration of their power, but still more their possession of military force. The senatorial provinces being without troops counted for nothing in such a period of civil war as the terrible year of the three emperors (A.D. 69). 'The unarmed provinces with Italy at their head were exposed to any kind of slavery, and were ready to become the prize of victory,' says Tacitus[1]. The only exception to the rule that a proconsular was divorced from a military command was Africa; and even here, in cases of special emergency, we find the governor appointed by the emperor. Still as a rule, in the reign of Augustus and Tiberius the proconsul of Africa disposed of troops, and was not elected by the emperor; a contradiction to the usual state of things which was sure before long to awake the susceptibilities of a jealous emperor[2]. Caligula in fact, on his accession, at once put an end to it, took the troops from the proconsul, and gave them to the legate whom he established by his side, with the exceptional title, explained by the exceptional circumstances, of *legatus Augusti pro praetore legionis*[3]. Henceforth the legate was continually encroaching upon his rival, whose position of superior dignity and real weakness exposed him to the most galling affronts. The legate felt that he was the emperor's man, and was sent there to assert his supreme authority in his own person. Caligula had made disputes inevitable. 'The patronage was equally divided between the two officers. A source of disagreement was thus studiously sought in the continual clashing of their authority, and it was further developed by an unprincipled rivalry. The power of the legates grew through their lengthened tenure of office, and perhaps because an inferior feels a greater interest in such a competition[4].' Even if actual violence was not shown (Piso was put to death

---

[1] Hist. i. 11. Their unarmed condition is illustrated by Hist. ii. 81 and 83.

[2] Cf. Cicero's expressions about Africa, Pro Ligario, 7 : 'Africam, omnium provinciarum arcem, natam ad bellum contra hanc urbem gerendum.'

[3] Tac. Hist. iv. 48, a very interesting and important chapter.

[4] Hist. iv. 48.

by Festus' order, A.D. 70 [1]), the proconsul was always liable to the interference of the legate in the internal affairs of his own province. The emperors made it their special business to look after the roads both in Italy and in the provinces [2]. So if a road was wanted from the boundary of Numidia to a place far within the senatorial province, the legate was commissioned to superintend the making of it; and his officers must have been constantly on the spot while his soldiers were engaged upon the work [3]. The yearly tenure also of the proconsul must have gone far to put him into a subordinate position. 'Between this annual proconsul, this governor of a dozen months who put in an appearance at Carthage, and was scarcely arrived in his province before he was gone again, and this legate who on the contrary settled himself in Africa, and from his camp at Lambesis saw the proconsuls pass and disappear, what a difference in real authority, what inequality in power [4]!'

If the legate was the emperor's man, still more was this the character of the procurator. There were no quaestors in the imperial provinces, all the accounts being kept and money matters in general being managed by one of these officials. But we also find them in the senatorial provinces. While the whole field of finance was committed to them in their own proper provinces, moneys pertaining to the fisc were managed by procurators in all provinces alike without distinction. They were practically independent of the senatorial governor. 'In any question of fiscal moneys, which concerns the procurator of the prince, the proconsul will do best if he keeps clear of it [5].'

The imperial procurators.

---

[1] Hist. iv. 50.

[2] The epigraphic evidence on this point is very large. The following references may be given: Suet. Aug. 30; Mon. Anc. § 20; Mommsen's Mon. Anc. p. 59; Kandler, No. 524; Bergier, i. 64–67.

[3] e.g. the road from Carthage, the capital of the proconsular province, to Thevesta was made by the legate (A.D. 124), and in the inscription which commemorates it there is no mention of the proconsul; Boissière, p. 254.

[4] Boissière, L'Afrique Romaine, p. 252. I have made much use of M. Boissière's admirable discussion of this subject.

[5] Dig. i. 18. 9; Marquardt, i. 414, note 4.

Such taxes as the *vicesima hereditatum*, when applied to the provinces, were under the superintendence of a procurator, whose powers extended over several provinces at once[1]; and in a later period of the Empire there were procurators to manage every conceivable source of income.

These officials as constituted by Augustus had, properly speaking, no judicial authority. But they began to presume upon their position as the emperor's nominees from an early date. Under Tiberius a procurator of Asia was accused by his province, and the emperor supported the accusation, vehemently asseverating that the authority which he had given him extended only to slaves and to his own private moneys[2]. It was however doubtless found inconvenient in practice that officials entrusted with such important duties should not have wider powers; and at Claudius' request the Senate gave them authority[3] to decide suits,—a power which must have extended at all events to all cases connected with the fisc. In the imperial provinces it is possible to trace a similar process of encroachment. Here their position corresponding to that held formerly by the quaestors, legitimately gave them wide powers, which they took care to maintain and increase. 'A single king once ruled us; now two are set over us; a legate to tyrannise over our lives, a procurator to tyrannise over our property.' Such is the complaint which Tacitus puts into the mouths of the Britons[4]. The rapacity of a procurator goaded Britain into rebellion[5]; and when Galba was governor of Tarraconensis he was obliged to witness similar conduct on the part of his procurator, apparently without the power to check it[6]. It was so regular a thing for the legate and the governor to

---

[1] Henzen, 6940, is a good instance; Marquardt, ii. 305, for a full account.

[2] Tac. Ann. iv. 15.

[3] Suet. Claud. 12. Claudius seems to have been a great patron of the procurators. Cf. Suet. Claud. 24.

[4] Tac. Agr. 15. [5] Tac. Ann. xiv. 32.

[6] Plut. Galba, 4. As Galba sympathised with the Spaniards, it is to be supposed he would have done so if he could.

quarrel, that Tacitus specially praises Agricola for having had no 'contention with his procurator' when he was governor of Aquitania; and so sharp was the dissension between Suetonius the legate of Britain, and his procurator, that Nero sent a freedman to endeavour to arrange the difference between them. It is significant that the upshot of their business was that a substitute was found, not for Classicanus, but for Suetonius[1]. The fact is that the procurator seems to have been designedly used, at all events by bad emperors, as a spy upon the legate, and, if need were, as an instrument against them. Being in theory nothing but the emperor's stewards[2], and being wholly dependent upon his favour for success in their career[3], they were absolutely devoted to his interests. A legate might revolt against his master, a procurator never. It is the procurator who lets the emperor know of rebellious movements in his province[4], and it is in the procurator that the emperor confides if he wants a legate put out of the way[5]. At least one instance occurs of a senatorial governor being actually put to death by his procurator[6]. The whole tendency is for the authority of the procurator to extend and strengthen itself till he and the legate are left confronting one another as almost equal powers. That they could, in emergency at all events, dispose of military force is proved by the appeal of the Romans of Camulodunum to Catus Decianus[7]; and in times of disturbance we find them only too ready to try their hands at military measures[8]. It is not at all inconsistent with what has

---

[1] Tac. Ann. xiv. 38.   [2] See Hirschfeld, p. 242.
[3] A Spanish inscription (C. I. L. ii. 556) shows how these procurators were sent all over Europe.
[4] Tac. Hist. i. 12.
[5] Suet. Galba, 9: 'Nam et mandata Neronis de nece sua ad procuratores clam missa deprehenderat.'
[6] Tac. Hist. i. 7.
[7] Tac. Ann. xiv. 32. They asked him for military aid. He sent only 200 men. Tacitus' language implies blame for this conduct; therefore he could have sent more if he had chosen.
[8] e.g. the procurator of Corsica; Tac. Hist. ii. 16.

been said that in settled times and under good and capable emperors the procurators were obliged to maintain their proper subordinate position; and had for instance to request a testimonial from the governor to the emperor on leaving the province [1].

Procurators as governors. Besides these officials of the imperial exchequer there were also a certain number of provinces ruled directly by a procurator, possessing the powers of an ordinary governor. Pontius Pilate was one of these minor governors [2]. These governorships were of a provisional character, and when the countries to which they had been applied had been thoroughly Romanised, or had lost the peculiarities which had made an exceptional treatment advisable, we find them organised like ordinary provinces. This happened for instance in the case of Thracia, Rhaetia, and Judaea itself [3]. Such provinces as these formed a class by themselves. In one passage Tacitus puts together a number of them,—' Mauritania, Rhaetia, Noricum, and Thrace, and the other provinces governed by procurators [4];' and we are also able to point to procurators of Cappadocia [5], of the Maritime Alps [6], and of the Alps of Savoy [7]. It was however understood that these procurators were subordinate to the regular governor of the neighbouring province [8]. This subordination was natural enough, seeing that though they had some sort of military force—perhaps a few cohorts or a legion [9]—enough to protect their persons

---

[1] Pliny, Ep. x. 36.

[2] When Finlay, i. 36, argues to the irregular and arbitrary character of the government from the case of Pontius Pilate he does not seem quite to understand the exceptional character of these procurators. They were in fact governors, and we find the procurator of Judaea also called *praepositus*; Suet. Vesp. 4.

[3] Marquardt, i. 413.   [4] Hist. i. 11.

[5] Ann. xii. 49.   [6] Hist. ii. 12; iii. 42.

[7] 'Proc. Alpium Atrectinarum et Poeninarum;' Orelli, 3888; Mommsen, *Schweiz*, 6.

[8] See Zumpt, Comm. Epig. ii. 127, 133.

[9] Pontius Pilate certainly had troops, which would be very necessary in an unruly province like Judaea.

and assert their authority within the province, they yet had nothing that could be called an army, and could not defend their province against attack from without. So under Claudius, when an incompetent procurator of Cappadocia raised auxiliary troops and ventured to meddle with the very *crux* and mystery of Roman foreign policy, the crown of Armenia, he was promptly recalled to his senses by the arrival of a lieutenant with a legion from Quadratus the governor of Syria. In this case it is the governor of Syria who interferes; but as a rule it was the legate of Galatia who was responsible for Cappadocia[1]; while Judaea was under the special control of the governor of Syria. Judaea however was definitely annexed to Syria on the death of its last king Agrippa[2]; and the constant inroads of the barbarians compelled Vespasian to substitute a consular legate with troops for the equestrian procurator in Cappadocia[3].

The government of Egypt was analogous to that of such provinces as these, but was in many points wholly exceptional. Julius Caesar had deliberately abstained from making a province of the country[4]; and when Augustus added it to the Empire after Actium[5], he subjected it to an altogether exceptional treatment. The country was his private property, or rather the emperor's private property; it passed as a matter of course, that is, from emperor to emperor[6]. Augustus appointed a praefectus to represent him in the province, just as in earlier times the urban praetors had sent prefects to represent them in the municipalities of Italy[7]. This prefect

Egypt.

---

[1] Perrot, *Galatia*, p. 98.

[2] Ann. xii. 23 (A.D. 41); and again put under a procurator from 44 to 70. See Marquardt, i. 335.

[3] Suet. Vesp. 8; Perrot, ib.

[4] Suet. Jul. 35: 'Veritus provinciam facere, ne quandoque violentiorem praesidem nacta novarum rerum materia esset.'

[5] 'Ægyptum imperio populi Romani adjeci;' Mon. Anc. § 27.

[6] That is, it was patrimonium Caesaris, but not res familiaris. See Marquardt, ii. 249, 300; i. 284.

[7] Other praefecti are those of islands—already mentioned—of Mesopotamia under the later Empire, of Berenicis; Marq. i. 413, note 2; Strabo, iv. 6. § 4.

was of equestrian, and not the highest equestrian rank[1]; no senators were admitted into the province; and the greatest jealousy was shown of the smallest interference with it[2]. By the side of the praefect were two other high officials, the *idiologus*[3] or imperial procurator, and the *juridicus* of Alexandria[4]. The name of the former was that which had been held by the steward of the Ptolemies; and the latter was a municipal magistrate with very exceptional powers, appointed directly by the emperor, as Napoleon III directly appointed the mayors of important French country towns. The reasons for the special jealousy of Egypt shown by Augustus and his successors were partly the great defensibility of the country, partly its immense importance as the granary of Rome. 'It was an accepted principle with our fathers,' says Pliny[5], 'that our city could not possibly be fed and maintained without the resources of Egypt.' Egypt did in fact feed Rome for four months in the year.

The governor's subordinates.

Of the subordinates of the governors either in the senatorial or imperial provinces it is not necessary to say much. The *juridici* that occur in different parts of Spain and in Britain were assistants of the imperial legates, not appointed by the legates,—for how could a deputy appoint deputies?—but directly by the emperor[6]. The legal council mentioned under the Republic as assisting the governor became a regular body under the title of assessors[7]. The comites still existed, and

---

[1] Ann. xii. 60, ii. 59. His powers were great; cf. Hist. i. 11.

[2] Ann. ii. 59.

[3] Marquardt, ii. 300. He is mentioned in the decree of Tiberius Alexander: πρὸς τῷ ἰδίῳ λόγῳ τεταγμένου. Cf. Strabo, xvii. 1. § 12, where Strabo makes him to be only procurator a caducis.

[4] Henzen, 6924, 6925.   [5] Pliny, Panegyr. 31.

[6] Henzen, 6487, 6489, 1178. 6490, 7420, and a complete list, Marquardt, i. 411, note. They occur of course only in imperial provinces, and are quite distinct from the juridici of Italy (instituted by M. Aurelius), as from the Juridicus Alexandriae. For the whole subject, see Zumpt, ii. 40-55; Henzen, p. 113 of his indices, where are full references, and p. 297.

[7] Plin. Ep. x. 19. See an inscription given by Boissière (unfortunately only in a French translation), p. 241, note.

though doubtless under better control, are sometimes complained of in much the same terms as they were under the Republic[1]. The quaestors still performed their duties in the senatorial provinces; but were thrown into the shade by the rapid rise and great extension of the class of procurators. The cases which sometimes occur of governorships being given to centurions[2] or even to ordinary veterans[3] are in each case so obviously due to special circumstances as not to require a closer examination.

The great and beneficent change which resulted from Augustus' arrangements was the much stricter control in which the governors were now held. The emperors made it their business to make themselves well acquainted with their Empire; of the eighteen years after the battle of Actium Augustus spent eleven out of Italy[4], and the only two provinces which he had not visited were Africa and Sardinia[5]. It was not their interest to tolerate misgovernment or oppression. 'Everywhere it is the rule that the owner spares the soil, while the tenant exhausts it[6].' Undisturbed by domestic politics they had leisure to devote their unwearied industry to the interests of the Empire as a whole[7]. The governors were regularly paid[8], and consequently lost the excuses for exaction which they could have offered under the Republic. It was expected that the governors should regularly report to the emperor on any matters of importance that occurred in their province[9]; and the number of questions referred to his decision was constantly on the increase. At the end of the decree in which he regulates an immense amount of details

The emperor as supreme head of the provincial administration.

---

[1] Hist. iv. 14: 'Gravi quidem comitatu.'
[2] A centurion governed the Frisii; Ann. iv. 72. Batavi apparently; Civilis complains of it; Hist. iv. 14.
[3] Tac. Ann. ii. 66.
[4] Duruy, iii. 230.   [5] Suet. Aug. 47.   [6] Boissière, p. 121.
[7] Cf. Suet. Vesp. 21; Plin. Ep. iii. 5, for Vespasian's labours.
[8] Dio, lii. 23, liii. 15; Suet. Aug. 38; Marquardt, i. 416; Merivale, iv. 25. The proconsul of Africa had an income of a million sesterces.
[9] Euseb. H. E. ii. 2; Marquardt, i. 417.

connected with the financial administration of the country, Tiberius Alexander, prefect of Egypt under Galba, says he will not decide a particular question himself, but 'I will write to the Emperor Augustus, and I will make known to him any other points of consequence, as he alone can wholly eradicate such abuses.' Boundary disputes [1], petitions for the right of sanctuary [2], petitions for the restoration of a temple [3], all such and many more were referred to his decision. All such matters would previously have been settled in a summary manner by the governor, and their reference to Rome shows the tendency to limit and define his absolute authority. The extent to which Pliny when legate of Bithynia refers to Trajan for directions is almost painful. To strengthen and secure this direct and immediate control of provincial affairs Augustus established an elaborate postal system, by which he might be informed with the greatest possible celerity of everything which occurred. Such misgovernment as had been frequent under the Republic was in part due to the remoteness of the governors from Rome; and to the inadequacy of the communication. The telegraph and the steamship have immensely strengthened the control which a modern country can exercise over its dependencies. Augustus had not these, but he made the best use of what facilities he had, and everything points to the much readier and speedier communication [4] between the provinces and Rome. And the emperor exercised this control not only over his legates, but, in virtue of his proconsular power, over the senatorial governors as well. The emperor's will overrode the edicts of the governors [5]; and where large questions arose connected with the administration of a province, an imperial 'constitution' laid down the rule to be followed, and so, in a sense, constituted its *lex provinciae* [6]. A special

---

[1] Ann. iv. 43. Cf. Vespasian's letter to the Vanacini in Sardinia; Bruns, p. 173.
[2] Ann. iv. 14.
[3] Ib. iv. 43.
[4] For the new postal system, see Suet. Aug. 49; Marquardt, i. 418.
[5] Plin. x. 109.
[6] Ib. x. 71, 72.

body was set aside for the hearing of provincial appeals[1]; and the Senate, so far as it had any authority left, was busied almost entirely with their administration. In exceptional cases the emperor, without superseding the governor, sent a special official to examine the affairs of a province[2]; and, where there was a peculiar need, could appoint a peculiar governor[3]. If there were mistakes in this supreme administration, they arose not from mere laxity and incompetence as under the Republic, but from excessive interference and over-centralisation. New organs were developed on all sides to meet the necessities of Empire. Thus the emperor was assisted by his cabinet; and his secretaries for the conduct of the different branches of the administration became ministers of state.

The provinces which were directly in the emperor's hands appear to have been particularly well governed. The splendid career open to a legate of capacity who was favoured by the emperor would be endangered if not forfeited by yielding to the mean covetousness which had disgraced the governors of the Republic. A man had more to gain by keeping his hands clean than by fouling them. Staying as they did for a period of years in the province, of which they were often natives, the legates did not regard their period of government as a banishment, as Cicero had regarded it. They became familiar with the needs and peculiarities of their province, and ruled its inhabitants as one of themselves. So much better was the condition of the imperial provinces than that of the senatorial ones, that when Achaia and Macedonia begged for relief from their burdens (*onera deprecantes*), their prayer was thought to be sufficiently answered by their transference from the rule of the Senate to that of the emperor. The legates were as a rule men of great

The government of the imperial provinces.

---

[1] Suet. Aug. 33; Marquardt, i. 403.

[2] Ann. xiv. 39. Not that this freedman of Nero did or was meant to do any good, but if the system was used once it was probably used often in better circumstances.

[3] When the cities of Bithynia were in trouble Trajan sent Pliny there as legate, instead of the usual proconsul.

capacity, equally at home in the camp and in the business of civil government, and to read a bare list of the commands which many of them held is enough to justify the expression of a modern writer when he calls them 'the glory of the Empire[1].'

Bad governors. It is not to be supposed that there were no bad governors under Augustus and his successors. A Licinius and a Lollius are there to undeceive us. But the danger which was now run made such governors the exception instead of the rule. Putting together the accusations of provincial governors mentioned in the Annals and History of Tacitus and in the Letters of Pliny, we get a complete list of twenty-seven[2] governors thus accused; of these seven were acquitted and twenty condemned. Augustus himself showed great severity to guilty governors, banishing Cornelius Gallus, and actually drowning the tutor and other attendants of the young Caius in Asia[3]. The case of Licinius is a less favourable one; but, as has been said, if it shows that in exceptional cases a governor could rob with impunity, it shows that it was at all events impossible to make a profit of the robbery[4].

---

[1] Prof. Seeley in his Essays, p. 20. I subjoin a *cursus honorum*, one of hundreds of similar ones, taken from Renier, *Mélanges*, p. 79: 'T. Caesernio Quinctio Macedoni Quinctiano consuli, sodali Augustali, curatori viae Appiae, praefecto alimentorum, legato legionis Piae fidelis, comiti divi Veri per Orientem, praetori candidato inter cives et peregrinos, tribuno plebis candidato, legato per Africam Mauretaniam, quaestori candidato, tribuno militum legionis trigesimo Ulpiae Victricis, triumviro auro argento aeri flando feriundo, patrono coloniae, decreto decurionum. Servilius . . . amico optimo.'

As a rule a man's whole life can be traced on these inscriptions, as they commonly begin with the first office he held, and go on in chronological order. In this case the office last held and of highest rank comes first, probably because the man had just been made consul, and his friend wished to flatter him by drawing special attention to the honour.

The case of Vespasian is an interesting one; Suet. Vesp. 2 and 4; cf. Suet. Tit. 4.

[2] Twenty-one in the Annals, of which sixteen were condemned, five acquitted. One in the Histories,—condemned; five in Pliny, of which three were condemned and two acquitted.

[3] Suet. Aug. 67. 4. [4] Duruy, iii. 227.

The regular court for trying cases of repetundae was still in form kept up, and cases might occasionally be referred to it, if the Senate did not wish to try them[1]. But as a rule all such accusations came before the Senate, who had the power to decide them, but no doubt settled each case in accordance with the known wishes of the emperor. The province could request the Senate to give them this or that advocate to plead their cause[2], and in some cases appear to have relied upon the talents of their own orators. Thus in one case the 'most eloquent orators of Asia[3]' pleaded before the Senate, probably in Greek, as the use of that language was specially permitted[4]. Now that the Senate had little else to do, these trials were the chief business that came before it, and it is no wonder that very special attention was paid to them[5]. Pliny in his letters gives far fuller and more elaborate accounts of these trials than he does of any other matter; and to judge from his description they must have presented striking and impressive scenes[6].

Accusations of provincial governors.

Above all, Augustus was the great peace-maker. This is the light in which he is most proud to represent himself[7]; and when on his return from Spain and Gaul the Senate consecrated an altar in the Campus Martius to *Pax* Augusta, they paid him the best and most appropriate of compliments[8]. This is the final justification of the Empire as against the Republic, that it succeeded in this first duty of securing peace. Even under Nero we read, 'never had there been so profound a peace[9];' and it was in this aspect that the Empire most powerfully impressed both Romans and provincials[10]. The fault was that the peace did not last long enough. After all, the Romans ought not to have failed in keeping back the barbarians.

The Empire secured peace.

---

[1] This seems to be made out from Pliny, Ep. iv. 9.
[2] Pliny, ii. 12, iii. 9; Marquardt, i. 416, note 9.
[3] Ann. iii. 66. [4] Marquardt, i. 47.
[5] This is Zumpt's remark; Comm. Epig. ii. 51.
[6] See esp. Plin. Ep. iii. 9.   [7] Mon. Anc. § 13.   [8] Ib. § 12.
[9] Ann. xv. 46.
[10] Strabo, iv. 6. § 9, and passim in Books iii and iv; Tac. Hist. iv. 74; Pliny, N. H. iii. 6.

Perhaps Augustus was wrong when he dissuaded any attack upon Germany[1]; for if that country had once been held and civilised, the balance of power would have inclined to the side of the Empire, and not to the side of the Northern races which overwhelmed it. But the fault lay deeper, and was one inseparable from any despotism however well planned and skilfully administered. Ideally Rome's true aim should have been to prepare the peoples to stand by themselves, to civilise and organise them so as to be fit for freedom. The wholesome tendency was in the direction of independence, the dangerous and fatal tendency was in the direction of a bureaucratic centralisation. It was however inevitable that the latter tendency should prevail. The power of self-government can only be got by use and practice; and there was no self-government except in the towns. On one side the central government, on the other side the municipia; those were the only centres of political life. 'A Roman province with its municipal life was far above a satrapy, though far below a nation[2].' That is very true, but municipal towns without federation have little power of self-defence, and will fail in the hour of need. The provinces could not have defended themselves without Rome; for 200 years Rome defended them; but if a wiser system had been used, if the provincial councils had been made into real parliaments instead of kept to their so-called religious duties; above all, if there had been a regular and organised representation of the provinces in the central government, Rome and her provinces together might have defended themselves for a thousand years instead of two hundred. It is however idle to ask what might have been; and a Roman statesman might complain that we were trying his country by transcendental standards, that the debt of the modern world to Rome is already

---

[1] The question is discussed by Mignet, *Introduction de l'Ancienne Germanie dans la société civilisée*; De la Berge, *Trajan*, p. 66; Congreve, *Roman Empire of the West*, p. 38.

[2] Goldwin Smith, *The Greatness of the Romans;* Contemporary Review, May 1878, p. 333.

sufficiently great, and that no other people would have done better in their place. It is impossible for us to be sure how far the policy of Rome was dictated by military necessities. It is very possible that a Roman might have doubted the safety of such a treatment of the provinces. Above all he might have doubted the fitness of the provincials as a whole to be entrusted with self-government and a share of Empire. It is hard, as we see by India, for the conquerors to regard themselves as equal to the conquered; and though the provincials as a whole were more nearly on a level with the Romans than the Hindoos are with their English rulers, still the Romans felt that it was they who ruled, organised and civilised, and that they had proved their capacity, while their subjects had not. The weakness of those who have conquered and ruled with eminent success, is to be sceptical with regard to the fitness of others to do a similar work; and a Roman governor would probably be as incredulous if you spoke to him of a genuine parliament at Lyons or Corduba as an Indian official would be if you suggested a Hindoo parliament at Delhi.

The unacknowledged character of the despotism which Augustus created was a more indisputable evil. It retarded the admission of the provincials within the Roman circle; and it prevented a rational settlement of the succession. If Julius really aimed at a hereditary monarchy he was wiser than his successor, whose ultra-Roman pedantry sought to maintain intact all the forms of the constitution after they had lost their vitality. The only excuse for Augustus is that men are often far readier to give up the reality than the name of freedom, and that the disregard of forms is often a greater offence than the disregard of rights. As the work of Augustus consisted to a large extent in a return to the old Roman exclusiveness in politics and religion, he fostered all the ideas which regarded the Romans as a peculiar people, and made it difficult for an emperor to be liberal with the franchise. In the first century, at all events, the prestige of Augustus' example was so great that one of the signs of a 'good' emperor was this obsolete

Evils of the unacknowledged character of the early Empire.

and preposterous *Romanism*[1]. Still more important was the way the succession was settled, or rather unsettled. To leave it in form to the Senate and people as did Augustus, while really confining it to the members of one family, was an arrangement by which neither the advantages of an elective presidency nor of an hereditary monarchy were secured. A nominal consent of the people and a real consent of the army was a very bad basis for any government[2]. A strictly hereditary system is to a certain extent a safeguard against revolution, and a strictly elective system is a safeguard against being ruled by a Caligula or a Nero. 'We must not forget that it is to the entirely Roman system of adoption that we owe the century of the Antonines[3].' Perhaps Augustus might have made this system the principle of the succession. Too much depended upon the character of the individual emperor to make the hereditary principle a safe one. Some system which would enable the Senate and emperor together to name the heir, as the Senate and Nerva together named Trajan, would perhaps have been the best solution. But it must be remembered that even when the principle of adoption was tolerably established, a wise man like Aurelius was blind enough to let a Commodus succeed him. And as there was practically no check upon the emperor, there was nothing to prevent his yielding to merely personal feelings in this all-important matter. The real evil lay in the very nature of the imperial rule; and the history of the Empire is only another instance of the shallowness of the dictum which would make a good and permanent administration independent of forms of government[4].

The military character of the Empire becomes prominent with Tiberius. Julius possibly[5], and Augustus certainly, had

---

[1] See Freeman's Essays, Second Series, p. 321.
[2] Duruy, iii. 390, note 3.
[3] Ib. iii. 374.
[4]   'For forms of Government let fools contest,
      Whate'er is best administered is best.'—Pope.
[5] Mommsen scouts the notion of Caesar having sought to establish a

kept this aspect of it in the background; but Tiberius while pretending to leave everything to the Senate, at once took upon himself the direction of the army[1], and guarded his person with troops. The last case of a general being saluted as Imperator occurs in his reign[2]; and when Germanicus won his victories across the Rhine, it was not he, but Tiberius as commander-in-chief, who was so saluted. Tiberius was himself a consummate soldier, who had won his own laurels in a series of difficult and dangerous campaigns; and his intimate familiarity with the different parts of the Empire, derived partly from his long exile at Rhodes and partly from his campaigns on the Rhine and Danube, fitted him to become a capable and beneficent administrator.

Tiberius' reliance on the army.

Whatever we may think of the life and character of Tiberius as a whole[3], there can be no question of the excellence of his government of the provinces. He had shown himself a friend of the provinces even before he was emperor[4]; and his reign did not belie the hopes then raised. Tacitus himself commends his choice of governors[5], and his habit of leaving his governors for exceptionally long periods in their provinces, though disparaged by Tacitus[6], was viewed very differently by the provincials. Tiberius, says Josephus[7], permitted those governors who had been sent out to their governments to stay there a great while out of regard to the subjects who were under them.' That is, as he explains, the temptation to make a rapid fortune by extortion would be lessened. The governors were under the strict control of a man who detested misgovernment and disorder, and was sure to punish with severity[8]. Even

Tiberius' administration of the provinces.

---

purely military despotism, and maintains that he abhorred it; but Suet. Jul. 26 hardly squares with the theory.

[1] Ann. i. 7.   [2] Ib. iii. 74.
[3] The question was apparently first started by Duruy; see his History, iii. 409, where he gives a full list of subsequent works, to which add Mr. Beesley's Essay, and a discussion by Messrs. Church and Brodribb, Annals, p. 419.   [4] Suet. Tib. 26, 32.   [5] Tac. Ann. iv. 6.   [6] Ib. i. 80.
[7] Jos. Antiq. xviii. 6; Church and Brodribb, Annals, p. 340.
[8] Philo, Εἰς φλάκκον, p. 965; Duruy, iii. 489, note 4.

Tacitus allows his care for the provinces. 'He was careful not to distress the provinces by new burdens, and to see that in bearing the old they were safe from any rapacity or oppression on the part of governors[1].' In circumstances of special necessity he showed special liberality. 'Decrees of the Senate were passed at his proposal for relieving the cities of Cibyra and Ægium in Asia and Achaia, which had suffered from earthquakes, by a remission of three years' tribute[2].' On the occasion of the still more terrible earthquake which destroyed twelve famous cities of Asia, he promised a million sesterces for the relief of the one which had suffered most, Sardis, and remitted its debts to the fisc or the emperor's privy purse for a period of five years. Eleven other towns or states were similarly assisted, and a special commissioner was sent to afford present relief[3]. In all this we see the brightest side of a paternal despotism.

Tiberius had seen too much of war not to be a peace-maker. His solicitude for peace was most genuine and even painful, and Piso's worst crime in his eyes was that he had 'carried war into a province[4].' At the same time as an old soldier he knew that peace can only be secured sometimes by energetic war; and the brigand Tacfarinas could not long commit his depredations with impunity even in the country which both Rome and France have found so unfavourable to regular troops. Even the worst evils of his rule were not evils to the provinces. The informers for instance were dangerous to Romans, but to the provinces they provided a means of avoiding much of the trouble and expense of a prosecution. The merciless severity of his punishments was all in their favour; and while the emperor felt himself hated by those immediately around him, he was all the more ready to give ear to their petitions or complaints. His own legates do not seem to have needed punishment[5]; the proconsuls had terrible

---

[1] Ann. iv. 6. [2] Ib. iv. 13.
[3] Tac. Ann. ii. 47; cf. Suet. Tib. 49. [4] Ann. ii. 64, iii. 14.
[5] All the accusations in the first six books of Annals are of senatorial

examples to warn them against neglect of duty, and if a province needed relief it was given by a simple transference to his direct command[1].

One of the most important events of the period was the revolt in Gaul, due, says Tacitus[2], to the burden of debt, but perhaps still more to the intrigues of two ambitious men. The loyalty of Gaul had been often proved under the early Empire[3]. Roman civilisation had penetrated here with wonderful rapidity. The wealth of Southern Gaul was notorious: 'those millionaires' a speaker in the Senate calls the Ædui[4]. Augustadunum (Autun), so famous a city under the later Empire, was already the centre of culture and civilisation[5]. Here the noble youth received a liberal education, and were taught to be Romans, as Sertorius had taught the Spanish youth at Osca. A generation later we find the works of the younger Pliny in request at Lyons, almost immediately after their publication[6]. The people paid for this perhaps too rapid and immature bloom by the loss of the manlier virtues. We often hear allusions to 'Gallic effeminacy[7]' and to the country's 'wealthy and unwarlike population[8].' 'As for the Gauls,' says Civilis, 'what are they but the prey of the conqueror[9]?' But their immense material prosperity is too well attested to allow us to take the protestations of Florus quite seriously, and he is inconsistent with himself when he contrasts the vigour of Gaul with the exhaustion of Italy[10]. But no doubt the passage may be taken to prove that the trade of the negotiator was not eradicated by the Empire; and indeed under Nero we hear complaints of the 'boundless usury' by which Seneca 'exhausted the provinces'

The revolt in Gaul.

---

governors, except of Capito, a procurator, with whom Tiberius seems to have been more than usually angry.

[1] The case of Achaia and Macedonia.   [2] Annals, iii. 40.
[3] Cf. Tac. Ann. i. 34, 43, xi. 24.
[4] Ann. xi. 23; cf. Ib. xi. 18, 24, xiii. 43, 46.
[5] Ib. iii. 43.   [6] Ep. x. 11.   [7] Tac. Germ. 28.
[8] Ann. xi. 18.   [9] Hist. iv. 76.
[10] Ann. iii. 40; Duruy, iii. 451.

and accumulated his enormous wealth. It is significant however that the word *negotiator* loses in this period its strict meaning, and becomes applied to legitimate merchants[1]. It is in this sense that it is probably used when we are told that London was 'frequented by crowds of negotiatores.' Florus' complaints of the tribute are to a certain extent supported by the more peaceable but not less urgent complaints of Syria and Judaea[2]. The immense sums left by Tiberius in the treasury were perhaps larger than they should have been for the welfare of the provinces[3].

Caligula. Caligula, that best of slaves and worst of masters[4], is an instance of the saying of Tacitus that bad emperors are most fatal to those in their immediate neighbourhood[5]. It was Rome that suffered from his hideous eccentricities of cruelty; and it was on Rome and Italy that he inflicted new burdens of taxation[6]. Of the features of his government of the provinces we know little. Perhaps his most important measure was the one already mentioned, the establishment of a legate in Africa by the side of the proconsul. His pretended campaigns against Germany and Britain merely exposed his own insane vanity and incompetence.

Claudius. Far more important as a ruler of the provinces was the despised and perhaps underrated emperor who succeeded him. Claudius' liberal treatment of the provinces, if in part due to mere placid good-nature, must in part be ascribed to a deliberate and statesmanlike intention. His governors were kept in excellent control[7]; and by arranging that there should always be an interval between two provincial commands, an opportunity was secured for bringing any accusations that

---

[1] Ernesti; see supra.   [2] Tac. Ann. ii. 42.   [3] Suet. Calig. 31.
[4] Ib. 10.
[5] 'Saevi proximis ingruunt;' Tac. Hist. iv. 74.
[6] He began by remitting the ducentesima rerum venalium (it had been reduced from 1 to ½ per cent. by Tiberius), Suet. Cal. 16, but laid on a great number of new taxes afterwards; Ib. 40.
[7] Dio, lx. 24, 25; Ann. xii. 22; Jos. Ant. xx. 5.

might be necessary¹. In granting immunity² or autonomy³ to provincial towns he was very liberal, and if in some cases a town secured such privileges for very inadequate reasons, in others the help met a real need⁴. But it is with regard to the franchise and to the admission of provincials into the Senate that his action is most interesting and important. If a passage in Seneca⁵ is to be taken seriously, he had the widest designs in regard to the bestowal of the franchise. 'He had determined,' Clotho is introduced as saying, 'to see all the Greeks, Gauls, Spaniards, and Britons in the toga.' He was very severe to those who pretended unlawfully to the possession of the citizenship⁶; as was natural, considering that the payments exacted for it, where it was not either given by the emperor or secured by passing through the stage of the Latin right⁷, must probably as early as this have formed a regular source of income⁸. But he was himself liberal in bestowing it. A decree of his, of the year A.D. 46, on the franchise claimed by the Anauni has been found at Trent. It runs as follows: 'Of the Anauni, Tulliassi, and Sinduni (now 'Non,' 'Dolas,' and 'Saone,' near Trent) I am informed that part have been attributed⁹ to the Tridentines, part however not. I know that the Roman franchise of these people

---

¹ Dio, lx. 25: ὅπως δὲ μὴ διακρούοιντο οἱ τοιοῦτοι τοὺς θέλοντάς σφισι δικάζεσθαι οὐδένι ἀρχὴν ἐπὶ ἀρχῇ παραχρῆμα ἐδίδου.

² Ann. xii. 58; Suet. Cl. 25; Ann. xii. 60.

³ e.g. Rhodes; Ann. xii. 22; Jos. Ant. xx.

⁴ e.g. Byzantium; Ann. xii. 63. This case looks bad for the taxation, but the circumstances appear to have been exceptional.

⁵ De Morte Claudii, 3.

⁶ Suet. Claud. 15 and 25.

⁷ Plin. Paneg. 35: 'Seu per Latium in civitatem seu beneficio principis venissent.'

⁸ Acts xxii. 28; Suet. Vesp. 16, 18; Finlay, i. 45. A passage in Dio Cassius, lx. 17, shows that these payments were introduced at all events as early as Claudius.

⁹ The verbs *attribui, contribui* are used indifferently in the sense of minor towns or peoples attached to a more important town, which gave them the law, and raised taxes from them, and with which they in process of time, as here, tended to amalgamate. I shall return to this subject.

does not rest on a very sound foundation[1], but what with long usurpation and what with long commingling with the Tridentines, from whom they could not be separated without injury to that splendid municipium, I allow them to retain the franchise they claim; and am the more induced thereto because some of these people are soldiers in my praetorian guard, others have been centurions, and some have judged in the decuriae[2] at Rome[3].' Still more interesting is the debate recorded in Tacitus as to whether the Aedui and other Gauls of Gallia Comata should be allowed access to the Senate, and so become eligible for the Roman magistracies. Claudius himself made an elaborate speech in favour of the proposal, which is not only reported in Tacitus, but was engraved on brazen tablets, one of which by a fortunate chance was discovered at Lyons in the sixteenth century[4]. It is a specimen of those imperial orations which the emperor used either to deliver himself in Senate or to get delivered by his quaestors—*Principis Candidati*. At first they needed a senatus consultum to be law; but this was soon dropped. The Codex Theodosius formally gives them the force of law, but they had had it in practice long before. There were two kinds of such orations, one a mere outline which the senatus consultum filled up, and the other giving reasons for the law and full heads of it. To this latter class belongs the oration of Claudius. That such orations were commonly engraved on bronze we know from a passage in Pliny[5]; and copies were no doubt procured by or sent to any states or cities which such orations might concern. Of all such orations this of Claudius is the only one in existence. The account of Tacitus[6] shows that the immediate occasion

Claudius' oration in the Senate.

---

[1] 'Non nimium firmam id genus hominum habere Romanam originem.'

[2] Cf. Orelli, 3805, Judex ex v. Decuriis, and 3877. Augustus made four decuriae, Caligula raised them to five.

[3] Bruns, p. 172.

[4] In 1528 or 1529. The tablet was broken into two parts, and is only a fragment of the whole. Published by Spon, 1673; Menestrier, 1696; Monfalcon, 1853; Zell, Opuscula, 1857.

[5] Plin. Paneg. 75. [6] Tac. Ann. xi. 23–25.

for the Aedui putting in their claim was the fact that Claudius had just ejected a number of members from the Senate, and that there were therefore vacancies to be filled up. It must not be supposed that Claudius gave all Gallia Comata the *jus honorum*, but only the men of rank and wealth who had previously got the franchise [1]. The chief men of the Aedui were given it first, after them the notabilities of the rest of Gallia Comata; but it would be an absolute error to suppose that the common people obtained the same privilege. Else how explain the passage of Pliny where, writing after Claudius, he divides Gaul into the regular classes of allied, Latin, and Roman towns? Of those who had the franchise some had either themselves won it or had received it from their fathers—were in fact 'freeborn;' others had it as being members of Roman towns—of which latter there were four, Lugdunum, Colonia Agrippina, Colonia Equestris (Nyon), and Augusta Rauracorum (Augst near Basle). The worst of it is that we only know the status of Lyons for certain—it undoubtedly had full Roman right. It is a mistake to suppose that Augustus gave all Gaul the franchise, apart from the *jus suffragii* or *jus honorum*, for all that Dio [2], who is the only authority, says, is that Augustus gave some cities liberty and the franchise and took it away from others. Augustus probably gave the franchise without the vote to those Gauls who had deserved well of Rome; but there is no reason for ascribing to him any liberal or comprehensive measure, which besides would have been contrary to the whole drift of his policy.

The comparison of the real speech with Tacitus' version is very curious. Besides transposing and changing the order, Tacitus has cut out those deviations from the point and those needless and verbose displays of learning in which the antiquarian soul of Claudius delighted and by which he wearied out even the slavish patience of his Senate [3]. In the Annals the

The real speech not given by Tacitus.

---

[1] Zell, p. 109.   [2] Dio, liv. 24.
[3] Zell, p. 117. For Claudius' defects as an orator see Dio, lx. 2; Juvenal, vi. 620; Suet. Cl. 39, 40; Seneca, de Morte Claudii, 4.

speech is an admirable specimen of simple and statesmanlike eloquence. Of the character of the real speech something can be made out from the following fragments.

In the first column he defends himself against those who might accuse him of being an innovator. 'Why, our history is full of innovations!' To prove which profound thesis the imperial antiquary plunges with great zest into a regular chronicle, beginning with the early kings: if he went on with the same fulness for the whole history of Rome he would have kept the Senate day and night. It is the oddest, most eccentric, most characteristic production that was ever engraved on bronze; interspersed with such remarks as 'this too is a disputed point among the historians;' or, 'if we follow our own authorities;' or, 'if we follow the Etruscan writers,' &c., &c.; and with little parentheses to show his command of Tuscan (nam tusce Mastarna ei nomen erat) or his knowledge of the world. Even here he begins to think he is getting a little lengthy, and asks, 'Why now should I mention the discovery of the dictatorship, &c.; why the transference of power from the consuls to the decemvirs, &c.; why the partition of the consular power among several, and the so-called military tribunes with consular power, six of whom, and often even eight, were appointed (this last touch is delicious in its inconsequence); why the sharing of office afterwards with the commons, and that not only of the regular magistracies, but even of the priesthood?' Why indeed? A few lines further on the bewildered reader, who imagined he was going to study a speech on giving the *jus honorum* to the Gauls, is relieved by lighting on the word *civitatem;* but this time the bronze plays us false, and the rest of this column of the inscription has perished. Turn we now to the remains of the other column that are left us.

It seems to begin by alleging the example of Augustus and Tiberius in favour of his design. This is an interesting sentence: 'It was the wish of my uncle Tiberius that all the flower of the colonies and municipia everywhere, that is, of the men of standing and means (bonorum scilicet virorum et locupletium), should be in this curia.' He goes on: 'What then? Is not an Italian senator preferable to a provincial? When I shall commence to justify to you this part of my censorship, I will show you by acts what I think about that matter[1]. But I do not think that even provincials should be rejected, if only they can adorn the curia. See for how long a time the most beautiful and powerful colony of Vienna contributes senators to this curia.' He mentions L. Vestinus, a native, and inveighs without naming him against L. Valerius Asiaticus[2], 'who,' he says, 'was consul before his native colony had received the full privileges of Roman citizenship[3].' At this point the Senate naturally get impatient and interrupt: 'It is time, Tiberius Caesar Germanicus, that you should reveal to the conscript fathers what your speech is aiming at, for you have already reached the furthest boundaries of Narbonensis.' Whereupon Claudius continues: 'All these noble young men[4] whom I see before me are no more to be ashamed of as senators, than is that noble Persicus, my friend, ashamed to read the name of Allobrogicus among the images of his ancestors. And if you grant this, what further do you require than that I should prove to you by pointing my finger that the country of itself beyond the boundaries of Narbonensis is already sending you senators, since we are not ashamed of having senators from Lugdunum[5]. With trepidation indeed, patres conscripti, I have transgressed the accustomed and familiar boundaries of the provinces; but now without disguise I must plead the cause of Gallia Comata. And if any one objects that these same Gauls waged war for ten years against Divus Julius, let that man put over against that fault the unchanging loyalty of 100 years and an obedience

---

[1] The Latin is untranslateable : 'quid de ea re sentiam rebus ostendam.'

[2] For whom cf. Tac. Ann. xi. 1-4 ; Dio, lx. 29.

[3] Meaning perhaps the *jus honorum*, or *jus Italicum* ; Zell, p. 134.

[4] *Insignes Juvenes* could hardly mean senators. Perhaps it means equites who had the right of attending the Senate ; in fact the equites illustres ; cf. Ann. xi. 4; Dio, lx. 11 ; Zell, p. 186.

[5] *Ex Lugduno.* It is not possible to name any. Perhaps Claudius means *himself* as born at Lyons. It would be just his way.

more than tried in many of our dangers. It was they who, when my father Drusus was subjugating Germany, kept a safe and sure peace in his rear, and that, though he had been called to war from the conduct of the census, an operation then new and unfamiliar to the Gauls. And how difficult and perilous to us is this business of the census, although all we require is that our public resources should be known, we have learnt by an experience only too considerable.'

The imperial freedmen.

I have already mentioned the new power and privileges bestowed by Claudius on the procurators[1]. This was a very questionable policy: still worse were the extravagant powers bestowed on the imperial freedmen. At all times the freedmen were 'a widely diffused body; from it the city tribes, the various public functionaries, the establishments of the magistrates and priests were for the most part supplied, as well as the cohorts of the city guard; very many too of the knights and several of the senators derived their origin from no other source[2].' But it was Claudius who made them ministers of state and governors of provinces; and Nero imitated his example. As it was not exceptional ability but merely a turn for subservience, a certain talent for intrigue and an eye for the weak sides of human nature which raised such men as Pallas or Narcissus or Polyclitus to their position, they did not justify the lowness of their origin by any excellence of their administration. They accumulated fabulous wealth; Pallas could refuse a present of 15,000,000 sesterces without self-denial; and it was not wealth obtained by good means. Felix before whom St. Paul appeared was one of these freedmen, and Tacitus describes him as 'indulging in every kind of barbarity and lust,' and as 'exercising the power of a king in the spirit of a slave[3].'

Accessions of territory under Claudius.

No less than five provinces were added to the Empire in this reign. Claudius was no soldier himself, but he chose his generals well. Besides the two new provinces in Africa[4],

---

[1] Suet. Claud. 12, 24; supra, p. 110. [2] Ann. xiii. 27. [3] Hist. iv. 9.
[4] Mauretania Zingitana, Mauretania Caesariensis.

Thrace[1], which had long been held in semi-subjection, was put under a procurator; Lycia, in which there had been some disorders, was added to Pamphylia[2]; and Southern Britain was conquered and made into an imperial province under a legate[3].

---

[1] There is a good summary of the relations of Rome and Thrace in Church and Brodribb, p. 411.

[2] Dio, lx. 17: Τοὺς δὲ Λυκίους στασιάσαντας ὥστε καὶ Ῥωμαίους τινὰς ἀποκτεῖναι ἐδουλώσατο, καὶ ἐς τὸν τῆς Παμφυλίας νομὸν ἐσέγραψεν.

[3] I subjoin a summary of the epigraphic evidence as to Britain,—made out from C. I. L. vii, with the help of Hübner's introductions and notes.

Inscriptions of early date in Britain are very rare. Those of the first century A.D. as rare as those of the Republic in an ordinary province. There is one of Nero's reign; and there are leaden bullets with the names Claudius, Britannicus, Nero, Vespasian, Domitian. A few milestones of Hadrian and Antoninus Pius. A few military inscriptions also probably belong to the first century. Very few others of any sort. The local distribution of the inscriptions proves that the South was thoroughly conquered and occupied even in the first two centuries—excepting Devonshire and Cornwall, whence we get hardly any inscriptions, though that country had been visited by Gauls for lead and tin. The original capital probably Camulodunum— Colonia Claudiana. But even from the first London was probably a sort of second capital. Also the inscriptions of the South are older than those of the North and East; so we gather how slowly and painfully the island was conquered. By the time of Trajan Eburacum seems to have been the capital and seat of government. The inscriptions in York neighbourhood are of the middle or end of the second century. Hadrian's wall not far north of York; that of Antoninus Pius was where Agricola had reached, i.e. between Clyde and Forth. This was the limit of Rome, Ireland was not touched. The Silures were never really conquered; no inscriptions from Wales. But on their borders were the garrisons of Isca (Caerleon), Deva (on the Dee), Segontium (just south of Bangor). And these cities supply only inscriptions of the end of the second and beginning of the third century, which looks as if the Roman hold in these parts was considerably strengthened about that time. That Septimius Severus and his son Antoninus fought both in this district and in the North is shown by inscriptions. Hardly anything of Diocletian: nothing of Carausius and Allectus, though they were British emperors in a sense, and though we have plenty of their coins. No Christian inscriptions of the fourth or fifth century. From fifth to eighth century Christian inscriptions are found in Cambria, also in the country of the Dumnones.

Britain was an imperial province, under a consular; Tac. Agr. 14; Ann. i. 60. Hübner has made out a list of them—mainly from Tacitus—in Neu Rhein. Mus. vol. xii. 1857, p. 46. No consular or praeses of the Con-

Claudius and the Druids.

Another noteworthy feature of this reign is the determined position of hostility taken by Claudius against the Druids. As their religion had a political significance [1] the Romans never regarded them with the same tolerant indifference as they did other creeds. Augustus had incorporated Hesus and their other deities in the Roman Pantheon, but the Druids would not come forward and accept the priesthoods under Roman direction and control. Claudius persecuted them in Gaul, and perhaps his expedition to Britain was caused by the desire to uproot the last stronghold of their preponderant influence [2]. In another part of the Empire, a famine in Greece serves to point out that country as still the least prosperous part of the Roman dominions [3]. On the Rhine the establishment of the Colonia Agrippina marks the birth of the city which is still famous as Cologne [4].

Nero.

Nero, who was only a boy when he became emperor, started

---

stantine period can be named. Besides the governor and legates of legions we also find a procurator provinciae. Hadrian created juridici, here as elsewhere, of whom four are known from inscriptions in other provinces. Britain was divided into two provinces, Superior and Inferior, by Sept. Severus, according to Herodianus, iii. 8. 2. Perhaps confirmed by Dio, cap. lv. 23, and by two inscriptions found in Britain, and one at Lambesis in Africa. One cannot tell where the boundaries were; but *Superior* probably was the southern province, though an inscription found north of York with *Superioris* on it is against this view.

Speaking generally,—hardly any inscriptions of municipal life; hardly any colonies, and those military. Of the towns which were either *castella* or *mansiones* we do not know the status. London was a municipium. Camulodunum was a colony; Tac. Ann. xii. 32. So was Lindum (*Lincoln*) and Eburacum (Inscrip. 248). Plenty can be gathered about the legions on the other hand: four was the regular number; after Hadrian, three. There were also auxiliary troops, also a fleet; Tac. Agr. 25; Hist. iv. 79; Inscrip. No. 18. 374.

There was a native coinage in Britain long before the Romans,—imitations of the Macedonian stater. Probably the earliest in Britain are from 200 to 150 B.C. (Evans, p. 26). Church and Brodribb are wrong on this point (Annals, p. 405).

[1] Suet. Claud. 25.   [2] Duruy, iii. 526.
[3] Duruy, iii. 537, note 2, and his authorities.
[4] Ann. xii. 32.

with excellent professions. He 'was for relieving the allies;' he started a wild scheme of abolishing all indirect taxes, and along with them the publicani[1]; and Josephus testifies to the justice of his decisions[2]. He issued an edict to prohibit any provincial governor from exhibiting shows of gladiators or other such entertainments, as it was found by experience that this was only a form of bribery[3]. But the intoxication of power was too much for that vain head and cruel heart; and the rest of his rule was not consonant to the fair promise of its beginning. After the great fire of Rome he sent some of his freedmen on an excursion to get what they could out of the provinces. Acratus in particular distinguished himself by the forcible robbery of statues and pictures; and when Barsa Soranus, who governed Asia like a Scaurus, did not punish the people of Pergamos for their violent resistance to the freedman's impudent depredations, he incurred the bitter enmity of his master[4]. Nero openly told his governors that he expected them to plunder[5]; and the revolt of Britain was due in part to the burden of the taxes, and partly to the 'boundless usury' of the money-lenders[6]. The circumstances of this revolt, in particular the treatment of Boadicea and her daughters, show what the rule of the provinces could still be under a bad emperor.

But if a newly-conquered province could still be thus treated, it is impossible to mistake the general growth in prosperity and influence of the provinces as a whole. It would be easy to ascribe too much importance to the gift of freedom which the well-flattered emperor made to the province of Achaia[7]. The immunity from taxation which generally went with this gift of freedom was a positive boon enough, but it was revoked by Vespasian; and if Pliny tells a friend of his who was appointed

General prosperity of the provinces.

---

[1] Ann. xiii.   [2] Josephus, Antiq. xx. 8. § 11.
[3] Tac. Ann. xiii. 31.   [4] Ibid. xvi. 23.   [5] Suet. Ner. 32.
[6] Tac. Ann. xiv. 32, xiii. 42.
[7] Suet. Nero, 24. See Finlay, i. 46, 48, 63; Freeman's Essays, 2nd Ser. p. 322.

to the province that he was 'sent to a society of men who breathe the spirit of true manhood and liberty[1],' it is to be feared that he is only indulging his natural love of phrases. The gift of the Latin rights to the people of the Maritime Alps[2] was one much better worth having. These rights implied all the privileges of the Roman franchise except the jus suffragii; and moreover opened a regular access to the full franchise, as all magistrates of Latin towns became ipso facto Roman citizens[3]. 'It likewise enjoys the rights of the Latin towns, so that in Nemausus you meet with Roman citizens who have obtained the honours of the aedile and quaestorship,' says Strabo of the present town of Nismes[4]. The extension of these rights to the provincials began when Pompey's father, Pompeius Strabo, gave them to the Transpadanes[5]. Caesar had a plan of extending them to the whole of Sicily, and Augustus was apparently more liberal with this minor privilege than with the full franchise. It is easily intelligible that when a town had once gained as much as this, it had good hopes of gaining the full privilege[6]. Such concessions as these show in which direction the stream was going; and there are other indications of the rapid gain of the provincial upon the merely Roman element. Many of the provincial governors were themselves provincials; and all the governors seem to have been really controlled by the wishes of the people they had to rule. No wonder men of the old school, like Paetus Thrasea, complained of 'the new insolence of provincials,' and that votes of

---

[1] Plin. Ep. viii. 24. [2] Ann. xv. 32.
[3] Cic. ad Att. v. 11; Merivale, ii. 100. It is a curious fact that a Latin who built a ship for the corn traffic got the franchise; Suet. Claud. 19.
[4] Strabo, iv. 1. § 12. See also § 21 of the Lex Salpensana.
[5] Merivale, ii. 99.
[6] I have not mentioned two distinctions which are yet of importance— (1) between Latin Coloniarii and Latin Juniani, the latter being a particular class of freedmen who were given Latin rights by a Lex Junia Narbona (A.D. 19); and (2) Latium Majus and Minus, the former being when a magistrate got Roman franchise only for himself, the latter when he got it for his 'parents, wife, children, and grandchildren on the male side;' § 21 of Lex Salpens. See Marq. i. 57 and 61.

thanks to ex-governors were forbidden by senatorial decree, when a rich provincial could boast his power to decide whether or no a governor should receive such a vote, and when the governors were seen going about at the latter part of their time 'seeking votes like candidates[1].' That the inflexible and tyrannous Roman governor should be turned into a complaisant popularity hunter was a change indeed. The wealth of the provinces is sufficiently shown by such facts as that, when Laodicea was overthrown by an earthquake, the inhabitants without any relief from Rome rebuilt the town by their own resources[2]; and that on the occasion of the great fire, Lyons alone offered a subscription of four million sesterces. Southern Gaul was in fact more prosperous in this than in any period of its history. There was an immense marine trade, an active internal navigation, and the towns reached a great size and were inhabited by a dense population[3].

Nero was not one of those who extended the boundaries of the Empire. The Alpes Cottiae which had been under the nominal rule of a client prince were made into a province, and put under a procurator[4]. This may have still further strengthened and secured the communication between Italy and Gaul, but could otherwise have been of little consequence. More interesting is the addition of the Greek city of Tyras to the province of Moesia, an event which occurred in this reign[5]. In this part of the world the policy of Rome was one of beneficent encroachment. The few Greek towns which showed like bright centres of civilisation amidst the clouds of barbarism could hardly keep their own unaided, and the services rendered by Rome were of the most real and precious kind.

Accessions of territory under Nero.

---

[1] Ann. xv. 20, 21; cf. Plin. Pan. 70, which shows that such votes were used for elections at Rome. Pliny, Ep. vi. 13, illustrates the freedom of the Bithynians in the Senate. Cf. Suet. Vesp. 4.   [2] Tac. Ann. xiv. 27.

[3] See some interesting remarks in Lentheric, pp. 232, 401, 433, 441.

[4] Suet. Nero, 18.

[5] Henzen, 6429; Marquardt, i. 150. For an interesting letter of Severus and Caracalla to the people of Tyras in answer to a claim of immunity they had set up, see Bruns, p. 176.

The three pretenders.

The fearful year of civil war which followed the death of Nero could not of necessity be of much consequence for the provincial administration. It is noticeable, however, that Italy suffered very much more than the provinces[1]: the sack of Cremona[2] recalls the worst horrors of Corinth or Magdeburg. The time was gone by when it was Asia or Greece that was the battle-field and the prey of the conqueror, and the turn of Italy was now come. It is impossible to say which of the three pretenders would have made the best emperor. All three had distinguished themselves as provincial governors[3]. Galba was too old and too narrow in his views (he was very chary of giving the franchise[4]) to become a great emperor; but he was certainly an honest man. Vitellius was profusely extravagant in bestowing such privileges as remissions of tribute, immunity, the Latin rights, and the privileges of treaties[5]; but there seems to have been no settled plan in this, any more than in other parts of his conduct after his head had been turned by the prospect of Empire. Perhaps Otho, notwithstanding his profligate youth, showed the most promise of the three. His bestowal of the franchise on the Lingones looks as if he would have been a liberal emperor.

Vespasian. When Vespasian became emperor he succeeded to all the difficulties bequeathed by the civil war. He himself declared that there was need of 4000 million sesterces to let the State exist; and if he found any such deficit as that, it is hardly wonderful that he was a hard master in regard to the taxation. The tribute of all the provinces was increased, of some doubled; and he is even accused of deliberately appointing rapacious procurators, in order to squeeze them afterwards[6]. The same absolute necessity of getting money was the motive for an act which must have been in the highest degree invidious and un-

---

[1] Tac. Hist. ii. 56, 87; iii. 49. [2] Hist. iii. 33.
[3] Galba in Africa and Tarraconensis; Suet. Galba, 7, 9; Hist. i. 50. Otho in Lusitania; Suet. Otho, 3; Hist. i. 13. Vitellius in Africa; Suet. Vit. 5.
[4] Suet. Galba, 14. [5] Hist. iii. 55.
[6] Suet. Vesp. 16 for all the statements in the text.

gracious. He deprived of their freedom Achaia, Lycia, Rhodes, Byzantium, and Samos[1]: that is, he obliged them to pay taxes as before. His general administration, however, was much better than some of his previous acts would have led men to expect[2]. He was an enormous worker[3], and animated with the best intentions. There can be no doubt that he did much to secure a stable administration, which Domitian did not overturn, and which was strengthened and consolidated by the Antonines. An interesting feature of his rule was his bestowal of the Latin rights upon the whole of Spain[4]; while the most important event connected with it was the siege and capture of Jerusalem.

Titus did not live long enough to fulfil the promise of his first years of empire; and though we are tolerably acquainted with the life of Domitian, our knowledge refers rather to his cruelties in Rome than to his administration of the provinces. We know however that, at all events in the first part of his reign, he was very severe to his governors, and that they never ruled better than when under him[5]. His campaigns on the Danube were without permanent result, but are interesting as anticipating the advent of a more vigorous conqueror. 'There may be great men even under bad emperors[6];' and Agricola in Britain carried the Roman arms north of the Cheviots, and secured the whole country by a mixture of clemency and force. The policy which his father Vespasian had commenced in Spain was carried out in detail under Domitian's rule. It is to this date that the existing laws of the municipia of Salpensa and Malaga and of the colony of Ursao belong; and it is very probable that all the cities of Spain after they had received the

Domitian.

---

[1] Suet. Vesp. 8.
[2] Cf. Hist. ii. 84. As to his governorship of Africa, Suet. Vesp. 4, and Tacitus, Hist. ii. 97, are in absolute contradiction.
[3] Suet. Vesp. 21; Plin. Ep. iii. 5.   [4] Plin. N. H. iii. 4, fin.
[5] Suet. Dom. 8: 'Provinciarum praesidibus coercendis tantum curae adhibuit ut neque modestiores umquam neque justiores extiterint.'
[6] Tac. Agr. 42.

Latin rights from Vespasian had been ordered to make public their municipal law [1].

Trajan.

The most important act of Nerva's brief reign was the choice of his successor. Trajan was a good administrator as well as a consummate soldier, and no choice could have been more fortunate. With him begins the long line of warrior emperors, who spent most of their time upon the frontiers. He added four new provinces to the Empire, and in one case at all events his departure from the policy of Augustus proved a signal success. Though perhaps a little too exclusive in his views as to Italy and the provinces [2], he yet showed a genuine solicitude for all parts of his Empire. His campaigns had given him a great experience of the most different provinces [3]; and the modest scale of his journeys was a great contrast to the barbaric progresses of Domitian [4]. There were bad governors in his reign—the African Classicus [5] plundered Spain, and the Spaniard Marius plundered Africa [6]—but Marius was banished, and Classicus either died too soon for punishment or anticipated his sentence by suicide. His correspondence with Pliny shows at any rate that unwearied and constant application to details which marks a successful administrator. Nor is the charge of over-interference, often brought against him, well founded. The circumstances under which Pliny was sent to Bithynia as legate instead of the ordinary proconsul were wholly

---

[1] That the law of Salpensa was published under his rule is plain from § 24, 25, 26, and § 29 of Malacitana. And as the title of Germanicus is not given, they must have been published between 81 and 84; cf. C. I. L. ii. No. 1945, where the magistrates of Aluro (Alora) thank Domitian for having attained the franchise through their duumvirate. The law of Ursao is of a much earlier date, but the character of the writing shows it to have been formally published at this time.

[2] Perhaps Dean Merivale, followed by Mr. Freeman, states this view too strongly. The argument is the establishment of Alimenta in Italy, and will hardly bear the weight put upon it. The whole of Pliny's letters leaves a different impression. De la Berge is of a different opinion.

[3] Plin. Pan. 15.   [4] Ibid. 20.   [5] Plin. Ep. iii. 9.

[6] Plin. Ep. ii. 11; Juv. i. 45. The Spaniards made a grim joke on the maltreatment of themselves and Africa by an African and a Spaniard respectively.

exceptional, and we have no right to argue from his conduct in this case to his conduct in other provinces[1]. The cities of Bithynia had got into financial difficulties, due partly to mismanagement, partly perhaps to such dishonesty of their magistrates as that which Cicero mentions in Cilicia under the Republic[2]; and Pliny was sent there for the express purpose of inquiring into their municipal affairs, and, if possible, putting them upon a satisfactory footing[3]. He was welcomed with gratitude; and even an allied town, though in right free from any interference of the governor, was glad to subject its affairs to his examination. It is very natural therefore that in these novel and untried circumstances the governor should refer more largely than usual to the supreme decision of the emperor; and the sense and tact with which Trajan answers Pliny's sometimes rather unnecessary questions excites our admiration. It is noteworthy, for instance, that he refuses to sanction any rough and ready measure of general application to all the cities of the province, but insists on a particular examination of each case by itself[4]. His jealousy of all associations, though it seems to us excessive[5], was probably dictated by a consideration of the welfare of the towns themselves as much as by the desire for an untroubled administration. His great strictness in giving leave to private persons to travel by the public post[6] must certainly have been welcome to the provincials. The great work of Trajan's reign was the conquest of Dacia. 'The Dacian descending from the banded Danube[7]' had long been an object of some fear to the Romans. 'A people which can never be trusted' is Tacitus' description of them[8]; and when they had consolidated themselves into a nation under a powerful

---

[1] This is well stated by De la Berge, p. 120.
[2] A law of Trajan (Dig. xlviii. 13. 4. 57) made such thefts peculatus; De la Berge, ib.   [3] Plin. Ep. x. 41.   [4] Ib. Ep. x. 14.
[5] Ib. Ep. x. 43, 94, 97. Caesar abolished all guilds.
[6] Ib. Ep. x. 14, 121. Trajan did much for the postal system; see Merivale, viii. 53; De la Berge, 122; Hudemann, p. 19, foll.
[7] 'Conjurato descendens Dacus ab Istro;' Virgil, Geo. ii. 497; cf. Horace, Od. iii. 6. 13.   [8] Hist. iii. 46.

chief, they showed themselves really formidable. Domitian won very little glory from his campaign against them, and is said to have paid them a regular tribute [1]. Trajan's two campaigns ended not so much in the conquest of the people as in their annihilation; and their place was taken by immigrants from all parts of the Empire [2]. The Romanisation of the province was extraordinarily rapid and permanent. There was only one town in the country when Trajan conquered it,—the royal residence, Sarmizegathusa. He established four colonies—Apulum, Napoca, Dierna, and another at the old capital; and Dacia is one of the provinces in which the growth of the town system is most obvious and most interesting. To this day the language of the Roumanians testifies to their origin. The country still remains an integral part of the Latin world, though isolated from the rest, and profoundly modified by its after history. 'The two names which are still the most popular in all the valley of the Lower Danube are those of Trajan the victorious organiser and Justinian the great constructor [3].' Trajan's dispossession of the prince of Armenia and substitution of a legate was not a measure of much consequence. It was changed by Hadrian, who also gave up his conquests beyond the Tigris, on the principle by which Cato conceded freedom to Macedonia. His new province of Arabia was a more important and more permanent acquisition; and Roman civilisation seems to have made considerable strides in this quarter. The two most important towns were Bostra and Petra, of which the former appears to have received special benefits from Trajan, and the latter from Hadrian [4].

Hadrian.

Hadrian has been called 'the first emperor who really cared for the provinces [5].' Perhaps this is unjust to Trajan; but the

---

[1] Dio, lxvii. 6; Merivale, viii. 26; De la Berge, 37.

[2] Eutrop. viii. 6; De la Berge, 59. For Galatians at Napoca, see Marquardt, i. 155. [3] Desjardins, *Les Antonins d'après l'épigraphie*, p. 654.

[4] Marquardt, i. 275.

[5] Freeman's Essays, Second Series, p. 334. I have said something about this already, but must add a speech of Trajan to the man whom he intended to make his successor: 'Commendo tibi provincias, si quid mihi

praise which it implies is well deserved. Hadrian had the most intimate familiarity with all his dominions. 'No emperor traversed so many countries at such a rate[1].' To read the sketch of his life by Spartian is like watching a panorama which carries you from one end of the world to the other. After he had returned from the East to Rome on the death of Trajan, his first journey was to Gaul and Germany[2], where he made himself remarkable by the strictness of his discipline. Then he crossed to Britain and built the wall known by his name[3]. Returning to Gaul he built a splendid basilica at Nemausus (Nismes), crossed the Pyrenees, and remained the winter at Tarraco[4]. His next journey was to the Archipelago, Asia, and in particular Achaia, in which province he especially favoured Athens—being himself so fond of Greek learning as to be nicknamed *Graeculus*[5]—and conferred many benefits upon it. The next resting-place was Sicily; from whence he crossed to Africa, and did much to improve the condition of the African provinces. Thence he returned to Rome, but hardly halting there, made his way again eastwards, passing through Athens, to dedicate the temple he had commenced on his previous visit, and Asia[6]. Passing through Syria, where the insolence of Antioch earned the people his hearty aversion[7], as it did afterwards that of the gentle M. Aurelius[8], and through Trajan's new province of Arabia, he came to Egypt, thus completing the circle of the Roman provinces.

The immense knowledge thus acquired was made available for the purposes of an excellent administration. Notwithstanding his liberal remissions of taxation[9], he yet introduced so excellent and economical a management of the exchequer[10], that the great expenses of his buildings in the provinces[11] do

Hadrian's administration.

---

fatale contigerit.' I seem to detect in these words a full consciousness of his responsibilities and none of that merely Roman sentiment which has been ascribed to him.

[1] Spartian, 13. [2] Ib. 10. [3] Ib. 11. [4] Ib. 12. [5] Ib. 1.
[6] Ib. 13. [7] Ib. 14. [8] Capitol. 25. [9] Spartian, 6, 7, 21. [10] Ib. 20.
[11] 'In omnibus paene urbibus et aliquid aedificavit et ludos edidit;' Spar-

not seem to have exceeded his means. Bad governors were severely punished [1], and in particular the procurators, who seem to have done their best all through the Empire to act the part of the publicani they had supplanted, were kept in check by a strong hand [2]. He imitated Trajan in keeping his freedmen in their due subordinate position [3]; discouraged informers, and showed an almost excessive complaisance to the Roman Senate [4]. He was liberal in his bestowal of the Latin rights [5]; and one of the best measures of his reign was to ameliorate the wretched lot of the slaves [6]. His establishment of the four consular judges in Italy [7] shows the commencement of the tendency to treat Italy much like a province [8]; for the evidence goes to prove that these magistrates were not merely judges, but discharged general executive functions as well [9].

Hadrian's foreign policy.

As already mentioned Hadrian gave up Armenia and Mesopotamia, and thought, according to Dio, of giving up Dacia. His was a peaceful reign, and the military measures which he took were generally those of self-defence. Besides his wall in Britain, he built a similar fortification to protect the Agri Decumates on the North, and so shut them off from the German tribes. This triangular piece of land needed special defence, as it was the only place where it was possible for the barbarians to press into the Empire without crossing either the Rhine or Danube; and the soldier-like Probus imitated Hadrian in driving a wall from stream to stream. The country had its name in all probability from the payment of a tithe by the inhabitants to Rome, and Roman civilisation seems to have held its own there for at least two centuries [10].

---

tian, 19. A facetious Frenchman has said that Hadrian had ' la maladie de la pierre.' Several towns were called after him simply Hadrianopolis, in token of gratitude, as he did not like honorary inscriptions.

[1] Spartian, 13.   [2] Ib. 3.   [3] Ib. 21.   [4] Ib. 8.   [5] Ib. 21.
[6] Ib. 18.   [7] Ib. 22; Capitol. Antonin. 2.
[8] Already under Trajan Pliny, Ep. iii. 7, calls Campania a 'province.'
[9] There is a list of these juridici drawn up by Mommsen in Lachmann's Gromatici Veteres, ii. 192.
[10] By 369 at all events the Rhine was again the boundary; Marquardt, i. 125.

The successor whom Hadrian had chosen, M. Antoninus Pius, imitated and perhaps even exceeded his solicitude for the provinces. He was however no traveller like him, and preferred to rule the Empire from what was still its centre—Rome. 'With such diligence did he rule the subject peoples that he cared for all men and all things as his own. All the provinces flourished under him[1].' Such is the express testimony of his biographer, and this though the disasters of the time were numerous[2]. As a means to this end he kept good governors long in their provinces, some for seven or even nine years[3]. The procurators were kept in order, as they had been by Hadrian[4]. The municipal towns were assisted with money to commence new buildings or restore old ones[5]; the decay of the municipia, mainly owing to the bad state of their finances, is a melancholy change of which the traces are beginning to appear. In foreign policy an interesting feature is the support given to the Greek cities of the Euxine against the barbarous Scythians[6]. Olbiopolis was so effectually succoured that the tribe which had attacked it were forced to give hostages for their good behaviour. The revolt of Egypt[7] at the commencement of the reign was no doubt due to the unruly turbulence of the Alexandrians, who were the first to urge their governor to rebel against the ruling emperor; and if they could not seduce him from his loyalty, would still revolt on their own account[8]. The fact that all Gaul had received the franchise by the end of this reign shows how rapidly the Empire was tending to uniformity[9], and the decree of Tergeste throws an interesting light upon the interior of a municipality during the period[10].

Administration of Antoninus.

---

[1] Capitol. 7.
[2] Famine, earthquakes in Rhodes and Asia; fires in Rome, Narbo, Antioch, and Carthage; Capitol. 9.
[3] Ib. 5.   [4] Ib. 6.   [5] Ib. 8.
[6] Capit. Anton. 9.   [7] Ib. 5.   [8] Cf. Preuss, p. 71.
[9] Mowat, *Une inscription inedite de Tours*, p. 28.
[10] Tergeste (Trieste), a Roman colony in the tenth region of Italy; cf. Pliny, iii. 18. Velleius however, in his list of colonies in Italy (i. 15), does not mention it; so not founded before 100 B.C. But Appian, Illyr. 18,

M. Aurelius. With the accession of M. Aurelius we first find that partition of powers between more than one emperor which was

mentions it as a Roman colony, and apparently it can be made out to have been such from Caesar, Bell. Gall. viii. 24. So somewhere in the twenty years between B.C. 55 and B.C. 35 Augustus strengthened Tergeste as an important post for his campaigns in this region; Gruter, p. clxvi. No. 6. Augustus also attributed the Catali to it—meaning that they got justice from Tergestine magistrates, and paid a regular vectigal. See Suet. Aug. 46: 'Italiam xxviii coloniarum numero deductarum ab se frequentavit operibusque ac vectigalibus plurifariam instruxit;' Zumpt, pp. 13-15.

The decree has been separately edited by Zumpt. My translation is in the main from his text, correcting him here and there by reference to Henzen, 7168, who has utilised the work done by scholars, especially Mommsen, on the inscription since Zumpt's time, and omitting merely periphrastic and complimentary expressions.

'Hispanius Lentulus and Vibius Nepos, Duoviri juri dicundo, spoke to the following effect:

'That Fabius Severus, vir clarissimus, had previously conferred great benefits upon our Republic, for he had pleaded and won many causes of the highest importance before the emperor Antoninus Pius, without any charge to our treasury, in such a way as to bind his country and all of us to him. But at the present time he has done the Republic so great and permanent a benefit as to throw all his previous good deeds into the shade; and therefore, although our gratitude cannot equal his services, yet we must reward as we can his benevolences, not in order to make him the readier to do us future services, but that we may show ourselves duly grateful and worthy of his protection.

'Whereupon the following proposal was made at the motion of L. Calpurnius Certus:

'Since Fabius Severus has always shown his devotion to his native place, and aimed at senatorial rank, chiefly that he might do it services, by pleading before judges assigned by Caesar, and before Caesar himself in public suits, which, partly by the justice of the emperor, partly by his own talents, he has always carried in our interests; and since of late more especially, as is shown by the celestial letter of Antoninus Aug. Pius, he has so happily represented our wishes before him by obtaining from him that the Carni and Catali, attributed by Divine Augustus to our Republic, should, in proportion as they deserved it by their lives and incomes, be admitted into our curia through the aedileship[1], and thereby attain Roman citizenship; and since he has thus enriched our treasury, and filled up our curia, and

---

[1] The aedileship was the most expensive office in a municipium, with least real power. See Zumpt's note on the passage.

to be made the basis of the imperial system by Diocletian[1]. Lucius Verus, however, does not seem to have contributed anything to the dignity and welfare of the Empire, and his sudden death relieved M. Aurelius from a compromising associate. M. Aurelius was a good ruler of the provinces[2], liberal to the municipia, and ready to give exemptions from taxation in case of need[3]. If his lot had been cast in times of peace he would probably have thrown his energies into the details of the administration, and done something more to merit his popularity with the provincials[4]. But the hard necessities of his time kept the man who, above all men, would have loved a life of peace and quiet study, engaged in arduous and unceasing warfare against ever-gathering masses of the barbarians. A great internal movement seems to have begun among the trans-Rhenane and trans-Danubian peoples in this period. The northern races were pressed down southwards by still

---

amplified our whole Republic with excellent citizens[2] by admitting to a share in office and in Roman citizenship the best and richest individuals, so that those who previously only paid a tribute[3] now pay twice as much, owing to the honorarium, and at the same time share with us the *munera* of the decurionate, which are burdensome to a few:

'To show our gratitude for all this we erect to him an equestrian gilded statue in the most crowded part of the forum, with a suitable inscription, and we call upon Fabius Verus, the father of Severus, to thank the latter in our name. Passed[4].'

[1] Capit. 7. All inscriptions consequently in which Augg. instead of Aug. occurs are at all events not earlier than A.D. 161.
[2] Capit. 17. [3] Ib. 23.
[4] Ib. 26: 'Orientalibus provinciis carissimus fuit.'

---

[2] So Zumpt. The stone appears to read *cum egminiis*. Mommsen conjectures *fomentis* (?), which Henzen accepts.
[3] Perhaps this is too strong a word. The Latin is—*In redditu pecuniario erant.*
[4] It may be asked why the inscription does not simply say that the Catali by favour of the emperor received the Jus Latii? Because the Jus Latii included not only the attainment of Roman franchise through a magistracy, but also the commercium with Roman citizens. See Ulpian, lib. xix. 4. So when it was conceded to the Catali that they should become Roman citizens by holding a magistracy at Tergeste, nothing whatever was given to the rest of the tribe, who held no magistracy. So their status was inferior to that of the twenty-four towns attributed to Nemausus (see Pliny, iii. 4; for they had all Latin rights, according to Strabo, iv. 1. 12, p. 187). See Zumpt's note, p. 15.

fiercer nations in their rear, and being thus compelled to become invaders they attacked all who refused to give them a refuge[1]. M. Aurelius appears to have led the Roman armies with constancy and ability, and was greatly beloved by his men[2]. According to his historian, his conquests were considerable enough to allow him to think of making a new province or provinces out of his principal enemies, the Marcomanni, Hermunduri, Quadi, and Sarmatae; and he would have carried out his idea had it not been for his too early death[3]. However this may be, he certainly inflicted some severe defeats upon the barbarians, and was able to transplant a number of them to Roman territory, thus employing the system of *Coloni*, which is so important a feature of the Empire under Diocletian[4]. But the beginning of the end had come. It was not only on the Rhine and Danube that the Roman Peace was rudely interrupted. The Moors devastated all parts of Spain, and though Aurelius' legates fought against them with success, yet the depopulation of the country had to be met by an infusion of Italian blood[5]. There were disturbances also among the Sequani in Gaul[6], and in Egypt[7]. Aurelius' necessities were so pressing and the ravages of the plague had been so fearful, that he was obliged to make soldiers of slaves and of the brigands of Dalmatia, and to hire German mercenaries to help him to destroy the Germans[8]. From this time forward the Imperial rule becomes strictly military in character; emperors are chosen exclusively for their qualities as soldiers; and reforms are dictated solely by military necessities.

Summary of the period.

. These two first centuries of the Empire were for some countries the flower of their history. Asia Minor was rich and

---

[1] Capit. 14. [2] Ib. 27. [3] Ib. 24, 27. [4] Ib. 24.
[5] Capit. 21 and 11: 'exhaustis Hispaniis.' The cause is not mentioned, but is probably the one stated in the text. Perhaps the plague too had its share. Spain had apparently been prosperous under Trajan; De la Berge, p. 125. For the invasion of the Moors, see Boissière, *L'Afrique Romaine*, p. 289.
[6] Capit. 22. [7] Ib. 21. [8] Ib. 21.

populous[1], and studded with innumerable cities. The immense sums which these cities voluntarily spent upon their aqueducts, amphitheatres, and other public works, were perhaps excessive and extravagant, but attest a grandeur of conception and a superb indifference to economy which could only have sprung from a great material prosperity. The same facts appear in Syria. There were 200,000 Christians alone in Antioch in the fourth century. Jerusalem had a population of 600,000. Egypt was inhabited by seven and a-half millions of people, 300,000 of whom were settled in Alexandria[2]. Strabo and Pliny give similar testimony as to Spain and Gaul[3]; and Africa in particular enjoyed a prosperity which has never fallen to its lot before or since[4]. The Danubian provinces were equally well off, and the towns both more numerous and more important than they are at present, while those that are still the most considerable, for instance Widdin, Sistova, Nicopolis, and, further south, Adrianople, are all Roman foundations.

I have already spoken of the fundamental defects which made it impossible for the rule of Rome to be permanent. And it should also be mentioned that the taxation, though lightened as far as possible under the rule of the many capable and well-meaning rulers of this period, still pressed heavily upon the people[5]. The frequent remissions and exemptions granted in

Fundamental defects of the Roman rule.

---

[1] Cf. what Pliny says of the province of Bithynia, which was certainly not one of the most prosperous of the peninsula; Plin. Ep. x. 50. For Nicomedia, see Preuss, 118. Pergamum had a population of 120,000. Caesarea, in Cappadocia, of 400,000. The facts about the theatres, etc. are interesting. The theatre at Syracuse seated over 30,000; the amphitheatre at Arles 25,000, and the theatre 16,000; ditto at Nismes; Stephan, *Das Verkehrsleben in Alterthum*, p. 24. For Ancyra, the capital of Galatia, see Perrot, *De Galatia*, p. 76 foll. For some interesting figures of the population of Spain, see Pliny, N. H. iii. 4, sub fin.

[2] Marquardt, ii. 117, and his authorities. For Alexandria in particular, Marquardt, i. 297, 304. Strabo calls it τὸ μέγιστον ἐμπόριον τῆς οἰκουμένης.

[3] For Gaul, see esp. Plin. N. H. iii. 5, init.

[4] Marquardt, i. 403; Boissière, L'Afrique Romaine, passim.

[5] Cf. the case of the little island of Gyarus, whose scanty population of fishermen had to pay more taxation than they could afford, Strabo, x. 5. § 3.

special cases show this clearly enough, and the day was coming when all such means of relief would be done away. Then when the barbarians were thundering at the frontiers, and the tax-gatherers demanding the means for an administration which ruled but did not protect, the provinces were all the more wretched by the contrast with the former brilliance of their prosperity. Rome had undertaken an impossible task, that of ruling an immense Empire without federation and without a representative system, where the only sources of power were the supreme central government and the army. It would be puerile, however, to blame her for not having grasped and applied ideas which were foreign to antiquity, and which have only been worked out by the slow experience of centuries. We should rather wonder at what was achieved by 'the weary Titan,' as we see her

> 'Staggering on to her goal
> Bearing on shoulders immense
> Atlantean, the load
> Well nigh not to be borne
> Of the too vast orb of her fate.'

NOTE ON ROMAN SWITZERLAND[1].

There is no such thing, strictly speaking, as a Roman Switzerland. Different parts of it belonged to different border countries. Geneva was in the district of Vienna, and so belonged to Provence. West Switzerland, including Nyon, the lake shore and Rhone valley, belonged to Lugdunensis. East

---

[1] A great subject is often best seen by a close examination of some small portion of it. It may be of interest therefore if I subjoin what can be made out of a little country which formed part of several different provinces, and the account of which should throw light on several points of interest. I refer to Switzerland. My account is obtained from Orelli, *Inscriptiones Helvetiae*; Mommsen, *Schweiz in Romischer Zeit*; Troyon, *Monuments de l'Antiquité dans l'Europe barbare*. The inscriptions have also been collected by Mommsen. The collection of them now being published by Hagen, and of which the first part, containing the inscriptions of Aventicum, has just appeared, will supersede all others.

Switzerland was part of Rhaetia; Tessin belonged to Italy. A special administrative district was made out of the Rhone valley and part of Savoy, under a governor called *Procurator Alpium Atractianarum et Poeninarum*[1]. For some purposes of administration the whole of Gaul, including West Switzerland, formed a unit, e. g. there is a uniform mile-stone system over the whole area, from which we may argue to a uniform road and postal system and a central administration of them. Also all Gaul had one system of tax and customs, and as part of this there was an important custom-house at Zurich, another at St. Maurice, and at Conflans in the valley of the Isère. The Zurich *statio* was connected with the Julier Septimer and Splugen routes from Milan; that of St. Maurice with the Great, that of Conflans with the Little St. Bernard[2]. So there was a ring of posts at the edge of the Gallic frontier, directly behind which edge is Western Switzerland. Also there were probably Swiss representatives at the great religious festival of Lyons.

By the later arrangements of Constantine, West Switzerland comes under the minister of Gaul, Spain, and Britain; while East Switzerland went with Italy, Illyricum, and Africa.

The military importance of Switzerland rested on its being part of the frontier. The chief military station was at Vindonissa, a very strong position on the high point of land between the Reuss and the Aar, commanding the roads from Como by the Splugen, &c., and that from Avenches coming over the Great St. Bernard. Augusta Rauracorum (Augst) and Augusta Vindelicorum (Augsburg) enabled it to connect itself easily with the Rhine and the Danube. The transit of the Rhine at Zurzach was secured by a bridge, and thence the road went to Coblenz. Vindonissa also communicated with the head-quarters at Mayence, and this road crossed the Rhine at Breisach, which was guarded by a detachment of the troops quartered at Vindonissa[3]. Later on we find Vindonissa connected with the Danube through Zurzach, Rottenburg on the

---

[1] Mommsen, *Schweiz*, 6.   [2] Ib. 8.   [3] Ib. 10.

Neckar, and Ratisbon[1]. Switzerland flourished for about 250 years, but about 260 A.D. the Alemanni invaded it and burnt Aventicum. A few years afterwards Augusta Rauraca was burnt. The frontier line now became the Rhine, which was guarded more carefully than ever. There was a Roman fleet on Lake Constance. But no coins of Augusta are found later than the end of the fourth century, and in that time we must put the victory of the barbarian deluge[2]. The same thing applies to coins found all over Switzerland, and the last inscription is of the year 377[3]. By 395 all connexion between Italy and Gaul was at an end. In Switzerland the Valais remained Roman longest, and was not overrun till Italy was[4]. Latin was the official and common language. But West Switzerland was much more Romanised than East. The Rhone valley was Romanised fully and completely, owing to the great trade route over the Great St. Bernard; so was Geneva, as part of Provence. There are very few inscriptions in East Switzerland, and when we find names of Helvetii or Rauraci occurring, they are very barbarous and un-Roman. The same thing occurs on the North French coast, where inscriptions are very rare. The present divisions of Switzerland explain themselves by these facts. For the Burgundians in West Switzerland found an old civilisation already, and got Romanised, while the Alemanni in the East started on quite new ground[5].

Gaul fell naturally into *pagi*. There were eight of these in Switzerland, of which the Nantuates were the most important.

The first considerable town was Nyon[6], belonging to no *pagus*, but wedged in between the Sequani, Helvetii, and Allobroges. Other towns are Baden near Zurich, Vindonissa, Turicum, Salodunum, Lousanna[7]. But by constitution these were never

---

[1] Mommsen, 11. [2] Ib. 12. [3] Ib. 13. [4] Ib. 13. [5] Ib. 17.

[6] The *Colonia Equestris* of Noviodunum was a very considerable place, much larger than the present Nyon. See Troyon, p. 481.

[7] At Lausanne have been found a bronze Diana, bust of Cato, medals of Victorina, Trajan, Zenobia; Troyon, p. 485. The remains of Roman columns were employed in building Lausanne Cathedral; ib. 487.

regular municipia. No duoviri or quattuorviri occur in any of them. Under the Empire however we get important towns, e.g. Martigny, Sion, and St. Maurice, with Latin right. Augusta Rauraca and Aventicum were Roman colonies, and the surrounding *pagi* were subject to their jurisdiction[1]. Citizens of Aventicum were scattered about the country, and their interests were well looked after. As to the natives, they probably got the *civitas* of the place in time, and therefore Roman *civitas* also—as was the ordinary procedure with natives. Apparently these citizens of Roman colonies were exempt from military service. But troops were got out of the rest of the country,—an *ala* was raised in Valais, and the Helvetii must have contributed at least two cohorts of infantry.

Commerce was very unimportant in early times. But the foundation of Aosta and consequent extension of the Great St. Bernard as a trade route changed this. From Martigny the road went down the Rhone valley to Nyon, or diverged from Vevey to Solothurn and Augst[2]. After this we find articles of commerce passing through Switzerland from Germany and Flanders, and Switzerland exporting its own cheese, timber, &c., and importing oil, wine, &c.

---

[1] Mommsen, 19.

[2] Between Vevey and Solothurn discoveries of Roman remains have been pretty frequent, e. g. at Moudon; Troyon, 492. An immense deal has been discovered at Avenches—frescoes, ib. 495; aqueducts, temples, statues, ib. 497. It had a patron, ib. 498; an amphitheatre, ib. 502; fragments of statues, Hercules and Faun, Apollo, ib. 503. Remains also at Yverdon, ib. 505; Orbe, ib. 506.

CHAPTER IV.

The Period of the Later Empire.

THE period from the Antonines to the accession of Constantine is the least known of any period in the history of the Empire; and is yet of vast importance for our subject. The praises of a rhetorician[1] and the invectives of a sworn opponent[2] are the chief materials for the history of an emperor whose reforms effected a revolution in the whole system of administration. It is in a sense fortunate that the emperors between M. Aurelius and Diocletian effected so little, even in the best cases, but a successful resistance to the barbarians on the frontiers. At all events it makes us the less regret that the materials for their history are so scanty. It would be tedious and superfluous to collect every scattered notice of each emperor that flits across the theatre and is gone. I will only attempt to give some account of the chief administrative changes, especially those effected by Diocletian, and of the material condition of the provinces.

Bestowal of the franchise on all provincials. The Edict by which Caracalla in the year A.D. 215 bestowed the Roman franchise upon all provincials must not be regarded as a measure peculiarly honourable to its author. Dio[3] distinctly informs us that Caracalla's reasons were purely financial. Under the existing system the land-tax was paid by the provincials and the legacy-duty by the Roman citizens in Italy who were exempt from the former impost. By giving the Roman franchise to all the provincials, Caracalla made them pay the *vicesima*

---

[1] Eumenius.   [2] Lactantius.   [3] Dio, lxxvii. 9.

hereditatum as well as and over and above the tribute. Thus the provincials had to bear a double burden, while Italy, though it paid the legacy-duty, was still left exempt from the heavier tax. Nor is it easy to say what definite privileges, except perhaps in securing the right of appeal, the provincials obtained by this concession. It is a melancholy feature in the history of the Empire that the needed reforms come too late to be of use, and that when they do take place, they imply new burdens rather than new privileges.

But the exceptional position of Italy was one that could not long continue. Now that Italy no longer gave her blood to defend the provinces, her privileged position was a monstrous and indefensible injustice. I have already remarked how the ideas of an absolute difference between Italy and the provinces had been fading in the course of the last century[1]; and it needed scarcely two generations after Caracalla before all difference between her and the provinces had ceased to exist. The country itself became a province, or rather a group of provinces, and the land-tax was imposed on it as upon any other part of the Empire. Henceforth we regularly find Italians designated as provincials, and Etruria and Campania as provinces[2]._ _Italy itself becomes a province._

The successor of Caracalla marks the advent of a new race to the direction of the Empire. There had been a succession of Spanish emperors; now it was the turn of another country, and Septimius Severus was the first African emperor; the next, and in some ways greatest series of all, was that of the Illyrian emperors. Severus was naturally a friend to his native country; he gave three of its cities—Carthage, Utica, and Leptis—the *jus Italicum*, or exemption from the land-tax[3]; and executed many works of permanent utility[4]. He it was also who created

---

[1] So under M. Aurelius in a letter of Fronto, bk. ii. epist. 11, to a juridicus of North Italy, we find him applying the term *provincia* to his friend's authority. See this point discussed by Zumpt, Comm. Epig. ii. 48. The *juridici* were practically much the same as provincial governors.

[2] Cf. Orelli, 3648; Henzen, p. 386.

[3] Boissière, L'Afrique Romaine, p. 292. [4] Ib.

the province of Numidia, and established in it as a regular governor the legate who had previously held that anomalous and invidious position by the side of the proconsul, which we have already endeavoured to describe[1].

The separation of civil and military functions.

The many short-lived emperors of this period spent their reigns contending against the barbarians; and it is only seldom possible to ascribe to this or that emperor some definite administrative change. It appears however that the separation of civil and military functions, which is commonly ascribed to Diocletian, must have been the work of some earlier emperor. An inscription of the time of Carinus (A.D. 281 circa) proves that the governor of Numidia at that time did not call himself legate, but simply by the civil title of *praeses*, and was not of higher than equestrian rank[2]. Another inscription of the year A.D. 261 testifies to the existence at that date of a legate of Numidia. So in the twenty years between 261 and 281 A.D. the change must have occurred. Now it would be absurd to ascribe any such change to the indolent and incompetent Gallienus, who let Gaul sever itself from the Empire because he would not take the trouble to protect it; and if we glance through the list of the other transitory rulers of the period, there is but one man who conceivably might have done it. That man is Aurelian, the same who established the new office of *corrector* in Italy; and it is very probable that we are to ascribe to him these new *praesides*, and also the creation of the new office of the *dux limitis Africae*, a military commander who about this period appears in Africa by the side of the *praeses*. Putting the facts together, it comes out plainly that the governor no longer was allowed to hold civil and military

---

[1] See p. 108.

[2] 'Viro perfectissimo, praesidi provinciae Numidiae.' Now *perfectissimo* is a title which could never have been used loosely, and always implied equestrian, just as *clarissimus* implied senatorial rank. *Praeses* was the generic title for any governor, and had been usurped by the procurators who governed provinces, as the only title open to them. But no legate would have called himself simply *praeses* from choice; cf. Boissière, p. 309.

powers in his single hand, but that with lesser dignity and inferior rank he was assigned the jurisdiction and other civil duties, while a new officer took the command of the troops. We may connect with all this the changes effected by Gallienus, who forbade any senator to leave Italy, and so precluded them from all provincial command. The emperors were jealous of their provincial governors, and were already casting about for means to diminish their authority. Under the existing system a successful provincial governor was sure some day or other to rebel against his superior, and we cannot wonder if the emperor regarded self-preservation as the first law of nature. In any case, whether Aurelian commenced this work or not, it was carried out and perfected by Diocletian.

During all this third century the barbarian invasions were ever becoming more formidable. The Alemanni pressed into Italy at its north-eastern corner, and reached Ravenna; the Goths spread over Greece and devastated the western coast of Asia Minor; while on the Rhine and Danube the Suevi, Alemanni, Marcomanni, Carpi, and many other tribes maintained an unceasing struggle with the defenders of the frontier[1]. In such a state of things an emperor had to do two things; to protect the frontiers, and to secure himself against the pretenders whom their military ability or their popularity with the soldiers were ever bringing to the front. It is not surprising therefore that already before Diocletian became emperor we see signs of change and transition. 'One is compelled to recognise in the whole of this third century an epoch of transition, and even of anarchy, but also of gradual elaboration of the new administrative system—a system which at first confused, and only with difficulty disengaging itself from the traditions of the past, did

The barbarians.

---

[1] A.D. 240, the Franks in Gaul; A.D. 256, the Alemanni before Ravenna; A.D. 258, Temple of Diana at Ephesus burnt by the Goths, who had previously burnt Trapezus and Nicomedia, and plundered Greece; A.D. 270, rise of the Persian monarchy under Shapur, defeat of the Roman army, and capture of the Emperor Valerian.

not reach its official development and definite consecration till the long reigns of Diocletian and Constantine[1].'

The period from Claudius to Diocletian.
With the deposition of Gallienus and the election of Claudius, A.D. 268, comes the beginning of a better time. Claudius won the name of Gothicus by defeating the Goths in a tremendous battle at Naissus; and his successor was a man of still greater vigour and capacity. His murder after five years' successful rule was not only a misfortune, but it showed very clearly that at all costs the tyranny of the soldiers must be done away. There was no hope for the Empire if after a capable man had been raised to the throne, and was giving promise of a great reign, it should then be in the power of a brutal and capricious soldiery to rid themselves of him with impunity. Any system which taught the soldiers to know their place would be a benefit to the Empire. That this was more or less clearly felt by the good and capable men of rank in the army itself is shown by the meeting of the generals at Milan, and their decision to leave the choice of an emperor to the Senate. This looks very much as if, weary of a mere military despotism, they wished to found something in the nature of a constitutional monarchy. But the solution of the problem did not lie here; and the gentle old man whom after eight months' delay the Senate at length appointed, was murdered by his troops before the year was over. This time the choice again reverted to the army, and Probus was elected (A.D. 276). During the years 275 and 276, encouraged probably by the brief interregnum during which there was no emperor, the Franks had made a fearful inroad into Gaul and burnt seventy towns[2]. Probus at once marched against them, inflicted a terrible defeat, and followed the fugitives across the Rhine. He resumed the Agri Decumates which had been given up by Caracalla, and built a still more powerful wall than that of Hadrian, to protect the country. On his murder in 282 he was succeeded by the Illyrian Carus. Carus sought to establish the hereditary principle, and when he died

---

[1] Desjardins, quoted by Boissière, p. 312.   [2] Preuss, p. 3.

fighting against the Persians, his two sons, Numerianus and Carinus, shared the throne between them. Numerianus was a respectable man of letters, but no soldier. He was probably murdered by his uncle Arrius Aper, and on his death the officers chose Diocles, an Illyrian who had fought his way from the lowest to the highest station, to succeed him as emperor, A.D. 284. They probably little knew how momentous a step they were taking, for this Illyrian was the great emperor afterwards known as Diocletian.

Diocletian spent the first years of his reign partly in a campaign against Carinus, whose murder by one of his own tribunes left him undisputed emperor; partly in driving back the Germans across the Danube from Pannonia. In the next year he took the memorable step of dividing the Empire with Maximian, assigning to him the Western, while he himself retained the Eastern provinces. The reasons for this measure were mainly, no doubt, military. Several distant parts of the frontier had to be protected at once. Part he could guard himself; but part could not but be committed to another general. The powers that general must have were too great for a subordinate; and it seemed therefore best and safest to give him at once a share in the throne. There was a close friendship between Diocletian and Maximian; both were Illyrians, and had been brothers-in-arms for many years. The measure was greatly facilitated by the sterling good sense of the rough soldier, who never mistook the moral superiority of the older emperor, and willingly carried out orders and consented to measures which sometimes perhaps he did not understand, or even actively disliked. *First years of the reign of Diocletian. Partition of power with Maximian.*

There was a great deal for Maximian at once to do. The state of Gaul demanded all the energies that could be brought to bear upon it. From Gallienus to Aurelian (A.D. 260-272) Gaul was sundered from the Empire, and governed by emperors of its own (Lollianus, Victorinus, and others), who resided at Trèves, and protected the country against the barbarians. They seem to have discharged this paramount duty *State of Gaul.*

with some success[1], but there was a good deal of *internal* disturbance under them, as was natural. Aurelian conquered the last of these emperors, Tetricus, but scarcely was the land quieted internally, than the Germans began invading it from without. In the interregnum between Aurelian and Tacitus these inroads were so bad that the whole country seemed lost; and scarcely had Probus driven out the barbarians when two generals—Proculus and Bonosus—raised the standard of revolt at Cologne. They were soon put down, but the Germans broke in again on Probus' death; the *Agri Decumates* were again lost; and at the same period unfortunate Gaul was visited by the Bagaudae[2]. The insurrections of these Bagaudae are to be compared to those of the Jacquerie in France in the fourteenth century; and an account of the causes which led to them will throw a good deal of light on the condition of the provinces.

The peasantry. The state of the peasantry was miserable in the extreme in the last centuries of the Empire. In Italy an eighth part of the rich Campania was untilled and desolate; and similar causes produced in the provinces similar results. 'Latifundia perdidere Italiam jam vero et provincias,' says Pliny already at the end of the first century[3]. Roman citizens often held large estates in the provinces, Agrippa for instance in Sicily[4], Rubellius Plautus in Asia[5]; the emperors in particular had domainlands in almost every province[6]. Plantations in Sicily, mines in Spain, cattle-pastures in Dalmatia, to give a few out of a long list, were all owned by Roman citizens, and all worked by

---

[1] Treb. Pollio, Trig. Tyr. 5, says of them: 'Quos omnes datos divinitus credo, ne quum illa pestis (Gallienus) inauditae luxuriae impediretur malis, possidendi Romanum solum Germanis daretur facultas.'

[2] Preuss, p. 24.

[3] Pliny, N. H. xviii. 7. § 3; Finlay, i. 54, 89.

[4] Horace, Epist. i. 12. 1: 'Fructibus Agrippae Siculis quos colligis, Icci.'

[5] Ann. xiv. 22.

[6] e.g. Nero in Spain; Plut. Galba, 5. The *procuratores rei privatae*, though strictly speaking only the emperor's bailiffs and appointed to look after these properties, were yet important officials.

multitudes of slaves[1]. In Africa, according to Pliny, six proprietors owned half the country.

With this increase of great estates and simultaneous increase in the number of slaves (so many Goths were made slaves by Claudius, to give one instance, that there was not a district without them), the small proprietors could no longer maintain the fruitless struggle, and, as a class, wholly disappeared. Some, no doubt, became soldiers; others crowded into the already overflowing towns; while others voluntarily resigned their freedom, attached themselves to the land of some rich proprietor, and became his villeins, or *coloni*. But this was not the chief means by which this class was formed and increased. When Savigny wrote his famous essay[2] on the *Coloni* in 1828, he asked: How did this class of coloni arise? a man might be born a colonus, and indeed a common name for the class as a whole was *originarii*; but how did the first and original coloni come into existence? After pointing out the evidence which proves that in some cases free men became coloni by their own act, he goes on to state that a constitution of the Codex Theodosius (A.D. 409), discovered shortly before he wrote, throws a new light on the matter. This constitution gives public notice that any landowner may apply to the praefectus praetorio for labourers from the newly-conquered Scyrians; which labourers are to be used not as slaves, but as coloni. 'Thus we have a very remarkable example, indeed the only known example, clearly pointing out the manner in which bodies of coloni on a large scale originated. The emperors might have sold the barbarians who had fallen into their hands, as slaves, but preferred (without doubt from politico-economical grounds) giving them away as coloni. Now one might conjecture that the whole class sprang up originally after the same manner, so that this single instance should be only a repetition of similar previous ones[3].' His final conclusion is that the

Extinction of small proprietors.

Formation of the class of coloni.

---

[1] Stephan, *Das Verkehrsleben in Alterthum*, p. 25.
[2] Translated in the Philological Museum, ii. 117-145.
[3] I quote from the translation in Phil. Mus. ii. 144.

class might no doubt have originated in this manner, but that on the other hand it might not, and that it is better not to be dogmatic on the point. But the careful examination which the subject has received since Savigny's time has left no doubt that the solution which his critical sagacity was the first to indicate is the right one. These transplantations of population and this peculiar tenure begin at an early date. Augustus settled the Triumpilini, an Alpine tribe, in Italy[1], and after him it became the regular practice, after having inflicted a defeat on a barbarian tribe, to transport them to some place far away from the frontiers and settle them on the land with the status of coloni. M. Aurelius made great use of this system. 'He settled an infinite number of men from the different barbarian peoples, on Roman soil,' says his biographer[2]; and succeeding emperors pursued the same policy. After a successful war these serfs were given, as is indicated by the passage of the Codex Theodosius, to landed proprietors without payment; and in this way not only was the class of free peasants diminished or altogether destroyed, but—a happier result—the slave system was directly attacked.

Distinction between the coloni and slaves.

The coloni themselves were not slaves. The codes directly distinguish them from slaves, and in several imperial constitutions they are called *ingenui*[3]. They could contract a legal marriage, and could hold property. It is true that a colonus had to pay his master (patronus) a certain sum of money for permission to marry[4], and that though he could hold he could not alienate property[5]. But a slave could contract no marriage at all in the eye of the law, and could not reclaim his property if deprived of it. On the other hand, the coloni were like slaves

---

[1] 'Venalis cum agris suis populus' is the expression of Pliny, N. H. iii. 20.

[2] Capit. 24; cf. Suet. Aug. 21, where we find Augustus settling Germans in Gaul; Suet. Tib. 9; Eutropius, vii. 9; Dio, cap. lxxi. 11; Kuhn, i. 260; Marquardt, ii. 234.

[3] Savigny, Phil. Mus. ii. 122.

[4] Ib. 130. The sum was not to exceed a *solidus*.

[5] Ib. 132.

in that they were liable to personal punishment[1]. What their exact position was is shown by a passage in the Codex where they are called *servi terrae*, 'slaves of the soil[2].' A colonus was indissolubly attached to the land, and could not get quit of the tie, even by enlisting as a soldier. The proprietor could sell him with the estate, but had no power whatever of selling him without it; and if he sold the estate, he was compelled to sell the coloni along with it. The coloni paid the proprietor a yearly rent for their land, generally in kind. The rent was settled by custom, and the proprietor had no power to raise it above what had been usual[3].

The position of these villeins was a very miserable one. Besides the rent payable to his patron for his bit of land, the colonus had to pay not only the poll-tax, which was levied on all who did not pay the land-tax, but also a tax on his corn, or cheese, or cattle, or anything else which he might sell at the market in the neighbouring town[4]. Then there were the extraordinary exactions, which could not be foreseen or calculated upon, and which caused endless misery. What was still worse, they had no protection against the arbitrary cruelties of their patron, who could scourge or imprison them, and at all times make their lives hateful to them by dreadful, hideous overwork. The patron was responsible for the poll-tax of his coloni, and we may be very sure that he exacted the last farthing out of them[5].

Miseries of the coloni.

So these coloni in Gaul, combined together, were joined by the free peasants still left, whose lot was not less wretched than their own, and, forming into numerous bands, spread themselves over the country to pillage and destroy. They were called

The Bagaudae.

---

[1] Savigny, Phil. Mus. ii. 123.   [2] Ib. 124.
[3] For all these statements see Savigny's Essay.
[4] Preuss, 26.
[5] Ib. and p. 27 for the statements in the text. It should be mentioned that our only full authorities for the coloni are of later date. But there is every reason to believe that what was true of the fourth century was true of the third; and the Bagaudae prove it.

Bagaudae, from a Celtic word meaning a mob or riotous assembly[1], and, under this name, recur often in the course of the next century both in Gaul and Spain. Their power rapidly increased; some towns were so wretched that they opened their gates willingly to them; and in the year 285 they set up two emperors of their own. Their head-quarters were in Northern Gaul, and their chief stronghold was built on a tongue of land at the juncture of the Marne and Seine[2].

The state of Gaul.

When Maximian was made emperor the first task entrusted to him was the reduction of these Bagaudae. This was quickly and easily accomplished; but the causes of the revolt were not removed. A good deal, however, was done both now and later by Constantius to remedy the depopulation of the country. Maximian planted large bodies of conquered barbarians in the parts of the country which had been desolated by the Bagaudae; and when Constantius conquered the Franks who had settled and absorbed the Batavi on the Rhone mouth, he planted such numbers of them over Northern Gaul, particularly in the districts of Amiens and Troyes, that all that part of the country must have been thoroughly Germanised. Attempts were also made, particularly by Constantius, to improve the material condition of the country. A good deal in particular was done for the gallant city of Augustodunum, which after having been captured by the usurper Tetricus, and given up to massacre and sack, had then suffered from the Bagaudae and the Franks[3]. But the whole country had suffered from many years of neglect, when men had neither the power nor the will to attend to anything but the protection of their lives and property against the barbarians. The water-courses were not looked after, and whole districts had sunk back into moor and morass; while others had become desert, and were inhabited only by wild beasts[4].

---

[1] Preuss, 30.   [2] Ib. 31.
[3] Preuss, 59–65, gives a very interesting account of the fortunes of Augustodunum.
[4] Eumen. vii. 6 and 7 (Gratiarum actio); Preuss, 63.

No sooner had Maximian crushed the Bagaudae, than he had to repel the swarms of the Burgundians, Alemanni, Heruli, and Chaviones, who had forced the frontier and poured into Gaul. In the next two years (287 and 288) he not only defeated them in Gaul, but drove them across the Rhine and made an inroad into Germany. Meanwhile the new confederacy of the Franks, whose devastations in Gaul some years before have been already mentioned, had formed a permanent settlement at the mouth of the Rhine, there learnt sea-faring from the Saxon races with which they had allied themselves, and became the pirates of the Channel. Carausius, whom Maximian sent against them, turned traitor, seized Britain on his own account, and took Franks and Saxons into pay. The sea campaign which Maximian conducted against him was a failure, and it was agreed that he should be recognised in his kingdom of Britain. Here, four years afterwards, he was murdered by his lieutenant Allectus, who sought to take his place; but Constantius won back the province to the Empire by a single battle in which the murderer fell. Perhaps Britain did not gain by the exchange [1]. Carausius had ruled it well, its commerce had flourished beyond all former precedent, and for the first time in its history the island had learnt to regard itself as mistress of the seas [2].

Meanwhile Diocletian was busy in the East. In the summer of A.D. 286 he was at Tiberias in Palestine. The Persian king Dahram II sent an embassy and asked for a treaty, being then at war with a rebellious brother, and so not venturing in any way to provoke Rome [3]. This state of things among the Persians permitted the Romans to recover their client-kingdom of Armenia. Tiridates, who had been brought up at Rome and was nevertheless a gallant soldier, was restored to his hereditary kingdom, and his subjects received him with enthusiasm [4]. After this fortunate settlement of the East Diocletian

Diocletian in the East.

---

[1] The rhetorician Eumenius has no doubt as to the benefits of the change. See Paneg. Const. 18 ; Schol. Rest. 18.
[2] Preuss, 40 and 56–58.   [3] Ib. 40.   [4] Ib. 42.

Military ability of Diocletian.

straightway returned to Europe, drove the barbarians out of Pannonia and Rhaetia, secured the frontier of both provinces, and then had an interview with Maximian. Probably at this interview it was settled that they should assume the surnames respectively of *Jovius* and *Herculius*, designations which well characterised their mutual relations, and which were at once seized upon by the Rhetoricians[1]. A great deal had been accomplished, but a great deal still remained to do. It was fortunate that just at this period the task of Diocletian was greatly facilitated by dissensions among the barbarians themselves. 'The Goths destroy the Burgundians. The Alemanni take up arms for the conquered. The Thervingii, another branch of the Goths, also rush to arms, with the help of the Taifali, against the Vandals and the Gepidae[2].' Rome had no wars with the Goths from this date till A.D. 323. This state of things left Diocletian free to direct his energies eastwards. In the year 290 we find him again in Syria. After defeating and capturing many of the Saracens who were making inroads on Roman territory, he straightway returned to Pannonia. 'Scarcely had Syria beheld him, when now Pannonia welcomed him[3].' At the beginning of the following year he met Maximian in a famous interview at Milan. Rome was carefully avoided, and the senatorial deputation sent to greet the arrival of the emperors on Italian ground learnt nothing of the purport of their interview.

Further partition of power.

It was probably at this meeting that the further partition of power was arranged which was made public in 293. The necessity of new wars for the security of the frontier, and the impossibility of Diocletian's leaving the East to conduct them, led to the nomination of the two new Caesars, Constantius and Galerius. Galerius was a Dacian, born not far from Sophia, and had been a cowherd, whence he was nicknamed Armentarius. He was an ardent persecutor of the Christians, and a man

---

[1] Preuss, 44.   [2] Mamert. Paneg. ii. 16, 17; Preuss, 46.
[3] 'Illum modo Syria viderat, jam Pannonia susceperat;' Mamert. Paneg. ii. 4; Preuss, 46.

of rough and even brutal character. Constantius was a man of good birth, and in every way a distinguished personage; modest however and kindly; and Gaul was well off under his rule. On March 1, 293, both were solemnly proclaimed as Caesar[1]; Galerius at Nicomedia, Constantine at Milan. Galerius married Diocletian's daughter Valeria; Constantius, Maximian's step-daughter Theodora. Young Constantine, Constantius' son, was summoned to the East, and there learnt the art of war under Diocletian and Galerius. *The two Caesars.*

To Constantius was assigned the task of recovering Britain. He accomplished this, as already mentioned, with celerity and success; and on his return to Gaul did his best to restore its former prosperity. It is a symptom of the advance of Britain and decay of Gaul in this period that when he recrossed the Channel he brought with him a number of British artisans and architects to help him to rebuild the towns of Gaul. The Franks were so badly beaten as not to reappear as invaders till the reign of Constantine; and a murderous defeat was inflicted on the Alemanni[2]. *Constantius recovers Britain.*

Maximian, besides the general control of the Western provinces, had Italy, Spain, and Africa committed to his special charge. His fixed residence was Milan, but we find him at one time at Aquileia, at another on the Rhine, at another in Africa[3]. When in 297 the Moors made a formidable inroad into Roman Africa, it was he who defeated them, captured a number of them, and settled the prisoners in other provinces. *Maximian in the West.*

From 293 to 296 Galerius was on the Danubian frontier. His enemies were the Jazyges, and more particularly the Carpi. The latter tribe he attacked and annihilated, with the exception of those whom he settled as coloni in Dacia. The Carpi do not reappear in history. *Galerius on the Danube.*

Above all, Diocletian had an arduous task before him in the reduction of Egypt. Though well and kindly treated, the Egyptians had always been insolent to their rulers, and always *Diocletian in Egypt.*

---

[1] Preuss, 51. [2] Ib. 65. [3] Ib. 66.

Egypt.

War with Persia.

ready to rebel. It was at this time a stiff-necked and obstinate race—not fit for freedom, and yet refusing to obey—which needed the lesson which Diocletian was not slow to give it. For ten years Egypt had been severed from the Empire and ruled by the usurper L. Elpidius Achilleus, a native of the country. When after a long siege Diocletian took Alexandria he punished it with terrible severity. He had determined to stop the spirit of rebellion once for all, and he set to work in the spirit of a Strafford. He also reorganised the administration, getting rid of Augustus' arrangements, and dividing the country into three provinces, Aegyptus Jovia, Aegyptus Herculia, and Thebais. While Diocletian was in Egypt the Persian king Narses seized the favourable opportunity of invading Armenia, drove out Tiridates, and seized the country. Diocletian entrusted the war to Galerius, who A.D. 296 rashly attacking without waiting for Diocletian to come up, was defeated with great loss, and he and Tiridates only just secured their own escape. The reception he met with from Diocletian at Antioch [1] was not such as to encourage him to a repetition of rash experiments. In the following year however he retrieved his character by the crushing defeat he inflicted on the Persians. The capture of Narses' wife and children was still more decisive even than the victory. Narses was willing to accept any terms to recover them, and after some preliminaries, peace was finally signed on the following terms:—1. The Tigris was made the boundary; so all Mesopotamia became Roman. 2. Rome relinquished her claim to lands on the north-east of the Tigris, the modern country of Northern Kurdistan. 3. Tiridates was reinstated, and compensated for the loss of the above-mentioned lands by a considerable share of Persian territory [2]. 4. The Iberian kings (who were of importance as holding the passes of the Caucasus) were to be dependent on Rome instead of on Persia [3].

Tiridates died after a long reign king of Armenia. No

---

[1] Preuss, 77.   [2] Ib. 82.   [3] Ib. 83.

Persian war occurs again till Julian. Then the defeat of the Romans 363 A.D. gave back all that Rome had by this treaty gained.

Peace had now been everywhere secured. The legions were no longer to be feared, for even if they wanted to mutiny, no general would dare to lead them against four different emperors. It was no mere hypocrisy if Diocletian was called 'restorer of the world,' or 'parent of the golden age[1].' With nothing to fear either from the army or the barbarians, he could now devote himself to the work of organisation. The first great change was the division of the supremacy among four Caesars. Before this there had been two emperors—M. Aurelius and Verus; and many emperors had named their sons Caesar or Augustus, so as to secure a peaceable succession. Similarly the army and Senate had made two Gordians, and had put Maximus and Balbinus on the throne together. But the success of these two last cases had not been such as to provoke imitation[2]. In 285 Maximian was undoubtedly given Gaul, Britain, Spain, probably also Italy and Africa; while Diocletian retained the rest of the Empire from the East to Rhaetia. All troops in the West were under Maximian's supreme command; victories were ascribed to his auspices; and he had power of life and death over all his military subordinates. He had also the supreme civil power; he administered his own treasury in his own provinces; supervised justice, and issued rescripts. In 293 the Empire was divided over again. Diocletian had the East with Egypt and Libya, the Island province, and Thrace. Galerius had Pannonia and Moesia, including East and West Illyricum, Macedonia, Greece, and Crete. Maximian had Italy, Africa, and Spain. Constantius Gaul and Britain. It is not easy to make out the exact relation between the Caesars and the Augusti. But when circumstances require it, the Augustus appears with troops in the Caesar's provinces and takes the command in chief. In 296 we find Maximian on the Rhine, in 293 and 294

Interval of peace.

Relation of the Caesars to the Augusti.

---

[1] Preuss, 83. [2] Ib. 86.

Diocletian at Sirmium; or, on the other hand, the Augustus invited the Caesar into his own province. But we never find Galerius in the West nor Constantius in the East. There are no constitutions or rescripts in the name of the single Caesars. Most of the coins and inscriptions bear the names of all the four. But the supreme legislative power lay with the Augusti, or in point of fact with Diocletian[1]. The Augustus sent the census officials into his Caesar's provinces, and also controlled the official appointments. It is a proof of Diocletian's pre-eminent position that he did not hesitate on occasion to send orders to the governors of Maximian's provinces; for instance, to those of Spain and Africa[2]. On the other hand, each of the four had large separate powers; made war and peace on his own account; and exercised supreme jurisdiction[3]. The general edict against the Christians was not carried out in Constantius' provinces, and those provinces did not suffer from the taxation as much as the rest[4].

Pre-eminence of Diocletian.

Diocletian was not satisfied with quartering the world. He further subdivided the provinces, making them much smaller and more numerous, and established a new official, the *Vicarius*, between the Caesars and the provincial governors. The whole Empire was divided into twelve dioceses, the smallest of which —Britain—consisted of four provinces, the largest—Oriens—of sixteen. Lactantius describes this subdivision as follows: 'The provinces also were cut into fragments. Many governors and more officials settled upon each single district, almost upon each single city[5].' The 101 provinces thus formed were under different governors of different rank. There was a *proconsul* in Africa, Zeugitana, and probably in Asia, Achaia, and Baetica.

Subdivisions of the provinces.

---

[1] Preuss, 89; Mommsen, *Über die Zeitfolge der Verordnungen Diocletians*, Abh. der Akad. der Wiss. zu Berlin, 1860, p. 419.

[2] Preuss, 91.   [3] Ib. 88.   [4] Ib. 89.

[5] Lact. de Morte Pers. 7: 'Provinciae quoque in frusta concisae, multi praesides et plura officia singulis regionibus ac paene jam civitatibus incubare, item rationales multi et vicarii praefectorum.' *Rationalis* is in this period used where *procurator* had been used; cf. Lampridius, Alex. Sev. 45, 'procuratores, id est rationales;' Marquardt, ii. 298.

Then came the *consulares* with rank of clarissimi. Then the *correctores*, some of whom had rank of clarissimi, others only of perfectissimi. Lastly, the *praesides* with the rank of perfectissimi. This title of praeses supplanted the old title of procurator [1]. The title of legate, if it had not ceased already, does not at all events occur after this reign.

Very important and permanent was Diocletian's arrangement of assigning a vicarius to each diocese. These officials had the rank of *spectabiles*, and the consulars, correctores, and praesides were their subordinates. What proconsuls there were however were of the same rank of spectabilis, and received orders direct from the emperor [2]. Whether the vicarius of Oriens was already at this period called comes Orientis and had a vicarius Aegypti under him is unknown [3].

The vicarii.

This system of titles and hierarchy of ranks, though commonly ascribed to Constantius, is a characteristic feature of Diocletian's arrangements [4]. He was the first emperor who is regularly and formally called *Dominus;* his titles were sacer and sacratissimus. He was greeted not by the customary embrace, as between equals, but by bending the knee as to a superior being. He dressed in silk and jewels, and ceremonial difficulties were made about audience. It would be absurd to ascribe all this to personal vanity. Such weaknesses were not part of the man's character, and on such a supposition his voluntary abdication and the simplicity of his after-life would not be easy to explain. It was part of his policy to surround the throne with an atmosphere of mystery. He wished the emperor to be neither citizen nor soldier, but equally above or remote from both. The last relics of the old Republican constitution vanished away. Diocletian paid no attention whatever to the Senate, and only once visited Rome during his reign. He resided at Sirmium, Antioch, most often at Nicomedia; and Maximian at Milan. The Romans did not like this, and there were conspiracies of senators and praetorians, which Maximian put down ruthlessly [5]. The praetorians

Undisguised absolutism of Diocletian.

Discontent of Rome.

---

[1] Preuss, 99. [2] Ib. [3] Ib. 100. [4] Ib.
[5] Lact. de Morte, 8 ; Preuss, 106.

were reduced in number and replaced by three Illyrian legions of whose absolute loyalty there could be no question. The praetorians still existed as a sort of police force in Rome till 312, when Constantine abolished them for ever [1].

Besides these great and far-reaching changes, there were a number of reforms effected by Diocletian in the different branches of the administration.

The formulary system replaced by cognitio. In A.D. 294 a law of Diocletian made a great change in the judicial process. The old system had been to try cases by means of a magistrate and a body of judices. The judices were now abolished, and the governors directed to decide cases summarily by themselves. Thus the *cognitio* or summary process, which had been the exception, became the universal rule [2].

The land-tax imposed on Italy. The process of levelling, the progress towards uniformity, had only gradually accomplished itself in the last three centuries. There were still special privileges and exemptions. Thus Italian land differed from provincial land, and there were different sorts of status for persons, according as a man was a Roman or a subject. Italy was free from the land-tax, as also were the towns outside Italy which possessed the Italian right. Such an exemption for Italy was impossible when it formed a diocese along with Spain and Africa; and Diocletian reimposed upon Italy the land-tax which it had not paid since B.C. 167 [3]. Lactantius has inveighed against a measure which was really just and necessary. The privileged position of Italy had been just when she paid for it with her blood; but now that she did not supply the army, it was unjust. The contemporaries of Constantine look back to the reign of Diocletian as a period when the taxation was moderate and bearable: it was only in the generation after him that it reached a ruinous pitch [4]. Another change of Diocletian's was to take the poll-tax off the towns. Previously it had been paid by every one who did not pay the land-tax, i.e. by the small artisans and workmen in the towns, by the coloni, and by women and children everywhere. The conse-

The poll-tax taken off the towns.

---

[1] Preuss, 107.   [2] Ib. 109.   [3] Ib. 110.   [4] Ib. 111.

quence was that by this change the tax pressed harder on the coloni; and if the modern historian of Diocletian maintains that this was not so [1], he must maintain that of the two alternatives— either that the treasury got less than before, or that those who still paid, paid more than before—the former is the more probable. A great deal was accomplished for the coinage, which had been getting lighter and baser ever since Nero. The government purposely issued bad money or plated bronze with silver, and under Gallienus the silver coinage was in reality nothing but plain pewter. Then it refused to take its own coins in payment of the taxes. Aurelian tried to introduce reforms, and quelled a mutiny of the monetarii which was apparently excited by his efforts, but died too soon to accomplish anything [2]. Diocletian made the silver pure again. The gold had not been debased:—'The public taxes and the tribute of the provinces were generally exacted in gold. It was therefore the interest of the governors to maintain the purity of the gold coinage [3] :'—but it had been terribly lightened; a state of things due to the fact that the government exacted the payment of the taxes by weight, but paid its own debts by tale. Diocletian fixed it at a weight which was maintained by a law of Constantine, and remained in force till the fall of the Byzantine Empire. Copper money had ceased to be coined. Diocletian coined two sorts—a larger coin, called *follis*, and a smaller, perhaps called *denarius*. Many of these coins were made at Alexandria. In the fourth century there were six regular mints in the West—Siscia, Aquileia, Rome, Lugdunum, Arelate, Treviri; and Diocletian is said to have started one at Nicomedia. These measures, though necessary and in the long run beneficial, probably helped to bring about the frightful dearness of prices which resulted in the *Edictum de pretiis rerum venalium*. There was also a failure of harvest throughout the East, and speculation had ruined the merchants. So the prices of necessaries octupled, and the soldiers could not live on their pay. Where-

---

[1] Preuss, 111.   [2] Ib. 112.   [3] Finlay, i. 49.

upon Diocletian issued an edict, great part of which has been found[1], to fix a maximum price for all necessaries. To sell at higher prices was punishable with death. The natural consequence was that the need only increased; a number of bloody punishments had no effect; and the edict had to be dropped[2].

Diocletian's object.

To get rid of the sham republican forms which were the legacy of Augustus and of the tyranny of the army was the main idea of Diocletian. He established the absolute monarchy undisguised. His subdivisions of the provinces were mainly evoked by the desire to secure the throne against possible usurpers; and though no doubt, from his point of view, necessary and justifiable, the bureaucracy thus established was not a benefit to the provinces. The increase of the official class was so enormous that the receivers of the public money seemed to be more numerous than the payers of it. 'Rectorum numerum terris pereuntibus augent[3].' The excessive centralisation thus established finally broke up the genuine municipal constitutions. The man who would have been previously content with a position as duumvir, would now compete for some petty post under government. Under Constantine the municipal offices were of importance only for purposes of taxation, and an unfortunate decurio was bound to his office just as the colonus was bound to his bit of land. Perhaps no other alternative was open to Diocletian. It was necessary that in some way the government should be made strong and permanent. The day had gone by for doing this by any means but an immense increase of centralisation. The great number of new wheels in the machine at all events enabled it to work smoothly, and prevented it being so easily stopped or damaged. But a machine the government was, and not an organism;

Great increase of centralisation.

---

[1] In Caria, 1709; another part in Egypt, 1807; fragments in Carystos, Megara, and Lebadea in 1860. Published by Mommsen, 1851; Waddington, 1864. The latter is the most complete edition. See Preuss' note, p. 115.

[2] Preuss, 114-117.

[3] Claudian in Eutrop. ii. 586; Marquardt, i. 423.

a dead thing working with a kind of fatal regularity, and with no healthy principle of life or growth. It was the weakness of Diocletian's intellect to think that everything could be accomplished by administrative machinery. He never reckoned enough on human wills and human hearts other than his own. It is characteristic of him that he should have tried to crush the new religion by an organised persecution, and should have failed to see the elements of superior strength and vitality which it possessed. Constantine saw what he did not see, that merely as a matter of policy it was better to make terms with the new power than to seek to crush it. In the same spirit he attempted to fix prices by a series of cast-iron regulations, without seeking to remove the causes of the evil; and though he crushed the Bagaudae he did not alleviate the miseries which had made them possible. But he was a man whose lot was cast in evil days, and perhaps he did all that was possible for any genius but the highest. He secured an interval of peace, and he relegated the army to its proper place. These were real benefits, and we must not blame him too severely if he failed to remove the roots of evils which had been growing for a hundred years.

All the evidence goes to prove that Diocletian considered his system of partition of power as one that should be permanent, and the model for succeeding reigns. He meant Galerius and Constantius to be the new Augusti, and had made Maximian promise to reign in their room at the same time as he did himself. But he ought to have seen that the circumstances which had made the system work well in his hands were quite exceptional. His own undisputed superiority and the loyalty of the other three to him were the main objects of its success; and was it to be expected that those necessary conditions should recur? Supposing the case of two emperors of equal age and equal claims on the throne together, who were not bound together by those ties of loyalty and affection which bound Maximian and the Caesars to himself, and it might have been foreseen that there would be a struggle. Here, as in

The system of partition of power breaks down.

some other parts of his policy, Diocletian did not reckon with human nature. Nor with respect to the accession did he even maintain a consistent and intelligible policy. When he and Maximian abdicated in 306, the two Caesars, Galerius and Constantius, naturally became the new Augusti. The only question was as to who should be the new Caesars. The logical and consistent arrangement would have been that each emperor should choose a Caesar. In this case of course Constantinus would have chosen his son Constantine, a man (for he was now thirty years old) who had given ample proofs of capacity, and who had a right to be dissatisfied if passed over. But Diocletian made the great mistake of thinking that his own Caesar, Galerius, was competent to play the same pre-eminent part that he himself had played. Diocletian had no doubt originally decided the choice of both Caesars, and that was natural enough. But it was not by any means equally natural that Galerius should appoint a Caesar for Constantius as well as for himself; and when Diocletian consented to such an arrangement he was responsible for the wars which followed. On Constantius' death the soldiers, with whom both father and son were popular, called Constantine to a share of Empire. After six years of divided rule, the battle of the Milvian bridge left him and Licinius joint emperors; and eleven years later the great battle of Adrianople left him the sole and the first Christian emperor.

NOTE.—I subjoin a list of the provinces according to the arrangements of Diocletian. See Preuss, p. 92 foll.; Marquardt, i. 336.

I. *Oriens* incl uded Egypt andLibya, and its sixteen provinces were: 1. Libya Superior, 2. Libya Inferior, 3. Thebais, 4. Aegyptus Jovia, 5. Aegyptus Herculia, 6. Arabia Petraea, 7. Arabia Augusta Libanensis, 8. Palestine, 9. Phoenice, 10. Syria Cocle, 11. Augusta Euphratensis, 12. Cilicia, 13. Isauria, 14. Cyprus, 15. Mesopotamia, 16. Osrhoene.

II. *Pontica* had seven provinces: 1. Bithynia, 2. Cappadocia,

3. Galatia, 4. Paphlagonia, 5. Diospontos, 6. Pontus Polemoniacus, 7. Armenia Minor.

III. *Asiana* had ten provinces: 1. Pamphylia, 2. Phrygia Prima, 3. Phrygia Secunda, 4. Asia, 5. Lydia, 6. Caria, 7. Insulae, 8. Pisidia, 9. Hellespontus, 10. Lycia.

IV. *Thracia* had six provinces: 1. Europa, 2. Rhodope, 3. Thracia, i.e. the district of the Upper Hebrus with Philippopolis, 4. Haeminontus, 5. Scythia, i.e. the Dobrudscha with Tomi, 6. Moesia Inferior.

All the above belonged to Diocletian.

Galerius had two dioceses:—

I. *Moesiarum* had ten provinces: 1. Dacia, 2. Moesia Superior, 3. Dardania, 4. Macedonia, 5. Thessalia, 6. Achaia, 7. Praevalitana, 8. Epirus Nova, 9. Epirus Vetus, 10. Creta.

II. *Pannoniarum* had seven provinces: 1. Pannonia Inferior, 2. Savensis, 3. Dalmatia, 4. Valeria, 5. Pannonia Superior, 6. Noricus Ripensis, 7. Noricus Mediterranea.

Constantius had three dioceses:—

I. *Britain* had four provinces: 1. Britannia Prima, 2. Britannia Secunda, 3. Maxima Caesariensis, 4. Flavia Caesariensis.

II. *Gallia* had eight provinces: 1. Belgica Prima, 2. Belgica Secunda, 3. Germania Prima, 4. Germania Secunda, 5. Sequania, 6. Lugdunensis Prima, 7. Lugdunensis Secunda, 8. Alpes Graiae et Poeninae. The four first under consulares; the four last under praesides.

III. *Viennensis* had seven provinces: 1. Viennensis, 2. Narbonensis Prima, 3. Narbonensis Secunda, 4. Novempopulana, 5. Aquitania Prima, 6. Aquitania Secunda, 7. Alpes Maritimae.

Maximian had the three last dioceses:—

I. *Italy* had fifteen provinces: 1. Venetia Histria, 2. Flaminia, 3. Picenum, 4. Tuscia Umbria, 5. Apulia Calabria, 6. Lucania, 7. Corsica, 8. Alpes Cottiae, 9. Rhaetia, 10. Campania, 11. Aemilia, 12. Liguria, 13. Samnium, 14. Sicily, 15. Sardinia.

II. *Hispania* had six provinces: 1. Baetica, 2. Lusitania, 3. Carthaginiensis, 4. Gallaecia, 5. Tarraconensis, 6. Mauretania

Tingitana. The two first under consulares; the four last under praesides.

III. *Africa* had six provinces: 1. Proconsularis Zeugitana, 2. Byzacena, 3. Numidia Certensis, 4. Numidia Tripolitana, 5. Mauretania Caesariensis, 6. Mauretania Sitifensis.

The first two of these was proconsular; the second and third under consulares; the three last under praesides[1].

---

[1] Preuss, 98.

CHAPTER V.

The System of Taxation.

SECTION I. *The taxes in the period of the Republic.*

WHEN in the year 167 the tribute was taken off Italy, the *Ager publicus in Italy.* expenses of the administration were undisguisedly supported by the taxation of the provinces. There was still a good deal of public land in Italy, particularly in Campania[1], and the Italian customs duties were a regular source of income; but by the end of the Republic all public land in Italy had vanished, and the customs duties were in abeyance, at all events for a period of fifteen[2] years. Before examining the chief taxes of the provinces it will be necessary to take a brief view of the numerous varieties of tenure subsisting in the provinces. Speaking generally, it may be said that free and allied towns paid no taxes; that Roman colonies and municipia did pay taxes, and were so far in a worse position than Roman colonies or municipia in Italy; that Latin towns paid; and that, lastly, the remainder of the provincials formed the great body of taxpayers, and were currently designated as stipendiarii. With these facts in mind it is possible to understand the Lex Agraria of 111, which, along with the Verrines, is our main authority for the provincial taxation under the Republic.

In this law three different tenures of land are mentioned.

---

[1] Cic. de Leg. Agr. i. 2. Cicero professes to attach great importance to the revenue from this land; de Leg. Agr. ii. 29. Cf. Phil. ii. 39.

[2] Cic. ad Att. ii. 16, for their abolition; Suet. Jul. 43, for their re-establishment by Caesar.

180   ROMAN PROVINCIAL ADMINISTRATION.

The lex Agraria of 111.

Land might be either *Ager privatus ex jure Quiritium*, or *Ager privatus ex jure peregrino*, or *Ager publicus populi Romani*. The first tenure was that of the colonists settled in Africa by C. Gracchus, to whom, after that reformer's laws had been abrogated and a curse laid upon the site of Carthage, the land was assigned over again, not as to members of a colony, but *viritim*[1]. The second tenure was that of the three cities—Utica, Thapsus, &c.—which aided Rome in the Third Punic War, and of the 2200 deserters who joined the Romans under Himilco Phameas. This land was the absolute property of the towns, which were no doubt *immunes* as well as *liberae*, and therefore paid no vectigal, and could not be touched by the tax-gatherer. The third tenure is the one which is important for our present purpose. This land was that which had either belonged to obstinate enemies like Carthage, or had been the domains of former kings. All the land of a conquered country became in theory Roman, but practically only that part was kept which came under one of these two categories. That, however, the *stipendiariae civitates* in any province were much more numerous either than the Roman colonies or municipia (which, however, themselves paid taxes unless specially privileged by the possession of the *Jus Italicum*), or than the free and allied towns, might be expected, and is proved by abundant evidence[2]. But I must not give the impression that all *Ager publicus* was necessarily tributary. It was further subdivisible into the following classes, all of which are mentioned in the Lex Agraria of 111:—Firstly, *Ager privatus vectigalisque*, that is to say, land sold by the praetor or quaestor at Rome, and alienable or bequeathable by the buyer. It paid a vectigal, but the amount was a nominal one, and only imposed to show that

---

[1] To have a claim to this land, however, each of these original colonists had to give in his name to the commissioners in order to be confirmed in the possession of his share; and it is to this *professio* that the first portion of the law refers. If a man's land had been sold *pro publico* at Rome, an equivalent amount was to be restored to him.

[2] Pliny, N. H. iii. 3, for instance.

the State still asserted its property in the land. We find land of this kind opposed to and distinguished from land really *vectigalis* by the gromatic writers. It approached very nearly in fact to being private property. As reasons for the creation of this class of land may be suggested that for an assignation of land a law was necessary, while for a sale a senatus consultum sufficed; and that it was a regular method of paying the interest due to the creditors of the State, to hand them over land under the fiction of a sale. Secondly, *Ager stipendiarius*[1]. This land, like the *Ager publicus* in Italy, was simply let out, and the Romans could resume it at any time at pleasure. It consisted of the old land restored to the old inhabitants under a tax; and included by far the largest portion of the provincial land. Thirdly, *Ager publicus populi Romani a censoribus locari solitus*[2]. In the case of Africa, this was the land of Carthage or other cities conquered by force of arms, excepting of course land actually within the walls of Carthage, or given to colonists, or sold, or granted to allies, or reserved for public uses, or let out to stipendiarii. Though of course these numerous exceptions embraced by far the greatest portion of the land, still a part was left which was let out by the censors at Rome. The tenants were probably in the main the original inhabitants, who now had their own lands let to them again, but revocable at pleasure. It was a mere life-tenancy, and there is no word in the law of the tenants being able to sell or bequeath. This land paid both *decumae* and *scriptura*, but there are indications that the author of the law was thinking more of pasture than of corn-land[3]. It is specially provided that the occupiers should not pay more to the publicani than had been arranged to be paid by the law of the last censors of B.C. 114[4]. So these tenants were better off than an ordinary tenant, in that they could not have their

---

[1] Cf. Cic. in Verrem, iv. 6.   [2] Ib. iv. 39, vi. 13; Marquardt, ii. 175.
[3] § 86 of the Law.
[4] § 85: 'Quantum vectigal . . . ex lege dicta . . . publicano dare oportuit, tantundem post hanc legem rogatam, qui agrum, locum in Africa possidet possidebit, publicano . . . dare debeto.'

rent raised on them. Fourthly, the roads, *viae publicae*, were and remained the property of the Roman people [1].

Ager stipendiarius.

The taxes, therefore, really lay on the second and third of these divisions; principally, of course, on the second. In strictness this *Ager stipendiarius* was the property of the Roman people, who, however, permitted its usufruct to the old inhabitants on payment of a rent. It had been the rule for the Romans to compel a conquered enemy, such as Carthage or Macedonia, to pay an indemnity for a term of years, allowing them to raise the money as they pleased, so long as they did raise it. Now what may be called a permanent indemnity was laid on each province, and the way it was to be raised was settled by the Romans themselves on the first organisation of a province. The chief tax is a direct one, and may be of two kinds, either levied on the soil, and generally a tithe of the produce—*decumae;* or a definite sum has to be paid, irrespective of the amount of produce levied partly on land and partly on personal property, and called *stipendium* [2].

Decumae.

Tithes were paid by Sicily and Sardinia; and, from the Gracchi to Julius Caesar, by Asia. There was no stipendium in these provinces as long as the tithes existed. In Sicily the Romans maintained the arrangements of the Lex Hieronica—by which the husbandmen in each community had every year to state the amount of their acres and of their seed sown, and then the decuma of a whole district was offered in Syracuse to any one who could undertake it. The man who offered the largest number of bushels got it, and he had to send to Rome the amount of bushels he offered. If it was an exceptionally good harvest, he would gain; if bad, lose. We find the towns

---

[1] In the particular case of Africa there still remain two classes of land: (1) *Ager publicus populi Romani ubi oppidum Carthago quondam fuit*, i. e. the land cursed by Scipio, which it was forbidden to cultivate; (2) *Agri publici regibus civitatibusve sociis permissi*. There are two mentions of this kind of land in the inscription,—that given to Masinissa's children, § 81; and that assigned to Utica (and no doubt other towns as well) by the commission of Ten created by the Lex Livia.

[2] Marquardt, ii. 178.

themselves in Sicily bidding for their own decumae[1]. Besides the ordinary tithes there was also the special *frumentum imperatum*, which, perhaps, only came on towns exempt from ordinary burdens.

These taxes would in all probability not have exceeded ability to pay, if it had not been for the illegal exactions of the publicani. But it has always been found that a system of tithes puts the cultivator at the mercy of the tax-gatherer; and the reform effected by Caesar when he changed the tithes of Asia, and probably also of Sicily, into a *stipendium* was necessary and beneficent. Decumae implied publicani.

We know of the existence of a regular stipendium or tributum in Sardinia, Spain, Gaul, Macedonia, Illyria, Achaia, Syria, Cyrene, Africa, and Egypt, and may take it for granted of the rest. Caesar fixed that of the three Gauls at forty million sesterces, Aemilius Paulus that of Macedonia at 100 talents[2]. In discussing this tax, about which there is much difference of opinion, the great thing is to bear in mind the conservatism of the Romans in regard to existing arrangements, to be prepared therefore for differences in taxation in the different countries, and not to expect a unity of organisation which did not exist[3]. The stipendium:

The stipendium might be paid in money or kind. It was money in Macedonia and the three Gauls; silphium in Cyrene; wax in the case of a tribe of Pontus, and hides among the Frisii[4]. Both land and persons paid stipendium; but to suppose that there were always the two normal forms of tributum soli and tributum capitis is not in accordance with the facts. Anyhow the main part of the stipendium came from the land: though here again it cannot be supposed that immediately a province was established a regular tributum soli was set on foot. For this would need a regular survey—which only subdivisible into the tributum soli.

---

[1] Cic. in Verr. iii. 42.
[2] Cicero mentions this tax in the most definite way. In Verr. iii. 6. 12: 'Caeteris impositum vectigal est certum, quod stipendiarium dicitur, ut Hispanis et plerisque Poenorum, quasi victoriae praemium ac poena belli.'
[3] Marquardt, ii. 186. [4] Ib. 186, notes 11 and 12.

existed, before the Romans did it themselves, in the one case of Egypt; or at all events a communal census, which only existed in Greek towns. Where was neither one nor the other, all that could be done was to charge about the same amount of taxation as the previous government had done. This was the course pursued by Paulus in Macedonia[1].

and tributum capitis.

As for the tributum capitis (φόρος σωμάτων), we cannot suppose that so rude an expedient as a mere poll-tax was intended by it; though that may have been used now and then in special cases, and is mentioned in Africa, Cilicia, Asia, Tenos, Britain. We may look upon such a poll-tax as a temporary expedient, employed for instance just after a devastating war, when any ordinary tax on property would be impracticable[2]. What the tributum capitis really meant was any personal tax, and under it were included *taxes on trades*, for instance on pedlars, shop-keepers, prostitutes, &c., or *income-tax*, paid by the richer classes (οἱ τὰ χρήματα ἔχοντες), while the poor only paid a poll-tax. This idea is confirmed by the word ἐπικεφάλαιον being used for a tax on trades[3]. So we find Appian[4] talking of the severity of the φόρος τῶν σωμάτων laid upon the Jews. This could hardly have been a mere poll-tax[5].

We gather, therefore, that the stipendium cannot be described as a regular tributum soli and a regular tributum capitis, but that the stipendium was as far as possible adapted to the pre-existing state of finance in the country. Supposing the ordinary stipendium was not enough, the income-tax came in as an extraordinary measure to supply the deficiency. It was essentially a supplement.

The portoria.

The chief source of our information as to the *portoria* or customs duties refers to the period of the Empire, but there is evidence enough to make it probable that besides the duties

---

[1] Marquardt, ii. 188.   [2] Ib. ii. 192.
[3] Arist. Oec. ii. 1. 3; Cic. ad Att. v. 16. 2.   [4] Appian, Syr. 50.
[5] Marquardt, ii. 195. These personal taxes were generally farmed out to publicani. Cicero speaks of the venditio tributorum; see ad Fam. iii. 8. 5; ad Att. v. 16. 2.

paid on goods crossing the frontier, for instance from Germany into Gaul, or from the far East into Syria, there were also duties levied in each province within the Roman dominions in this period. Thus Italy, for instance, had its own custom-houses, which no goods could pass without a payment of 5 per cent.[1] Nor was this all, for each free town had a right to levy its own dues. It is to these octroi duties that a disputed passage of Cicero, where he mentions the *portorium circumvectionis*, probably refers[2]. It was an important advantage of being a Roman citizen in the provinces that Romans were specially exempted from paying them.

Besides these ordinary legitimate taxes there were also such special imposts as that of the ship-money exacted from the cities of Sicily and Asia to pay for their defence against the pirates. This was imposed by a senatus consultum in the year of Cicero's consulship[3], and occasioned frequent complaints[4]. It is specially noteworthy that the free or allied towns which were exempt from the ordinary taxes were not exempt from the payment of ship-money[5]. *Ship-money.*

The mines, quarries, and salt-works did not belong exclusively to the State in this period. The most important ones, however, did; and were farmed out by the censors to publicani. Whether it was the mine itself which was thus farmed, or only the payments from the mine, is a point which is still disputed[6]. *Mines, &c.*

During the Republican period the only legal source of

---

[1] Cic. in Verr. iii. 72 and 75.
[2] Cic. ad Att. ii. 16. § 4; Watson, p. 75.   [3] Cic. pro Flacco, 12.
[4] Ib. and 14.
[5] Cic. in Verr. vi. 19. Other references for this ship-money are—for that of Asia, in Verr. ii. 35, v. 67; for that of Sicily, in Verr. vi. 17 and 24.
[6] Marquardt, ii. 240, maintains the former; Dietrich, p. 26 foll., the latter view. The bronze tablet of Aljustrel, which is probably to be ascribed to the latter part of the first century A.D. and which was found in Portugal in 1876, only mentions a *conductor vectigalis* throughout. Whence we should gather that it was only the sums paid for the privilege of working which were farmed. See Flach's edition of the bronze, p. 12.

Finance administration in this period. authority for this branch of the administration was the Senate. With its sanction the censors farmed out the domain lands, the indirect taxes, and the public buildings. The treasury was looked after by the two city quaestors, with a numerous body of clerks, for receiving and paying money and for keeping accounts. As the senators were forbidden by law to take part in any such business as that of farming the taxes, it fell to the equites, who, by their gains, constituted a class of capitalists. The word publicanus is used in a general sense for any one who accepts a contract from the State, but more properly and *The system of publicani.* narrowly for one who farms a vectigal[1]. Whether the Roman system of farming the taxes is to be traced, as Hübner thinks, to a Carthaginian, or, as Dietrich thinks, to a Greek influence, no one can say; but we may suppose that it naturally originated with the first enlargements of taxable territory. The conveniences of the system and the difficulties of the direct system caused by the short duration of the Republican magistracies would be reasons in its favour, while the great objections to it which might be raised in the interest of the payers were probably not foreseen. The publicanus binds himself to pay a definite yearly sum. So if the real results of the tax exceed the sum he binds himself to, he gains; loses if they are less. In this way the State was spared expense; but the provinces suffered for its convenience. As the taxes of a whole province were often all farmed together—for instance decumae, scriptura, and portoria all in a lump—societies had to be formed to take them—societatis publicanorum—the members of which got more or less according to the amount subscribed. Such societies of publicani are first mentioned in the twenty-third book of Livy, but go back to an earlier date, at least for buildings; and probably the taxes were farmed from the first in the same way as the buildings. It would be erroneous, however, to suppose that the farming of a tax by a single

---

[1] So Dig. xxxix. 4. 12. § 3: 'Publicani autem dicuntur qui publica vectigalia habent conducta.' See Marq. ii. 289.

person was expressly forbidden by law; under the Empire we certainly find a single publicanus for small transactions. But a single person might die before the contract was carried out, and the inconveniences of that, if nothing else, would bring these societies into existence[1]. The manceps of the society[2] offered for the taxes at the auction, made the contract with the censors, and gave the securities. The contract lasted a lustrum, regularly five years under the Empire, and began on March 15. The business manager of the society at Rome was called *magister societatis*, was appointed for a year, kept the accounts, and did the necessary correspondence; in the provinces there was a *pro magistro*, with a numerous class of officials, who were actually employed in tax-gathering. He had also his own tabellarii for correspondence, and slaves for accounts and other routine work. There were different kinds of publicani according as they farmed decumae, scriptura, or portorium. The first stood highest. Their arrangement was not to take over the actual tenth, but to contract before the harvest, calculating on the seed sown and on the average crop.

SECTION II. *The taxes under the Early Empire.*

The land-tax still remained the chief source of income under the Early Empire; and the survey and census of Augustus, already mentioned, made a rational and just apportionment of it possible. For the purposes of the census a survey was necessary, which should not only distinguish land by its legal title into private property, communal property, and state property, but also by its produce, so as to make a fair import possible. These differences of produce constituted seven different classes of land—ploughland, with the number of acres and average produce for a ten-year period; vineyards, with the number of

---

[1] I have made much use of Dietrich's Essay in this discussion.
[2] 'Mancipes sunt publicanorum principes;' Pseudo-Asconius ad Div. p. 113, or p. 290; Cic. in Verr. iii. 71.

barrels of wine produced; olive orchards, with the number of acres and trees; pastures, with the same arrangements as those used for ploughland; forests, fisheries, and salt works[1].

The annona. Besides this regular land-tax there was the *annona*, or payment in kind, originating no doubt in the *frumentum in cellam* of the Republican period. In the great majority of provinces it was called *annona militaris*, and applied to the maintenance of the officers, soldiers, and officials in the province. Egypt and Africa were exceptional in having to supply not only the *annona militaris*, but also the much more considerable *annona civica*. Egypt fed Rome for four months in the year[2], and therefore supplied an amount of corn which, estimated in money, would amount to about 2500 talents[3].

Income-tax. We hear of a poll-tax in this period, levied on trades. Merchants paid on ships[4], slaves, horses, mules, oxen, asses, in fact on their whole moveable property; and the whole artisan and shopkeeper class, hosiers, weavers, furriers, goldsmiths, &c., &c. (prostitutes paid in this class) also came under the operation of this tax[5]. In so far as this class of coloni existed in this period they paid a poll-tax; but their contribution to the revenue by no means attained the importance that it did under the Later Empire.

Ager publicus in the provinces. The domain-lands in the provinces became of considerable importance under the Empire. With the censorship the system of letting them by the censors (*censoria locatio*) came to an end; and the emperor took over the administration of the domains. Vespasian had them re-surveyed, and all cultivated domain-land *in Italy* sold or given away. When the provinces were divided into Senatorial and Imperial, the domains were also divided, and the vectigalia of those in the Senatorial provinces were paid into the aerarium, and those in the Imperial provinces into the fiscus. This lasted however only to Vespasian; after

---

[1] Marquardt, ii. 215. [2] Josephus, B. J. ii. 16. § 4.
[3] Marquardt, ii. 226, and his authorities. [4] Tac. Ann. xiii. 53.
[5] Marquardt, ii. 230.

whom all domains were under the emperor, and were called *loca fiscalia*.

Different from these lands were the private properties of the emperor in Italy and the provinces. Augustus owned all Egypt; the Thracian Chersonese was owned by the emperor up to Trajan. These lands were not always got in the most honourable manner. Tiberius, Caligula, and Vespasian took possession of the property of condemned persons, and in Christian times emperors 'conveyed' the private property of Pagan temples[1]. To manage this property the emperor had his bailiffs, like any other proprietor. These procurators were at first the emperor's freedmen, and must be distinguished from the regular procurators of the provinces, who were of equestrian rank. The technical name for all such imperial property was *patrimonium Caesaris*. Whether they belonged to the fiscus or the patrimonium, these lands are divisible into the three classes of arable land, pasture, and mines[2]. Private property of the emperor in the provinces.

Corn-land which was the private property of the emperor was looked after by his own slaves. For instance, we find a servus I. Caesaris Aug. Vespasiani villicus praediorum Pedureanorum. The fiscal lands were farmed out, and the money got in by procurators. During some time these contracts were for the regular five-year period; but later on we find hereditary farmers of the taxes, called *conductores domus nostrae*, or *coloni*— to be distinguished from the villeins of the later time. Administration of such lands.

The scripturarii ceased under the early Empire; but public pasture still existed, and was farmed by the procuratores of the fiscus. From these pascua the emperor got an income[3].

Mines had mainly belonged to private persons under the Republic. Under the Empire the most important were taken over by the emperor, part for the fiscus, part for the patrimonium[4]. This was not only the case in Imperial provinces, e.g. with the gold mines in Dalmatia and Dacia, silver mines in Pannonia Mines.

---

[1] Marquardt, ii. 249. [2] Ib. i. 414, ii. 249. [3] Ib. ii. 251.
[4] Cf. Suet. Tib. 49: 'Plurimis etiam civitatibus et privatis veteres immunitates et jus metallorum ac vectigalium ademta.'

Administration of mines.

and Dalmatia, lead and tin in Britain, iron in Noricum, Pannonia, Lugdunensis; but also in the Senatorial provinces, for instance with the copper mines in Cyprus and Baetica [1]. Quarries were withdrawn from private industry. Herodes Atticus owned those in Pentelicus; but most, and the famousest, both in Italy and the provinces, belonged to the patrimonium. Each mine was overlooked by a slave, later by a procurator; but there was no procurator for the whole number of them; and each mine or aggregation of neighbouring mines paid directly to the procurator patrimonii. Each procurator of a mine had under him a director of works, an inspector, and an engineer. This was if he managed the mine itself; but there are cases of his farming it out to a speculator or to a society of publicani. In either case he had to look after the accounts, and for this purpose had several clerks—four can be named—under him. The labourers were either slaves, or hired workmen, or soldiers [2], or convicts [3]. Such convict mines are mentioned in Palestine, Cilicia, Cyprus, the Lebanon; and after the conquest of Jerusalem part of the captured Jews were sent to work in the mines of Egypt [4].

The legacy-duty.

One of the quite new taxes which the emperors introduced was the legacy-duty. In the year A.D. 6 Augustus made the people of Italy pay their share of the State burdens, not by imposing a tribute, but by a vicesima hereditatum, or tax of five per cent. on legacies, only payable by Roman citizens in Italy. Near relations did not pay, nor legacies under 100,000 sesterces. So it was essentially a tax on the rich; and brought in large sums. Caracalla gave the Roman franchise to all provincials for the purpose of making everybody pay this tax, so that in future the wretched provincials had to pay the vicesima as well as the tribute. Till Caracalla did this it is probable that Romans in the provinces, paying as they did tributum, did not also pay the vicesima; for the original idea of the vicesima was that it

---

[1] Marquardt, ii. 253.   [2] Tac. xi. 20.
[3] 'Proxima morti poena metalli coercitio;' Dig. xlviii. 19. 28.
[4] Josephus, Bell. Jud. vi. 9. 2.

should be paid by those who did not pay tributum, and so put Italy upon a level with the provinces[1].

Of the indirect taxes the most important were the *portoria* or the customs duties. Under the Empire there was a thorough-going customs system on the frontiers. Some wares, especially iron, were absolutely forbidden to be exported; and all imported wares paid duty. Besides this there were special taxation provinces which were organised by themselves, and formed a smaller whole within the larger whole of the Empire. Sicily was such a unit; so were the Spanish provinces, Gallia Narbonensis, and the three Gauls. All imports paid two and a-half per cent. on crossing into the three Gauls—quadragesima Galliarum—and we can point out at least five custom-houses on their frontier—at Conflans, St. Maurice, Zurich, Coblenz, Statio Maiensis between Chur and Bregenz. Metz and Cologne are less certain. Britain also had its own import and export dues[2]. Moesia, with the Ripa Thracia, Pannonia, Dalmatia, Noricum, were all administered as a taxation unit, according to Appian, and the portorium Illyricum mentioned in inscriptions[3] may be supposed to have been dues levied on all goods crossing their frontier; so that, once this paid, goods could circulate freely through all this country without let or hindrance. Owing however to the fact that only one custom-house can be pointed out with certainty along this line of frontier, while several seem to be within it, Marquardt inclines to suppose that besides the general outer boundary for the whole, each of these districts also levied its own dues, or rather had its own dues levied for it. The portorium Illyricum was farmed, but the contractors for it have imperial procurators set over them. Asia had a quadragesima of its own; and Bithynia, Paphlagonia, and Pontus had one between them. Both were farmed, but here also were imperial procurators. Egypt was very important for these taxes. Most of the articles of Roman

---

[1] Marquardt, ii. 261.   [2] Strabo, iv. p. 200.
[3] C. I. L. iii. 752; Marq. ii. 264, note 6.

luxury came from the East through Syria or Egypt. Pliny[1] puts the yearly import of Indian goods through Egypt at fifty-five million sesterces; and the import of pearls by the same road at 100 million sesterces. Alexandria was the chief place these goods came to; but in all harbours of the Red Sea duties of twenty-five per cent. were levied on the landing of all Indian or Arabian imports. For Ethiopian goods there was a duty at Syene[2]; at Schedia near Alexandria an export duty was also levied, and in fact at all the mouths of the Nile.

Portoria varied in amount. The portorium was levied in the form of a percentage on the value of the goods. But this percentage differed; for instance, it was five per cent. in Sicily, two per cent. in Spain, two and a-half in the Gauls, Asia, Bithynia, and the Illyrian provinces. In the fourth century it seems to have risen everywhere to twelve and a-half per cent.[3] In other provinces there was a regular tariff for different wares; for instance, in Africa and under Commodus we find such a tariff for Eastern goods[4]. *Other indirect taxes.* Besides the portoria there were the following indirect taxes. *Centesima rerum venalium*, imposed by Augustus after the civil wars[5]. Tiberius reduced it A.D. 17 to ducentesima, but put on the old amount again A.D. 38. Caligula remitted it altogether, as we know from two authorities[6], who, however, disagree in the amount of it—Dio calling it ἑκατοστής, and Suetonius ducentesimam[7]. But the tax appears again and lasted the whole Empire through. We have no distinct testimony whether this tax was applied to provinces as well, but from Suetonius' phrase '*Italiae* remisit,' Marquardt infers that it was. And on the principle of the *vicesima hereditatum* we might infer that, after having been first applied only to Italy,

---

[1] Pliny, N. H. vi. 101.   [2] Marquardt, ii. 266.

[3] Cod. Just. iv. 61. 7, of the year 366: 'Quin octavas more solito constitutas omne hominum genus quod commerciis voluerit interesse dependat.'

[4] Marquardt, ii. 268.

[5] Tac. Ann. i. 78: 'Centesimam rerum venalium, post civilia bella institutam.'

[6] Dio Cass. lix. 9; Suet Calig. 16.   [7] Marquardt, ii. 269, note 8.

it came to be applied also to the provinces; the only objection to both arguments being that this is hardly likely to have happened so easily with the centesima, when it did not happen till Caracalla with the vicesima[1].

Another indirect tax was that of the four per cent. on all purchases of slaves (quinta et vicesima venalium mancipiorum) instituted by Augustus. Tacitus says it was taken off the buyers and put on the sellers, i. e. on the Asiatic slave-dealers, but that it came to the same thing in the end, as the tax was added on to the price. There was a bureau to look after this tax. The quinta et vicesima venalium mancipiorum.

Among the extraordinary sources of income the most important are the confiscated property of condemned persons (*bona damnatorum*), the lapsed legacies or *caduca*, and the so-called *aurum coronarium*.

Any capital punishment (in which term exile was of course included) was followed by such confiscation. The property falls to the aerarium, a system which lasted at all events to the end of Tiberius' reign; for Sejanus' property was so applied[2]. But cases also occur of the emperor's appropriating the money, and this became the accepted practice, so that these moneys fell regularly to the fiscus, and we find a *procurator ad bona damnatorum*. Besides unclaimed property (*bona vacantia*) these *caduca* were introduced by the Lex Julia et Papia Poppea. Properly the term means money left by will, but for some reason unclaimed; but the law made it impossible for bachelors to receive legacies, and so there were plenty of these caduca under the Empire. If not claimed by relations within the third degree such moneys fell to aerarium, after Caracalla to the fiscus. So Augustus failed to get people to marry; but his law brought in a good round income. Bona damnatorum.
Caduca.

---

[1] Marquardt mentions one of the Spanish inscriptions, which reads as follows, 'proc(uratori) Aug. prov(inciae) Baet(icae) ad ducem;' and says that the last two words may very likely mean ad ducentesimam. See C. I. L. ii. No. 2029; Marq. ii. 269, note 8.

[2] Tac. Ann. vi. 2.

Aurum coronarium.

The 'coronary gold' was originally a gold crown offered to a victorious general by provincials and allies to grace his triumph. But already under the Republic it was really a compulsory payment to the governor[1]. Under Augustus first we find *Italian* towns regularly giving him aureae coronae[2]; but on a previous occasion he had received an *aurum coronarium* from Italy[3]. Later on Augustus would only receive this from the provinces. In the later Empire it was paid exclusively by the decuriones. That this 'benevolence' was something considerable is proved by the sum mentioned in the Monumentum Ancyranum—35,000 lbs. of gold. It appears to have been regularly offered on the accession or adoption of a new emperor, both by Italy and the provinces; and Hadrian[4] and M. Antoninus[5] are mentioned as having done themselves credit by remitting a portion of it.

Sum total of the revenue.

It is impossible to say what a year's total revenue was at any period. We do not possess the necessary materials. In some provinces the expenses of administration absorbed all the revenues from it; for instance, Mesopotamia and Britain. Marquardt calculates the vectigalia in the time of Cicero at 200 million sesterces. And the following figures are known. The treasuries at the deaths of Tiberius and Antoninus Pius contained 2900 million sesterces. 'Nero had squandered in presents 2200 million sesterces[6].' Vitellius wasted 900 million sesterces in the course of a few months[7]. Under Hadrian the stipendium of Asia was 28 million sesterces. Gaul paid forty million sesterces immediately after its conquest; and under Constantine, Savigny thinks they paid 360 million sesterces. Sixteen years' arrears of that province before Hadrian amounted to 900 million sesterces[8].

According to Augustus' arrangements the whole field of finance administration was subdivided as follows:—

---

[1] Cic. in Pison. 37; de Leg. Agr. ii. 22; Dio Cass. xlix. 42.
[2] Dio Cass. xlviii. 4.   [3] Ib. xlii. 50.   [4] Spartian, 5.
[5] Capitol. M. Anton. 4.
[6] Tac. Hist. i. 20.   [7] Ib. ii. 95.   [8] Marquardt, ii. 288.

FINANCE ADMINISTRATION.

1. The *aerarium Saturni* had been the single treasury under The aerarium. the Republic. With the division of the provinces into imperial and senatorial, the *aerarium* became the senatorial treasury, into which, besides its previous sources of revenue, the taxes of the senatorial provinces were paid. The Senate had nominally full power over this[1], but really it came under the emperor[2]. The officials of the aerarium were appointed by the emperor, and we find them called praefecti—the regular name for imperial officials. After Nero the name for one of these two ministers was *praefectus aerarii Saturni*. So we find the emperor appointing extraordinary commissions to regulate the aerarium and to limit its outgoings. At the beginning of the Empire the aerarium was empty owing to the civil wars, and we find Augustus[3] and Claudius[4] lending to it. Generally speaking, the endeavour of the emperor was to draw all the more important revenues to the fiscus. This happened, for instance, with the revenues of the domains, with the income from aqueducts, with the *bona damnatorum*, and the *caduca*. By the time of Severus the distinction between senatorial and imperial provinces seems to have ceased; and all provinces paid into the fiscus. So the aerarium, which we find in existence as late as the beginning of the third century[5], became the treasury merely of the municipality of Rome.

2. The fiscus dates from Augustus. It was exclusively under The fiscus. the emperor[6]. In Greek the fiscus is called τὸ βασιλικόν, the aerarii τὸ δημόσιον[7]. Its chief expenses are—the support of the army, fleet, and war-material; the payment of officials; the supplying of Rome with corn; the cost of military roads; the post, and public buildings. The chief revenues were derived from the

---

[1] Suet. Tib. 30; Tac. Ann. ii. 37.
[2] See Dio Cass. liii. 16: λόγῳ μὲν γὰρ τὰ δημόσια ἀπὸ τῶν ἐκείνου ἀπεκέκριτο, ἔργῳ δὲ καὶ ταῦτα πρὸς τὴν γνώμην αὐτοῦ ἀνηλίσκετο: also lv. 22. Cf. Tac. Ann. vi. 2: 'et bona Sejani ablata aerario ut in fiscum cogerentur, *tanquam referret*.' Cf. Ann. vi. 19.   [3] Mon. Anc. § 17.
[4] Tac. Ann. xiii. 31.   [5] Marquardt, ii. 295, note 3.
[6] 'Res enim fiscales quasi propriae et privatae principis sunt;' Ulpian, Dig. xliii. 8. 2. § 4.   [7] Dio Cass. lxxi. 32.

imperial provinces, for which there were *procuratores*, the chief procurator in each province being a knight, the subordinate ones imperial freedmen. Also the fiscus asserted itself in the senatorial provinces; and we find there also procuratores; such officials looked after domain lands, *bona damnatorum*, and *caduca;* also superintended the different payments in kind, and personal services, demanded for the imperial magazines, for military support, equipments and transport, and for buildings[1]. Whether the fiscus also claimed its share of the regular stipendium and portoria of a senatorial province is unknown[2]. Anyhow the emperors disposed of these taxes as they pleased, as is clear from the case of Hadrian, who allowed Herodes Atticus—the corrector civitatium Asiae—to build an aqueduct at Troas, and assigned him three millions from the tribute for the purpose. But it cost seven millions, and the procuratores complained that the whole revenues of the province were employed on a single building. So we find a fiscus in every province— for instance, fiscus Gallicus provinciae Lugdunensis; fiscus Asiaticus. The fiscus in Rome is called simply fiscus without any such epithet, and its administration is called *summa res rationum*. The chief official was originally an imperial freedman, with the title of *a rationibus*. This post was one of great influence. Pallas occupied it under Claudius and Nero[3], Claudius Etruscus under Domitian[4]. He was also called procurator a rationibus, procurator summarum rationum; and, after Hadrian, was commonly a knight who had been procurator of several provinces before attaining this dignity, and who was afterwards advanced to the praefectura annonae or ab epistulis.

The patrimonium Caesaris.

3. The Patrimonium Caesaris also dates from Augustus. A numerous body of officials was wanted for its administration,

---

[1] Marquardt, ii. 296.
[2] Mommsen, Staatsrecht, ii. 937, note 2, conjectures that it did from the following passage of Tac. Ann. ii. 47: ' (Sardianis) quantum aerario aut fisco pendebant in quinquennium remisit.'
[3] Suet. Claud. 28.   [4] See Statius, Silv. iii. 3.

both in Rome and the provinces. They were the slaves and freedmen of the emperor; and were called *procuratores patrimonii*. The emperor controlled and directed them, and there was no one among them with a position anything like that of the *procurator fisci*. The emperor having the fiscus as well as this patrimonium at his absolute disposition, a question always arose at the death of every emperor as to what property he had a right to bequeath, and what part naturally descended to the State and to his successor. Egypt belonged to the patrimonium, and one of its highest officials was the ἰδιόλογος (which was the name of the king's steward under the Ptolemies), who as *procurator rei privatae* drew in taxes such as the *caduca*, which in other provinces belonged to the fiscus or aerarium. Of course it was understood that such *res privata* as Egypt passed on to the next emperor. So we want a new distinction, and we get it in that between patrimonium and *res familiaris*; the first being the emperor's official income,—just as the Chancellor of the Exchequer with us is given £5,000 a year for being Chancellor of the Exchequer,—and the latter his private means. Severus first clearly assigned them to different procuratores, and afterwards the procurator rei privatae became a very important personage, more so than the procurator patrimonii, and on a level with the procurator of the fisc. Res familiaris.

4. The *Aerarium Militare* was the treasury out of which the pensions to veterans were paid. Originally established by Augustus and endowed with 170 million sesterces[1], it was kept up out of the proceeds of the two taxes—*vicesima hereditatum* and *centesima rerum venalium*—which were regularly devoted to it. Also money came in to it now and then from extraordinary sources; for instance, the goods of the banished Agrippa Postumus[2]. Augustus put the fund under three men of praetorian rank, chosen by lot, and serving for three years. In Dio's time they were named by the emperor[3], with the title praefectus aerarii militaris. Their office lasted till the third century[4]. Aerarium militare.

---

[1] Mon. Anc. §. 17.   [2] Dio Cass. lv. 32.   [3] Ib. lv. 26.
[4] Tac. Ann. v. 8; Marquardt, ii. 302.

The system of tax-collecting in this period. The system of farming the taxes continued under the Empire, but was controlled and modified. The *decumani*, who under the Republic had formed the first and most influential class among the publicani, came to an end. But other taxes were still farmed[1], and during the whole Empire we find the system employed both by the State and by the municipalities[2]. After the decease of the censorship the locators were generally imperial procurators. So in Africa we find procuratores quattuor publicorum Africae side by side with conductores quattuor publicorum Africae[3]. The two tributes were no longer farmed by publicani, but got in directly, in senatorial provinces by the quaestor and his subordinates, in imperial by the procurator of the province and his subordinates. There was a *tabularium* (a sort of audit office) in each province, where the survey-documents and census-lists were kept; also in each province a *fiscus provinciae*, from which the governor paid the troops and officials in the province, and sent the surplus to Rome[4]. For all private revenues, which did not come into this fiscus provinciae, there was in each province a special imperial procurator, with a central bureau for them all in Rome.

Minor branches of the administration. Besides these main branches of finance administration there were a number of minor ones, about which indeed we are more completely informed (by inscriptions) than about the more important ones. For instance, we find a *procurator a caducis*[5], officials for aqueducts, public buildings, &c., for the *cura annonae*, and for the coinage[6]. With every separate detachment of troops

---

[1] Cf. Tac. Ann. iv. 6: 'At frumenta et pecuniae vectigalis, cetera publicorum fructuum, societatibus equitum Romanorum agitabantur.' See the important chapter, Tac. Ann. xiii. 50, where Nero thinks of abolishing all indirect taxes—a good passage for the use of the term vectigalia. Noticeable phrases are—'immodestiam publicanorum,' 'vectigalium societates,' 'publicanorum cupidines.'

[2] See the *Lex Malacitana*.

[3] See Henzen, 6648, 6650, quoted by Marq. ii. 303, note 2.

[4] Dio Cass. lvii. 10.   [5] C. I. L. iii. No. 1622.

[6] 'Procurator monetae in Tarraco;' C. I. L. ii. No. 4206. Also 'officinatores monetae.' See Orelli, 3226, 3227, 1090; Marq. ii. 304, note 3.

there was a *fiscus castrensis*, a *procurator castrensis*, and a commissariat official, *a copiis militaribus*. The *patrimonium* and the *res privata Caesaris* also employed numerous procurators to look after the emperor's private properties and receive the legacies left to him. We find them employed also for such matters as games, libraries, picture galleries, and the like[1].

There were also regular administration-districts for getting in the *vicesima hereditatum* and *vicesima manumissionum*; for instance, there was one for Pamphylia, Lycia, Phrygia, Galatia, and the Cyclades[2]; another for the two Pontus', Bithynia, and Paphlagonia[3]; another for Baetica and Lusitania; another for Hispania Citerior; another for Gallia Lugdunensis, Belgica, and the two Germanies; while in Italy there was one for Campania, Apulia, and Calabria; and another for Umbria, Tuscia, Picenum, and Campania[4].

SECTION III. *The taxation of the Later Empire.*

Diocletian's financial reforms took place under as yet unknown conditions. Caracalla had given the civitas to all the provincials. Diocletian imposed the tribute upon Italy. Diocletian divided the eastern part of the Empire into *juga*, that is, really existing divisions with definite boundaries, varying from five acres to sixty, but all alike of one and the same value. For instance, the five acres would be five acres of vineyard; the sixty would be sixty acres of indifferent corn-land. So that their money value would be the same. It has been a question about these juga whether they really existed or were only abstractions, ideal divisions for the convenience of reckoning. Savigny thought the latter. But a codex of A.D. 501—Eastern Empire—proves the contrary[5]; and we also learn from this

<small>The division into *juga*.</small>

---

[1] Orelli, 2417.   [2] Henzen, 6940.   [3] Ib.
[4] See Marquardt, ii. 305, note 5, where the authorities are given.
[5] The Codex is in the British Museum, published 1862 in Land's *Symbolae Syriacae*.

codex that a re-survey of the Empire took place under Diocletian for the purpose of this division into juga[1]. From these materials a kataster was drawn up giving in each district the number of juga, and the sum due from them. The decuriones in the capital of the district distributed this total among the landowners, and paid over the receipts, for which they were responsible. The lists which had to be kept have been found, and generally contain the name of the owner, the name of the property, its position, and the amount of tax payable by it in denarii. In case of a remission of taxation either the number of juga was reduced, or the amount payable by each province. So in the case of the Aedui, Constantine reduced the number of juga from 32,000 to 25,000[2]. It is not to be supposed that there was the same arrangement of these juga in all provinces alike. In Africa the jugum is called *centuria*, and consists of 200 acres. In Italy there is a larger unit called *millena*, whose larger size is easily explained by the existence of latifundia[3].

Increasing burden of taxation.

The coloni have been fully enough discussed already to make a furthur discussion superfluous. It was they who now were the chief payers of the poll-tax after Diocletian had taken this tax off the towns. The portoria were growing heavier during this period, till they reached the frightful rate of $12\frac{1}{2}$ per cent. in the fourth century. The new imposition of the legacy-duty on all provincials was bad enough; but it was the land-tax after all which was the crushing burden. It was this which made slaves of the municipal magistrates, and which made the hard-tasked victims of the terribly perfect machine of administration welcome the barbarians rather with hope than with despair.

---

[1] Marquardt, ii. 220.

[2] Eumenii Gratiarum Actio, ii; Sidonius Apoll. Carm. xiii. 19; Marquardt, ii. 222; and for the latter case, Lampridius, Vita Alex. Sev. xxxix. 6; Ammianus, xvi. 5, 14. Sidonius' expression is:—

'Geryones nos esse puta monstrumque tributum:
Hic capita, ut vivam, tu mihi tolle tria.'

[3] Marquardt, ii. 224.

CHAPTER VI.

Towns in the Provinces.

SECTION I. *Towns the basis of the administration. Increase of towns under Rome.*

THE use which Rome made of the towns in carrying out her administrative system has already been mentioned. When Cicero is mentioning the taxes of Asia, he speaks of them as the 'tribute of the cities' (tributa civitatum[1]). The towns formed the administrative means of raising the taxes. Each town comprehended a district of 'tributary lands' (fundi tributarii), the names of which and of their occupiers lay with the town magistrates, as for instance in Sicily[2]. When there were no towns we find 'homines stipendiarii' instead of 'civitates stipendiariae,' and in such cases the State itself had to look after the lists, and direct all that machinery of administration, which elsewhere was taken off its hands by the towns. Even under the Empire the tribute of a province was paid by a certain number of towns, and when we hear of remissions of taxes, it is to towns that the remissions are given. In all towns of Greek constitution a census already existed, and it is tolerably certain that the Romans introduced it wherever it did not, partly in order to introduce a timocratic constitution, partly to secure a fair apportionment of the taxes. Censors are expressly mentioned in Sicily and Bithynia, and no doubt existed everywhere[3]. It was at the towns also, of course, that justice was

Use of the towns for administrative purposes.

---

[1] Cic. ad Qu. Fr. i. 1. 8.   [2] Cic. in Verr. iv. 51.
[3] Marquardt, ii. 180 and 181.

administered. Fifty-five tribes, according to Pliny, had justice administered to them at Caesar Augusta in Spain, and sixty-five at Carthago Nova[1].

Could the towns act together?

A question naturally arises as to how far these towns had any capacity of united action. The general impression we get from a survey of the facts is that the opportunities of united action were limited and occasional, and that within any province the governor on the one side, and the municipal magistrates on the other, constituted the only two sources of power. But this impression is not absolutely exact, and a more particular examination of the *concilia* or provincial parliaments will correct it.

The provincial parliaments.

These parliaments, which are mentioned by Tacitus[2], were either older than the province itself, or were established under the first emperors, or, in the case of countries which did not till a late date become provinces, were at once introduced. The Romans at first dissolved all such assemblies, for instance in Greece, Sicily, and Macedonia; but afterwards permitted them to exist mainly for religious objects. These religious objects concealed a political object, for these parliaments formed a centre for the worship of the emperor. The high-priest of this worship (ἀρχιέρευς, or *sacerdos provinciae*) was, apart from the Romans, the most important personage in the province. He was elected by the deputies[3] of a certain number of the most important towns, and, like them, held his office for a year. He was elected from those who had either discharged all municipal offices in their town, or were of equestrian rank. He was exempt from taxation, and if a mission was sent from the province to the emperor he conducted it. The parliament met yearly, and after having taken part in the religious festival, re-assembled as a secular body. After settling any points connected with the temple, passing the accounts, and deciding any

---

[1] Plin. N. H. iii. 4.   [2] Tac. Ann. xv. 22.

[3] These deputies were not, and must be distinguished from, the municipal flamens; Marquardt, Ephem. Epig. ib. Flamen provinciae in the Inscriptions is another title for the high-priest.

proposal as to statues or other honours which might be brought before them, the high-priest for the next year was chosen. Then either a vote of thanks was voted to the outgoing governor, or, more important, a complaint was drawn up against him, and forwarded by special mission to the Senate or emperor[1]. This could be done without asking the governor's consent; and the emperor's reply was sent direct to the parliament. Thus we find Hadrian writing to the Council of Baetica, Antoninus Pius to that of Asia[2]. We may probably regard this as a regular means whereby the provinces exercised a control upon their governors, and as an element in the improvement of their condition[3].

But though in endeavouring to form a conception of the interior of a province it is necessary to assign a certain part to these parliaments, it still remains true that the single towns were of far greater importance when isolated than when thus combined. When the Romans had to organise the provinces they used towns wherever they could; and in countries of Greek or Phoenician civilisation, in Greece proper, Sicily, Western and Southern Asia Minor and Carthaginian Africa, they found towns with definite territory ready to hand. Where they did not find them in these parts of the world they would make a village into a town, or compose a town out of several neighbouring villages. Thus Orcistus in Phrygia was made into a town[4], and Aperlae, Simena, Apollonia, and Isinda in Lycia were made into one community with one Senate, and

Increase of towns under Rome.

---

[1] Cf. the phrases in Pliny, Ep. vii. 6, 'decreto concilii,' 'decreto provinciae,' in reference to an accusation brought against a governor.

[2] Marquardt, i. 371, note 5; Masdeu, *Historia de Espagna*, viii. 48.

[3] Most of the statements in the text are obtained from Marquardt, i. 365-377, and from the same writer's important essay on the subject in the Ephemeris Epigraphica. Mommsen, *Schweiz in Römischer Zeit*, p. 8, discusses the famous parliament of the sixty-four Gallic states at Lugdunum, which is mentioned by Strabo. But he speaks ironically of the right of complaint as if it were almost always negatived by a complaisant majority. The passages from Tacitus and Pliny, already referred to, hardly perhaps bear out this pessimistic view. [4] Marquardt, i. 17.

forming one δῆμος. The other provinces when conquered by Rome were in different stages of the development through which the Greek and Phoenician countries had long passed. Thus when Rome appeared in Spain the system of *pagi* or cantons, as opposed to the system of towns, was almost universal. In the statistics compiled by Agrippa and used by Pliny[1], we find 293 peoples enumerated in Hispania Tarraconensis, of which 179 dwelt in towns, while 114 had no town. We may be sure that this list shows an immense advance upon the number of real towns as opposed to mere strongholds, which existed before the commencement of the Roman rule; but a century later Ptolemy, writing under Antoninus Pius, shows us the rapid extension of the town system within that period, for he enumerates in the same province 248 towns, and only twenty-seven of these townless communities. So in Gaul there were before the Romans entered the country no real towns, with the exception perhaps of a few which were neither Greek nor Roman in the Narbonensis[2]. When Caesar conquered Gaul the country was divided among a number of tribes, each containing some 300 or 400 *pagi*. It was out of these that Augustus formed sixty-four states[3], each with a capital of its own. From these capitals arose some of the principal towns of France, for instance Amiens and Nantes. Lugdunum was the capital of all sixty-four states, and the centre of all administration, imperial and municipal. In the Transpadine districts the first care of the Romans was to found towns, to which they made the Gallic tribes subject. By the Lex Pompeia of B.C. 89 the peoples of the Eastern Alps were put under Tridentum, Verona, Brixia, Cremona, and Mediolanum, and the authorities of these towns had important duties connected with these populations, such as the levying of soldiers, the quartering of troops, the responsibility for envoys, the main-

---

[1] Plin. N. H. iii. 4.
[2] e. g. Illiberris, Narbo, Nemansus, Baeterrae; cf. Lentheric, Les Villes Mortes, &c. pp. 306, 390.
[3] Tac. Ann. iii. 44; Strabo, iv. 192; Marquardt, Ephem. Epig. p. 203.

tenance of the roads, and the exaction of the taxes[1]. Glancing through the other provinces, we see that in Pannonia important towns like Nauportus (Laibach) and Pellovia (Pettau) were of Roman origin[2]. In Dalmatia towns must originally have been very scarce, as even under Rome the circuits (conventus) were made up not of towns, but of *decuriae*. Important towns like Scardona were introduced by the Romans, and there were five Roman colonies in the country[3]. In Moesia the towns, such as Sistova, Varna, Istros, Tomi, are either of Greek or Roman origin; and in Dacia, as already mentioned, a number of flourishing cities were planted by the Roman conquerors[4]. The same policy was followed in Thrace, where the Romans founded many towns[5], and in those provinces of Asia Minor, such as Bithynia or Gallacia, which were not already covered with cities of Hellenic origin. Pompey made out eleven towns in Pontus, and twelve in Bithynia; other places were villages. In the course of time the number of towns considerably increased[6]. Galatia, inhabited by a brave and semi-barbarous people which did not yield to Rome without a struggle, was late in adopting the town-system, but when it did secure itself there it was a great success[7]. The number of towns in Cappadocia was originally four. This was considerably increased by the Romans, and from the Christian sources of the sixth century we gather that the Roman garrisons and stations on the military roads had gradually risen into towns, and were the seats of Christian bishoprics[8]. In Syria the town-system was begun by the Seleucidae and completed by the Romans, with aid from the Jewish kings, to whom were due such towns as Caesarea and Samaria[9]. In Africa the towns played a great part in civilising and Romanising the country. Of one tribe, which was yet untouched by Roman influence (the Musulamii), Tacitus informs us that they had 'none of the civilisation of cities[10].'

---

[1] Marquardt, i. 14. [2] Ib. 139. [3] Ib. 146.
[4] Marquardt, i. 155. [5] Ib. 159. [6] Ib. 199.
[7] Perrot, *De Galatia Provincia Romana*, p. 83.
[8] Marquardt, i. 216. [9] Ib. 270. [10] Tac. Ann. ii. 52.

But partly by means of direct colonisation, and partly by means of the gradual growth of towns from the villages of veterans, the 'civilisation of cities' was fully applied to the country, and with the happiest results. In Pliny's time there were in Africa thirty free towns, fifteen municipia, and six colonies[1]; and modern travellers notice with astonishment the ruins of what must have been flourishing cities far beyond the present limits of Algerian civilisation[2].

Gradual growth of a town.
The development of this town-system must in the majority of the cases have been gradual; it was not often that it was imposed full blown upon a country, as it was in the case of Dacia; and it is interesting to watch, where we can, the gradual growth of the garrison into the village, and the village into the town. The most natural way in which a town grew up of itself in a Roman province was from the surroundings of a Roman camp[3], and of course still more readily from the camp itself[4]. Even in the case of a temporary camp the settlers pitched their tents just outside the rampart[5]; and where the camp was permanent, as in Syria or Africa or on the Rhine or Danube frontier, these fortuitous aggregations of merchants and camp-followers soon grew into something like a town. 'It is well known that the *castra stativa* of the legions have in the majority of cases given birth to towns, some of which never had any name but that of the legion to which they owed their origin[6].' 'This inscription[7]' (of Troesmis in Lower Moesia) 'shows us how these towns came into existence.

---

[1] Marquardt, i. 317.
[2] Playfair, *Travels in the Footsteps of Bruce*, p. 69 and *passim*.
[3] Cf. Tac. Hist. iv. 22.
[4] Cf. the case of Lambesis in Africa.
[5] Caesar, B. G. vi. 37.
[6] e. g. Leon and Caerleon as mentioned *supra*.
[7] The inscription is as follows: 'Pro salute imperatoris Caesaris Trajani Hadriani Augusti, Gaio Valerio Pudente veterano legionis quintae Macedonicae et Marco Ulpio Leontio magistris Canabensium et Tuccio Aelio aedilibus, dono dederunt veterani et cives Romani consistentes ad Canabas legionis Quintae Macedonicae.'

Sutlers and merchants came to settle in the neighbourhood of the camp, and these built huts, *canabas*, the aggregate of which soon formed a village. When this village had attained sufficient importance to have an administration of its own—a *res publica* —it was given along with the title of *vicus*, the administration of a *vicus*, that is, one consisting of two *magistri*, two aediles, and a council composed of *vicani* or decurions[1].' Another inscription mentioning these canabae has been found at Argentoratum[2] (Strasburg), and three more at Apulum (Carlsburg) in Dacia[3]. We may suppose that the first canaba grew out of the legion known as VIII Augusta, which was stationed at Argentoratum, and the latter from that known as XIII Gemina, which was stationed in Dacia, and the name of which occurs on two of the inscriptions of Apulum. In one of the latter we find the phrase 'Kanabensium legionis XIII Geminae,' and we may suppose that, strictly speaking, *Canabae* or *Canabenses* was never a complete title by itself, but needed the addition of the name of the legion to become intelligible. Where however every one knew the name and number of the legion, they might very naturally

---

[1] Renier, *Inscriptions de Troesmis*, in the Révue Archéologique, xii. 414.

[2] M. Renier reads the inscription as follows: 'In honorem domus Divinae, genio vici cannabarum et vicanorum Canabensium .... Martius Optatus, qui columnam et statuam dono dedit.'

[3] I transcribe them from Ackner and Müller: (1) 'Fortunae Augustae sacrum et genio Canabensium L. Silius Maximus veteranus legionis I. adjutricis piae fidelis, magistras (sic) primus in Canabae dedicavit et Silvia Januaria et Silius Firminus' (No. 433 in Ackner and Müller). (2) 'Libero patri et Liberae Claudius Atteius Celer, veteranus legionis xiii. Geminae Gordianae (Severianae?) decurio Canabensium cum suis votum libens solvit. Locus datus decreto decurionum' (No. 358 in Ackner and Müller). (3) 'Pro salute Augusti Matri deum magnae sanctum Titus Flavius Longinus veteranus ex decurione alae II. Pannoniorum decurio coloniae Dacicae, decurio municipii Napocae, decurio Kanabensium legionis xiii. Geminae, et Claudia Candida conjunx et Flavius Longinus, Clementina, Marcellina filii ex imperio pecunia sua fecerunt. Locus datus decreto decurionum' (No. 387 in Ackner and Müller). Cannaba occurs twice in the Itin. Anton. pp. 189, 191, ed. Wesseling—in both cases on a Syrian road. I owe the reference to Ackner and Müller, loc. cit.

be omitted on the inscription, as it was not worth while spending time and labour to add them[1].

Relation of a town to the surrounding district.

However it originated, a town always included a considerable surrounding district; and in many cases the smaller towns were not themselves independent units, but were included in the territory of a larger city. Nismes and Marseilles had a great number of these smaller towns thus 'attributed' to them. Marseilles had at one time authority over Nice and Antibes, among others; and Nismes over no less than twenty-four smaller towns, each of which possessed the Latin right like herself[2]. In Italy itself the *regio Herculanensium* or *pagus Herculaneus* (it is called by both names[3]) was included in Naples; and Baiae stood in the same relation of subordination to Cumae[4]. Andes came under Mutina[5], and Cicero speaks of the 'many tribes which make up the municipia of Umbria[6].' The powerful colony of Vienna (Vienne) in Gaul 'included all the country of the Allobroges[7].' There were 293 states dependent on others in Tarraconensis[8]. In almost all provincial municipia and colonies there was no doubt a portion of the surrounding population thus attributed; the *contributi* are mentioned for instance in the Lex Ursonitana, and we learn from that law that they shared the military duties of the full citizen[9]. I shall have something to add upon this subject later. At present the ground has perhaps been sufficiently cleared to allow of an examination of the different classes of provincial towns,—the

---

[1] I have done nothing here but give a resumé of M. Renier's masterly discussion. While on this general question of the growth of towns I may refer to Marquardt, i. 273, for the case of Batanea, which was first a κωμή, then a garrison, then a town, and then a colony.

[2] Plin. N. H. iii. 4; Strabo, iv. 1. 12; Appian, B. C. ii. 26; Zumpt, Decr. Terg. p. 10. For Marseilles, Caesar, B. G. i. 35.

[3] Orelli, 3801 and 3795.

[4] Orelli, 2263. The official acting at Baiae calls himself *pro magistro* in his inscription; cf. Zumpt, Comm. Epig. ii. 54.

[5] Merivale, iii. 239.   [6] Cic. pro Murena, 20.

[7] Renier, *Mélanges*, p. 67.   [8] Plin. N. H. iii. 4.

[9] § 103 of the law.

non-Roman towns (including the free and federate states), the colonies, and the municipia.

Section II. *The non-Roman Towns.*

In the enumeration which Pliny gives of the 175 towns of Baetica he makes out nine colonies, eight municipia, twenty-nine Latin towns, six free towns, three federate, and 120 tributary (stipendiariae)[1]. In the list which he gives of the towns of Tarraconensis the numbers are different, but the proportions are precisely similar[2]. It appears therefore, and this is what might have been anticipated, that the unprivileged towns were far more numerous than those provincial towns which under the name of free or federate possessed autonomy and immunity, as well as those composed of citizens with either the full Roman or the Latin franchise. Unfortunately it is of this class that least is known. We possess a large amount of evidence as to the internal arrangements of a Roman colony or municipium, and something is known of the constitutions of the more important free or federate towns; but of the great mass of the 'stipendiariae civitates' our information is exceedingly scanty. It will be better therefore to set out what is definitely known of the free and federate states before proceeding to the discussion of the other far more numerous class of non-Roman towns.

Three classes of non-Roman towns.

1. Both the federate towns and those which were called simply 'free' might, if desirable, be grouped under the one head of 'free towns.' But it is convenient to separate them in practice, because though all federate towns were free, not all free towns were federate. The federate towns were those which had made a definite treaty with Rome, sworn to on both sides, and carved on brazen tablets, of which one was kept in each contracting city. Their position was the most favourable of all provincial towns, and of course as Rome acquired a position of absolute predominance, no more were made. But there were one or

---

[1] Pliny, N. H. iii. 3.   [2] Ib. iii. 4.

Federate towns. two in almost every province. There were three in Sicily; one in Tarraconensis; three in Baetica; one, Marseilles, in Narbonensis, besides whole peoples—the Remi, Ædui, Carnuti and Lingones—in *Gallia Comata*. Athens, Rhodes and Tyre were federate towns, and four others can be pointed out in Asia Minor. Cicero mentions it as an exceptional thing and as a stigma on Sardinia, that in all that island there was no town which was 'free and united by friendship with the Roman people[1].'

It is difficult to make out the precise relation of these towns to Rome. In every case the treaty expressly forbade an independent foreign policy. It was open to such a town to adopt the civil law of Rome or not, as it pleased; but it had no choice about ratifying or declining to ratify matters concerning the Empire, the wars, the safety or the victories of Rome[2]. All of these towns were exempt from the ordinary taxes[3]; and all had the right if they pleased of using their own laws. Even Romans living in a federate town pleaded before its courts in civil cases[4]. But, these common features apart, there were the greatest varieties in the position secured to the different federate towns by their treaties with Rome. Such treaties were regularly divided into favourable (aequa) and unfavourable (iniqua). An instance of an *iniquum foedus* is that made with the Helvetians and other barbarous peoples, in which it was expressly stipulated that no one of them should ever become a citizen of Rome[5]. The treaty of Heraclea on the other hand was so exceptionally favourable that its citizens were very doubtful as to whether they should accept the offer of the privileges of Roman citizenship[6]. In Sicily the treaties made with Messana and Tauro-

---

[1] Cic. pro Scauro, § 44. For the whole subject see Zumpt, Studia Romana, p. 315; Marquardt, i. 348.

[2] I almost translate from Cic. pro Balbo, 8.

[3] See Cic. in Verr. iii. 69, iv. 40, v. 9 for illustrations of this immunity; also de Off. iii. 22.

[4] Marquardt, i. 349.   [5] Cic. pro Balbo, 14.

[6] Cic. pro Balbo, 8 and 22; pro Archia, 4.

menium differed in the important respect that the people of Messana were bound to furnish a vessel at their own expense, while from this burden the Tauromenians were expressly excused[1].

Though in all cases the foedus laid down the exemption of such towns from the interference of the governor[2], and though they had a legal right to maintain any sort of political constitution they might think fit, we do as a matter of fact find them interfered with, and we may be sure that means were pretty generally taken to bring their constitutions up to the usual timocratic level. The answer which Pompey gave to the people of Messana when, on the ground of their treaty, they claimed exemption from his jurisdiction, must often have been given in such cases by the men of the sword[3]. In the case of Marseilles we know that the government was a very pronounced oligarchy[4]: perhaps this is one reason for the elaborate panegyric which Cicero more than once bestows upon the place[5]. Rhodes on the other hand had a peculiar kind of democratic constitution[6], which doubtless was one reason why the Romans found the place difficult to deal with, and why its privileges were ultimately taken away.

Interference in the internal affairs of these towns.

These towns owed their privileged position to services done to Rome in the past, and Rome looked to them to do if necessary similar services in the future. Cicero speaks of Marseilles almost as he speaks of Narbo[7], and its services were doubtless great. So it was the Remi who took the lead in peaceful measures when part of Gaul revolted under Civilis[8];

Services of these towns to Rome.

---

[1] Cic. in Verr. vi. 19.   [2] Ib. iii. 66.
[3] Plut. Pomp. 10: παραιτουμένων γὰρ αὐτοῦ τὸ βῆμα καὶ δικαιοδοσίαν, ὡς νομίμῳ παλαιῷ Ῥωμαίων ἀπειρημένα, Οὐ παύσεσθε, εἶπεν, ἡμῖν ὑποζωσμένοις ξίφη νόμους ἀναγινώσκοντες;
[4] Cic. de Republ. i. 27; Strabo, iv. 1. § 5.
[5] Cf. especially Cic. pro Flacco, 26.
[6] Cic. de Republ. iii. 35; Mommsen, ii. 306.
[7] Cic. pro Font. 20: 'Ea condicione atque eo fato se in iis terris collocatam arbitratur, ne quid nostris hominibus istae gentes nocere possint.'
[8] Tac. Hist. iv. 67.

and Gades from the time of the Punic wars had given many substantial proofs of loyalty[1].

These towns tend to become Roman.

It shows however how strong was the tendency to uniformity and how great the attraction exercised by Rome that we find almost all these towns, whose position seems so exceptional and so favourable, voluntarily renouncing it in order to become colonies or municipia. In Sicily, Tauromenium became a colony, and Messana apparently a municipium[2]. In Spain, Gades becomes a municipium, under the title of *municipium Augustum Gaditanum*[3]; and so also do Saguntum and Malaga, both of which had previously been federate. The latter case seems to show that an allied town would even accept the minor privileges of the Latin right in preference to its independent condition[4]. Similarly in Italy, both Heraclea and Neapolis became Roman municipia[5]. It was doubtless found by these towns that the advantages they enjoyed were not of a very substantial character, and that a more certain protection against tyrannical magistrates as well as a larger opening to ambition was supplied by their being incorporated into the Roman State, instead of their remaining outside it in semi-independent isolation[6].

Free towns.

2. The *civitates sine foedere immunes et liberae* differed for the worse from the federate towns in that their freedom was secured, not by the stipulation of a treaty, but by the voluntary gift of Rome, and could therefore at any time be taken from them. Towns which had sided with Rome in war, for instance Utica and six other towns in Africa, or which, like Troas, enjoyed the special

---

[1] Cf. Cic. pro Balbo, 17.
[2] Plin. iii. 8. He calls Messana 'civium Romanorum.'
[3] C. I. L. ii. 1313; Orelli, 3690, 3691.
[4] Zumpt, Studia Romana, p. 316 foll., will not believe that a federate town ever accepted merely the Latin franchise. But the law of Malaga is against him, though he explains away its difficulties very ingeniously (p. 318).
[5] Cic pro Archia, 5. § 10; ad Fam. xiii. 30.
[6] Strictly speaking, the free and allied towns did not belong to the province at all; cf. Mommsen, C. I. L. i. 99.

good-will of the Senate or the emperor, received the gift. A fragment of the Lex Antonia de Thermessibus which still exists shows that these towns had the right to use their own laws, to be exempt from soldiers being quartered on them, and to use their own customs duties[1]. They were also, like the federate towns, exempt from the taxation; but were of course also, like them, subject to the supreme disposal of the Senate. The difference then between them and the federate towns lying merely in their weaker legal position as against Rome[2], and not in any practical inferiority of privilege, we may expect to find much the same features visible in them, that we have already noted in the cognate class of towns. The same right of exemption from the jurisdiction of the governor appears in these as in the federate cities[3]. Piso had to bribe a tribune heavily to bring in a law to authorise him when governor of Macedonia to decide upon cases of debt in the free city of Byzantium[4]. But in the Greek cities at all events, which were always 'free,' it is very certain that taxes were exacted, and that the governor exercised the supreme jurisdiction[5]. It is of the cities in this part of the world that Tacitus is speaking when he describes them with a kind of irony as 'the allied nations and free states *as they were called*[6];' and we may infer from Strabo that the freedom of 'Corcyra the free' was not a matter of very much consequence[7]. Perhaps the freedom was sometimes badly used. Suetonius[8] says that Augustus deprived of their independence some of this class of states, 'which by their excessive licence were hastening to their own ruin.' Rome endeavoured to maintain control over them by favouring the aristocratic or

---

[1] C. I. L. i. 114, No. 204.

[2] '... die *civitates federatae* und die *civitates liberae* ... nicht so sehr in dem Umfang der Rechte sich unterscheiden als darin, dass das eine Verhaltniss rechtlich, das andere bloss factisch besteht;' Mommsen, Römische Forschungen, p. 363, note.

[3] Cf. Strabo, iv. 6. § 4; Pliny, Ep. x. 93.

[4] Cic. de Prov. Cons. 4. [5] See Mommsen's elaborate note, iii. 50.

[6] Tac. Ann. xv. 45. [7] Strabo, vii. fragment.

[8] Suet. Aug. 47.

rather timocratic element in their constitutions[1]; we find for instance the Areopagus apparently the chief judicial authority in Athens[2],—a strange return to the days before Pericles and Ephialtes. But the affairs of these states got into confusion, and such special missions as that of Pliny to the cities of Bithynia are of frequent occurrence[3]. A good governor was careful to show one of these towns special respect[4], but a Verres could disregard their privileges with impunity, and at all events one case occurs of a magistrate of one of these towns being scourged by a Roman governor[5]. It is no wonder therefore that the same causes which changed the federate cities into municipia should act still more powerfully here, notwithstanding that for a considerable period at all events there was much competition for the privileges of freedom[6], and that they were purchased with large sums of money[7]. A free town would naturally enough appeal to Rome for assistance in case of disturbance in its internal affairs. Thus the free town of Halesa in Sicily requested the Senate to regulate its constitution, which was done by sending C. Claudius Pulcher to the place as extraordinary commissioner[8]. Similarly Caesar when praetor in Spain regulated the internal affairs of Gades[9], and a free town of Bithynia, though asserting its right to exemption from all interference of the Roman governor, voluntarily submitted its

---

[1] Cf. Marquardt, i. 238, for Syria; i. 248, for Judaea; i. 578, for Tarsus and generally. The last is the important passage. The guard for the defence of Byzantium, Plin. Ep. x. 82, which 'protected its privileges,' is not easy to explain. Perhaps it was intended for the support of the aristocratic element against the plebs.

[2] Tac. Ann. ii. 55.

[3] Cf. Plin. Ep. viii. 24: 'Messius Maximus missus in provinciam Achaiam ad ordinandum statum liberarum civitatum.' Henzen, 6483: 'Legato divi Hadriani Athenis, Thespiis, Plateis, item in Thessalia . . . legato divi Hadriani ad rationes civitatum Syriae putandas.'

[4] Suet. Cal. 3; Tac. Ann. ii. 55, for Germanicus.

[5] Mommsen, iii. 67.

[6] Cic. ad Qu. Fr. ii. 11, for the refusal of freedom to Tenedos.

[7] Cic. de Off. iii. 22; Suet. Jul. 54.

[8] Cic. in Verr. iii. 49.   [9] Cic. pro Balbo, 19.

affairs to Pliny's examination[1]. This was a tendency which once begun would not stop before the assimilation of these towns to the regular municipal type. Thus Nero made Puteoli, which had been a free town[2], into a colony[3]; and we find the same change effected in the case of Hadrumetum, Hippo, and Parentum in Africa[4].

3. The great mass of provincial towns—civitates stipendiariae —possessed no special privileges. That however their internal affairs were not very largely interfered with, and that they to a large extent, at all events under a good governor, retained the use of their own laws, is proved by all the evidence. Temnos had five praetors, three quaestors, and four mensarii, names which we may no doubt regard as translations of Greek equivalents[5]. Thyatira had a βουλή and an ἄρχων, and its chief magistrates appear to have been στρατηγοί[6]. In Africa we even find Sufetes[7]. So we find a προάγορος at Catina in Sicily[8], and all the Sicilian cities had apparently their local Senates. Cicero frequently mentions that of Syracuse, and when speaking of it gives it its regular Greek name of βουλευτήριον[9]. The great change made by Rome was in the direction of abolishing the democracies; though we still find the popular assemblies of Asia Minor in some cases apparently the chief source of power, at all events up to quite the end of the Republic[10]. Under the Empire timocracies seem to have been everywhere established. Only those possessing a certain income were permitted the full

Civitates stipendiariae.

---

[1] Plin. Ep. x. 56. [2] Cic. de Leg. Agr. ii. 31.
[3] Zumpt, Comm. Epig. i. 458. [4] Ib.
[5] Cic. pro Flacco, 19.
[6] Perrot, pp. 5, 9 of *Inscriptions d'Asie Mineure*; pp. 8, 16, 23, 27 of *Inscriptions de la Mer Noire*.
[7] For Sufetes, see Orelli, 3056.
[8] Cic. in Verr. v. 23. [9] Ib. iii. 20, 21; v. 64, 65.
[10] Cic. pro Flacco, 6 *fin.*; Cic. in Verr. ii 27, for Lampsacus. But such a passage as Cic. ad Qu. Fr. i. 1. 8 is significant: 'Provideri abs te ut civitates optimatium consiliis administrentur.' A passage of Caesar, B. G. viii. 21, seems to suggest that the populace was always at first unfriendly to Rome, and that Rome made it her business to conciliate the nobles; cf. ib. 49.

Conversion of these towns into municipia. franchise of the place. So at Tarsus, besides a βουλή and a δῆμος, there was a 'no small multitude which stood as it were outside the constitution[1].' In this case the regular franchise could only be purchased at a cost of 500 drachmae. But the great change of all was the conversion of these towns into municipia by giving them the Roman or Latin franchise. The Greek towns offered a passive resistance to this change[2]; and though after Caracalla the *decuriones* were introduced everywhere, we still find officers like the ἄρχων at Athens, existing up to Constantine. What were the steps by which the different town constitutions changed into the regular decurional arrangements no one can tell[3].

Section III. *Roman Towns.*

There were three main classes of Roman towns,—municipia, coloniae, and praefecturae,—of which the praefecturae do not require our discussion, as, though frequent in Italy, and perhaps the original type of all municipal towns in that country[4], they were not carried into the provinces. But it must not be supposed that all Roman towns came under one of these three heads. There were also the smaller units of *fora* and *conciliabula*, which are mentioned along with the three more important classes in the Lex Julia Municipalis[5]. Both of these were in origin the meeting-places of the different pagi of a tribe, and lingered on till late in districts where there was no town.

---

[1] Πλῆθος οὐκ ὀλίγον ὥσπερ ἔξωθεν τῆς πολιτείας. Dio Chrys. ii. 43 R; Marquardt, i. 518.

[2] Naples, though a colony, still had its demarchus and phratries; Orelli, 3720, 3800, 3801. So there were astynomi at Velia, Orelli, 3804; agonothetae and episcopus at Nice, Orelli, 4024.

[3] Marquardt, i. 523. Under the later Empire an official called *defensor civitatis* was instituted to protect the plebs against the nobles of the place; Marquardt, i. 522. These must be carefully distinguished from the defensor reipublicae, defensor coloniae, &c., which occur at a much earlier period. See Orelli, 3908, 3909; Henzen, 7088, and his note.

[4] Festus maintains this; Marquardt, i. 43.

[5] §§ 26 and 27 of this law.

Fora occur in Gaul, and of course very frequently in the Trans- Fora. padane country[1]. They are always called after some Roman,— Forum Appii, Forum Sempronii, &c.,—and perhaps were in each case definitely established as markets by some Roman general. In course of time such country towns would be attributed to a neighbouring colony or municipium, or would themselves rise to an independent position. In the provinces the word *vicus* Vici. appears to be used where one of these more definite terms would be used in Italy; and we know that a vicus regularly had its own aediles[2], probably elected part of the municipal senate of the respublica to which it belonged[3], and could apparently be the client of its own particular patron[4]. But the history of such villages, where it can be traced, always shows a development into the regular municipal system. All these minor towns met with more or less recognition from Rome; but the *pagi* which Pagi. occur now and then in inscriptions had no such well-defined legal position. We never for instance find them mentioned in such general municipal laws as that of Rubrius or Caesar. But we find magistrates calling themselves 'magistri pagi,' an office which Egger compares to that of the village mayors in France. Thus we find the pagus Herculaneus decreeing the restoration of a covered walk with the consent of the *magister pagi*, Cn. Laetorius; and the chief official of the Canabae appears to have been given the same title[5]. Even the aedile of a pagus occurs[6]; and the decrees of a *pagus* are more than once mentioned[7]. In Italy these pagi by the time of the later

---

[1] Pliny, N. H. iii. 20, gives a list.

[2] Cf. supra on the Canabae, and Bruns, p. 84, for an inscription of the vicus Furfensis, which formed part of the respublica Peltuinum in Sabinum: 'Venditio, locatio, aedilis esto, quemquumque veicus Furfensis fecerint.'

[3] Cf. Zumpt, Comm. Epig. i. 91, and Marquardt's criticism of Zumpt, i. 11, note 4.

[4] Cf. an inscription of Yverdon, which was only a *vicus*, in Troyon, p. 523. A case of iiii viri in a vicus appears to occur in the case of Aosta; Orelli, 4029.

[5] Willmanns, No. 2409, and ii. p. 627. For Cn. Laetorius, Orelli, 3795.

[6] C. I. L. i. p. 252, No. 1279.   [7] Orelli, 3984.

Republic were a mere relic of antiquity, perhaps maintained for sentimental and antiquarian reasons; but in some parts of the provinces they would still be the channel by which the administration reached the people. Thus we find a prefect of the pagus of the Epotes (Upuys) in Gaul[1].

Colonies. Apart from all such minor and dependent communities as the above, there remains two great classes of Roman towns—the colonies and the municipia. In the course of Roman history we find colonies used for three different purposes,—as fortified outposts in a conquered country, as a means of providing for the poor of Rome, and as settlements for veterans who had served their time. The colonies established in Italy before the latter part of the second century were of the first class, those designed by Gracchus were to be of the second, and those founded by Augustus were of the third. But the first sense of the word never died out; Camulodunum for instance was founded exclusively for military purposes. Gracchus' great scheme of transmarine colonisation proved in his hands abortive, but it was not long after his death before a Roman colony with full rights was settled at Narbo (B.C. 118). It is not however till the latter part of the first century B.C. that the system of transmarine colonisation was extensively employed. Caesar settled 80,000 citizens in different colonies out of Italy, and Augustus in B.C. 14 founded a number in Narbon Gaul and Spain, and others in Sicily, Africa, Macedonia, Achaia, Asia, and Syria. In some cases Augustus expelled the existing inhabitants to make room for his colonists, and thus founded entirely new towns, and in others merely added his settlers to the existing population, the town then receiving the rank and title of a colony[2]. After Augustus the system was largely employed, but no doubt rather in the form of ascription of colonists to existing populations, than by making entirely new foundations. In many cases a place was given the rank and

---

[1] Orelli, 4025.
[2] Hyginus, De Lim. p. 177; Lachm., quoted by Mommsen, Mon. Anc. p. 41.

privileges of a colony without receiving any new citizens at all. Hadrian largely used this system of honorary colonies. In Sicily Lilybaeum and Panormus, in Spain Italica, in Africa Utica, and no less than eight towns in Narbonensis, became colonies during his reign [1]. Probably later emperors carried out the same system; we know from Aulus Gellius that municipia competed for the title of colony [2]; and Commodus is said to have thought of bestowing it upon Rome!

Honorary colonies.

The ceremonies usual at the foundation of a colony remained on the whole unchanged in all periods. The land was parcelled out into *centuriae* or squares of 200 acres each; and these again divided into allotments, *sortes*, the size of which differed in different colonies. In military colonies a man received a larger or a smaller share according to his rank [3]. From a comparison of the Mamilian Law with the law of the colony of Ursao, which was founded by Caesar, it seems probable that Caesar established a norm of law for all matters connected with the land of a colony, and that from this original model the separate colonies transferred what was needed into their own municipal law [4].

The land of a colony.

As the greater part of these colonists were added to existing towns, there were naturally frequent difficulties between the new settlers and the original inhabitants. Cicero mentions the disputes between the new settlers in Pompeii and the natives of the place, and part of the quarrel seems to have turned upon political questions [5]. In the provinces, where the colonists brought with them a distinct superiority of legal right, the natives must at first have been in a disagreeable position. But they probably very soon, if not at once, obtained equal rights

Relation of the colonists to the natives.

---

[1] Zumpt, Comm. Epig. i. 458.

[2] Aulus Gellius, Noctes Atticae, xvi. 13. M. Aurelius made the village where his wife died a colony; Capitol. M. Aurel. 26. Diocletian made Nicomedia a colony; Marquardt, i. 457. Caracalla or Sept. Severus Palmyra; Marquardt, i. 256.

[3] Marquardt, i. 458; cf. Tac. Ann. xiv. 27 for the differences of rank.

[4] Bruns, p. 105, note 3.   [5] 'De suffragiis;' Cic. pro Sulla, 21.

with the colonists. We find the *contributi* forming part of the local militia in the colony of Ursao; and where there were duties there must also have been rights. The new inhabitants and the old intermarried, as in the Colonia Agrippinensis[1]; and these connexions doubtless often extended far beyond the immediate boundaries of the colony[2]. On the other hand, the excessive claims which a colony put forward as the representative of Rome often, no doubt, provoked the jealousy and hostility of neighbouring municipia or other provincial towns.

<small>Jealousies occur between colonies and municipia.</small>
Thus there was a long-standing feud between Lugdunum and Vienna, and Tacitus[3] represents the citizens of the former place as saying to the soldiers of Valens' army: 'Go to avenge us and utterly destroy this home of Gallic rebellion' (this though Vienna was a municipium and had furnished senators to Rome). 'There all are foreigners and enemies; we are a Roman colony, a part of the Roman army, sharers in your successes and reverses.' This was so far true in that the idea of a colony was that it was another Rome, transferred to the soil of another country. Even in the form and aspect of the place Rome was imitated[4], and the Roman law, with all its formal usages, was transferred unchanged into the provinces[5].

<small>Municipia.</small>
The difference between a colony and a full Roman municipium was a difference of history and, to a certain extent, of rank[6], but not a difference of right or privilege. In regard to their internal arrangements and constitution, what is true of a municipium is true of a colony[7], and it is therefore possible

---

[1] Tac. Hist. iv. 65.   [2] Ib. iii. 34.   [3] Ib. i. 65.

[4] Lentheric makes this remark of Narbo.

[5] Cf. the Fragmentum Tudestinum, Bruns, p. 117. Compare § 102 of Lex Ursonitana (about limit of time for speeches) with Cic. in Verr. ii. 9; Plin. Ep. iv. 9; see also § 103 of law. Cf. § 29 of Lex Sulpensana, *fin.*; Lex Malacitana, § 54 *fin.*, § 64.

[6] In an enunciation of the different classes of Roman towns *in Italy* the order is always municipia, coloniae, praefecturae, &c. But *in the provinces* this is reversed, and the colony is always put first.

[7] The few inconsiderable exceptions to this are given by Marquardt, i. 481.

to discuss the municipal polities as a whole without having to distinguish between the two classes of towns. The word municipium was roughly used for the whole body of towns with Latin or Roman right, and Gellius expressly says that the citizen of a colony would habitually call himself 'municipem' and his fellow-citizens 'municipes[1].' We even find cases in which one and the same place was called colony and municipium at once[2], and had both duoviri and quattuorviri. Ordinarily, however, it is possible to say at once whether a place is a colony or a municipium, as the mention of duoviri puts it into the former, while that of quattuorviri puts it into the latter category[3]. A municipium may be defined as a provincial town—not a colony—which was in possession of the Latin or the full Roman franchise. The phrase so frequent in Pliny[4] to describe a town—quae jure Romanorum civium fruitur—is just as if he had said without periphrasis, 'which is a municipium.' The historical difference between a colony and a municipium is that which is made by Aulus Gellius, namely, that the municipia were taken into the State from without, while the colonies were offshoots from within. A provincial town became a municipium when its inhabitants accepted the Roman or Latin franchise, and when it had received the definite municipal constitution from a Roman governor or special commissioner. This constitution was just as necessary to make a place a municipium as the possession of the Roman franchise[5],

---

[1] Aul. Gell. xvi. 13.
[2] C. I. L. iii. 183, No. 95; Orelli, 3826, 3846; cf. 3686.
[3] There are however exceptions. We certainly find duoviri used now and then of the magistrates of a municipium. Renier particularly notices this in the inscriptions of Numidia (cf. Henzen, 7044, p. 416). In any case the distinction, though important as a key to the student of inscriptions, was one without a difference. In a colony as well as in a municipium there were four principal magistrates; only in a colony they were divided into *duoviri jure dicundo*, and *duoviri aediles*, whereas in a municipium they were all comprehended under the one name of *quattuorviri*. The powers and duties of each were precisely similar. [4] Pliny, N. H. iii. 13, 14, &c.
[5] Cf. § 53 of the Lex Mamilia, Bruns, p. 105; 'Quae colonia hac lege de-

and the occasional dictators, praetors, &c. which we find in Italian municipia[1] are exceptional in Italy, probably in the great majority of cases came to an end with the introduction of such measures as that of the Lex Julia Municipalis, and do not occur at all in the provinces.

<small>Origin and various meanings of the term.</small>

A municipium meant originally a community which was in possession only of the incomplete franchise. By derivation the word is probably referable to the jus hospitii existing between Rome and Italian towns[2]; but its actual usage was for a town possessing the civitas sine suffragio, that is the right of trade and intermarriage, but not the jus suffragii or the jus honorum[3]. Gradually these municipia acquired the full franchise; and as this happened the meaning of the word changed, and municipes came to mean men who were not actually born at Rome, but were full citizens, and included in a tribe. Thus Cicero was 'Civis Romanus, municeps Arpinas.' At what period the change took place which established the Italian municipia as independent communities under the central government of Rome, but no longer administered by a prefect sent from Rome, it is impossible to say. Mommsen ascribes this great change to Sulla. There is, however, no direct evidence for his view; and all that can be said is that after the Social War and the extension of the franchise to all Italy, some reorganisation of the Italian towns was necessary; that it had become obviously impossible to go on treating the towns as if they were but so many outlying fragments of Rome, and that

---

ducta quodve municipium, praefectura &c. constitutum erit;' § 30 of the Lex Julia Municipalis.

[1] Orelli, 3789, 3786, 3787. Milo was dictator at Lanuvium; Cic. pro Mil. 10; cf. Cic. de Leg. Agr. ii. 34.

[2] 'The receiving of a gift,' *munus capere*, i. e. Italians from Romans when sojourning in Rome, Romans from Italians when passing through any town connected with them by such a tie. See Marquardt, i. 27.

[3] Festus, p. 142 M: 'At Servius filius aiebat municipes initio fuisse, qui ea conditione cives Romani fuissent ut semper rem publicam separatim a populo Romano haberent, Cumanos, &c. &c., qui aeque cives Romani erant . . . sed dignitates non capiebant.' Marquardt, i. 28.

Sulla was the only statesmen of the period who seems to have had the head for reorganisation on a great scale. The great law of Caesar secured and defined this municipal independence, and was probably applied by Augustus to all municipia in the provinces. Roman towns had naturally grown up in the conquered countries—Italica, to name one instance, had so grown up in Spain; and now that the Italian municipia had been regulated, the same process must have been applied to them. The arrangements of the Italian towns had been taken over we may be sure without much change, and all that had to be done was to regulate and legalise them. Augustus was solicitous about the welfare of the municipia [1], and we shall probably not be wrong in ascribing to him a considerable share in the carrying out of the details of the Italian system into the provinces.

Transference of the municipal arrangements of Italy to the provinces.

Section IV. *Municipal Polity and Law.*

A number of inscriptions permit us to see clearly what were the constituent elements of a municipal town. 'The order' (this was the regular name for the municipal Senate) 'and the whole people [2];' 'the centumviri' (the Senates consisted of 100 members) 'and Seviri and Augustales [3] and municipal citizens [4];' 'the decuriones and the people [5];' 'the decuriones and Augustales and the commons [6];'—such is the classification which perpetually recurs in inscriptions recorded in the name of the whole municipality. The Senate of 100 members in which sat the magistrates constituted a government of a decidedly oligarchical character [7], and it is no wonder that we

Composition of a municipium.

---

[1] See Egger, p. 15.   [2] Orelli, 4045; cf. Henzen, 7171.
[3] These were religious bodies, without political importance—to be discussed later.
[4] Orelli, 3706.   [5] Ib. 3704.   [6] Ib. 3937, 4009.
[7] The knights whom Augustus made so common in the municipia of Italy at all events must have constituted a sort of ready-made aristocracy, and no doubt were all decuriones; cf. Suet. Aug. 46. The 'hastiferi civitatis Mattiacorum'—Brambach, Inscriptiones Rhenanae, 1336—are perhaps to be similarly explained.

sometimes find such bitter disputes between the 'order' and the 'commons' as that which Tacitus mentions as occurring at Puteoli[1]. The body of the citizens elected the magistrates of whom the Senate was composed, but had no further control over it. The decuriones formed a town council, with more power and less responsibility than town councils as we know them. But besides the Senate and the citizens there was also a class of settlers or incolae, commonly Roman or Latin citizens who had settled in the municipium, and who for all practical purposes counted as full citizens. We find a special curia set apart for their votes at the municipal elections[2], and they took their place in the municipal militia[3]. In inscriptions recording the statues or votes of thanks or other honours offered by a municipium to a benefactor, we frequently find the incolae mentioned along with the regular coloni or municipes of the place[4], as sharing in the vote, or as bearing their part of the necessary subscriptions; and cases occur of their holding office and becoming members of the Senate[5]. Of the contributi, or native population attached to a colony or municipium, I have already said something. It is only necessary to add that they paid a vectigal to the municipium, and pleaded in the municipal courts[6].

The incolae.

The contributi.

It used to be commonly supposed before the discovery of the laws of Malaga and Salpensa[7], that the magistrates were elected

---

[1] Tac. Ann. xiii. 48.
[2] Lex Malacitana, § 53. [3] Lex Ursonitana, § 103.
[4] C. I. L. ii. 2222-2226; Orelli, 3705.
[5] C. I. L. ii. 2135; Orelli, 3709, 3725.
[6] Suet. Aug. 46; Zumpt, Decr. Tergest. p. 15.
[7] The tablets were found together in a brick-pit near Malaga by two workmen, who sold them to a smith, of whom they were bought by the 'Marchioni di Casa Loring,' in whose possession they still are. Berlanga published an account of them in the *Rivista Pintoresca* of Malaga, a copy of which was sent to Vienna, and thence to Mommsen, who at once recognised its importance and published a paper entitled, 'Die Stadtrechte der Lateinischen Gemeinden Salpensa und Malaga der Provinz Baetica.' The authenticity of the bronzes was attacked by Laboulaye—'Les Tables de Bronze de Malaga et de Salpensa traduites et annotées'—but has not been

by the decuriones, or that at all events all popular elections in the provinces came to an end at the same time as they did at Rome, that is early in the reign of Tiberius. But these laws show this view to be a mistake, and that for the first century of the Empire at all events the elections were of a strictly popular character, and excited a good deal of emulation and a strong political interest. The chief magistrates were six in number; two duumvirs, two aediles, and two quaestors, and were changed annually. On the day of election the senior duumvir, or if he was prevented, his colleague, presided, and was required to see that the curies into which the citizens were divided should give their votes in accordance with the prescribed arrangements[1]. He had to put to the vote first the candidates for the duumvirate, then those for the aedileship, and lastly those for the quaestorship, all of them 'from that class of free-born men, concerning which this law has made provision[2].' No one was to be proposed duumvir who was under twenty-five years of age, or who had held the office less than five years ago. No one was to be admitted as a candidate for the aedileship or quaestorship who was less than twenty-five, or who had anything against him which, if he were a Roman citizen, would prevent him from being a decurio in a Roman municipium[3]. What these dis-

Popular character of the elections.

---

since impugned (Hübner, C. I. L. ii. p. 259). The peculiarity about the 'find' was that the bronze of Salpensa was discovered along with that of Malaga, though Salpensa was at some distance. Berlanga supposes that the Salpensans had to fly from a barbarian attack to Malaga, and brought their bronze with them; Mommsen that the Malagans lost or somehow destroyed part of their bronze, and instead of making another found it cheaper to buy up part of that of Salpensa, the latter place having already fallen into ruin. Hübner doubts Salpensa's having fallen into ruin so early, but allows that in any case we must explain the fact of the Salpensan bronze being where it was, by some extraordinary cause. Perhaps, he says, the bronzes got mixed up during the Middle Ages. As it stands the commencement of the law is wholly lost; §§ 21-29 are supplied by the bronze of Salpensa; §§ 51-69 by that of Malaga.

[1] Lex Malacitana, § 52. The part of the law containing these prescribed arrangements is lost.   [2] Ib. § 54.
[3] Ib. § 54 *fin.* The last four words which I have supplied are I think

qualifications were we may infer with some confidence from the great measure of Julius Caesar, where it is provided that no one should be competent to hold office or enter the Senate in any Roman municipium or colony who was engaged in any petty trade, like that of a public crier or an undertaker; no convict; no gladiator; no bankrupt; no exile; no one proved guilty of libel or collusive accusation; no one who had been degraded in the army, or expelled the army; no actor; no pimp; no infamously immoral man; no one who had conspired against the life of a Roman citizen[1]. If no candidates or too few offered themselves, the magistrate holding the elections had to make out a list of sufficient and fit persons. These involuntary candidates were allowed to name the same number of new candidates as they themselves amounted to (thus five could name five, and ten could name ten); and these latter again could name a similar number. Then the names of the whole number were to be posted, and the elections made from them[2]. The electors gave their votes by curies,—each curia in its own enclosure,—and three citizens were told off to receive the votes of each curia, and were bound by oath to count and report them honestly[3]. Before declaring a successful candidate elected the presiding magistrate made him take an oath of obedience to the municipal law[4]; and each candidate before the voting began had to name securities, who would go bail for him that during his year of office the public money would be safe in his hands. If the securities did not appear to the presiding magistrate to be sufficient, he could refuse to accept any man's candidature[5].

In this law the provisions as to the nomination of involuntary candidates have a bad air; but the rest of the evidence would lead us to conclude that this law, like other laws, was calculated to meet unusual emergencies as well as everyday circumstances, and that in the first century at all events candidates were by no

---

inferrible from the Latin. Perhaps they were understood to convey a reference to the Lex Julia Municipalis.

[1] See §§ 83-141 of the Lex Julia Municipalis.
[2] Lex Malacitana, § 51.   [3] Ib. § 55.   [4] Ib. § 59.   [5] Ib. § 60.

means slow to offer themselves for the municipal magistracies. Bribery and corruption by means of a good dinner is expressly forbidden in the law of Ursao, and the number of guests that a candidate may invite every day is positively laid down[1]. So in the well-known *Tabula Pisana* it is mentioned that at one time, 'owing to the quarrels of the candidates,' the place had no magistrates[2]; and some curious scrawls on the walls of Pompeii show us how the goldsmiths, and the fishermen, and others interested themselves in the elections. 'The fishermen want Popidius Rufus made aedile[3].' 'The whole body of goldsmiths propose C. Cuspius Pansa to be aedile[4].' 'Fortunata wants Marcellus[5].' The restrictions of age and other qualifications necessary for candidature could hardly have been maintained if there had been much difficulty in obtaining candidates.

The powers of some of these magistrates appear to have been considerable. The aedile was probably very much of the nature of an honorary post; it was ordinarily the one first held; and was no doubt, as at Rome, an expensive office to the holder. The quaestors had the charge of the revenue and expenditure of the municipium, and there were strict regulations as to the rendering of their accounts[6]. The duoviri, as their name implies, were in the first place magistrates for the administration of justice. All cases which were not of such importance as to come under the jurisdiction of the Roman governor were decided by them, and there is reason to believe that as a rule the governor left the municipia to manage their affairs as they pleased[7]. 'Let no one administer justice in this colony except the duumvir, the duumvir's prefect, or the aedile,' says the Lex Ursonitana[8].

The aediles.

Quaestors.

Duoviri.

---

[1] Lex Ursonitana, § 132. [2] Orelli, 643.
[3] Orelli, 3700: 'Popidium Rufum Æd. piscicapi faciunt.'
[4] 'C. Cuspium Pansam Æd. aurifices universi rogant;' ib.
[5] 'Marcellum Fortunata cupit.' Orelli puts this with the rest. Perhaps, after all, it is only the relic of a love affair.
[6] Lex Malacitana, § 67, I take to refer to the quaestors.
[7] Cf. what Strabo, iv. 1. § 12, says of Nemausus.
[8] § 94.

Judicial functions of the duoviri. According to the usual Roman system of administering justice the duumvir appointed the jury to try the case, but it lay with him to secure the presence of the witnesses, to put them on oath, and if need were to expedite the decision of a suit[1]. It was laid down that a duumvir should not take his seat before the first, nor keep it after the eleventh hour, except in cases which by the municipal law had to be decided in the course of one day[2]. If a decurio was accused of being unfit for his position, the duumvir was called upon to try the matter, and if he gave an adverse decision, that decurio ipso facto ceased to be decurio[3]. The duumvir, prefect, or aedile had the power of imposing fines, subject only to the right of appeal to the municipal Senate[4]. It seems however that a too despotic magistrate could be controlled by the interference of his colleague. Duumvir could interpose against duumvir, quaestor could interpose against quaestor, and aedile against aedile[5]. The duumvirs could also interpose against the aediles or quaestors, while they on the other hand had no power of interposing against their superiors. The same subordination of these magistrates to the duumviri appears from the fact that though the aedile could impose a fine, he was obliged to acquaint the duumviri with the amount of the fine he had imposed[6]. Nor were the duumviri confined solely to judicial functions. In case of any employment of the local militia, such as is mentioned in the law of Ursao, it was the duumviri who received authority from the Senate to command the troops[7]. It was they who were responsible for the appointment of the keepers of the temples, for the performance of the ludi circenses, sacrifices, and pulvinaria[8]; and they seem to have had considerable powers over what we should suppose would be the special business of the quaestors, the municipal finances[9]. If a man wanted to manumit a slave, he could do so by going through the ceremony in the presence of the duumvir[10]; and, at

---

[1] § 95.   [2] § 102.   [3] § 105.   [4] Lex Malacitana, § 66.
[5] Lex Malac. § 27.   [6] Ib. § 66.   [7] Lex Urson. § 103.
[8] Ib. § 128.   [9] Lex Malac. §§ 60, 63, 64.
[10] Lex Salpens. § 28.

all events in Latin municipia, the duumvir had the power of appointing a guardian to a ward[1]. In case of need the authority of a duumvir would be supported by the special interference of the governor of the province. Thus a letter is extant from Claudius Quartinus, governor of Tarraconensis in the time of Hadrian, to the duumviri of Pampelona, to the effect that they can carry out the powers of their office against malcontents— 'Jus magistratus vestri exsequi adversus contumaces potestis[2].' But if the power of the duumvir was assured as regarded the mass of the citizens, it does not seem to have been equally well defined as against the decuriones—a feature in which the municipia sufficiently resembled their great prototype, Rome itself. Apparently any decurio could request the duumvir to refer any matter concerning the public money, or as to fines or punishments, or as to public sites, lands, and buildings, to the body of the decuriones for investigation or decision, and whatever the decuriones determined was to have the force of law[3]. The duumvir seems to have habitually consulted the decuriones in regard to the more important details of the administration[4]; and it is expressly laid down that all duumviri, aediles, prefects, or decuriones of the colony are to obey the decrees of the decuriones, and to carry out whatever they may be ordered by decree of that body[5]. But it can easily be imagined that a man of resolution could exercise very extensive powers, and not refer more to the Senate than had been done sometimes by the Roman consuls. We find a duumvir at Vienna ordering the total abolition of the games, and although the matter was brought to Rome on appeal, and it was alleged that he had no powers for such an act, his order was maintained[6]. The men who, as in some cases, were magistrates of several important

Relation of the duoviri to the decuriones.

---

[1] Lex Salp. § 29.
[2] C. I. L. ii. 402, No. 2959.   [3] Lex Ursonitana, § 96.
[4] Ib. § 99. On the other hand, for a valid decree the presence of the magistrates was apparently essential; see the Tabula Pisana; Orelli, 643; Zumpt, i. 51.
[5] Lex Urson. § 129.   [6] Plin. Ep. iv. 22.

municipia at once[1], must have been persons of power and influence, and must to a large extent have escaped the control of the local Senates. It is worth mentioning in this connexion that in municipia or colonies which were near a frontier or otherwise of any military importance, we frequently find the municipal magistracies held by old soldiers or officers of the army[2], a fact which looks as if their authority must have been of a very practical kind.

The municipal praefecti.

The praefecti who so frequently occur in municipal inscriptions are to be regarded as taking the place of the duoviri. In the municipal laws the commencement of a clause often runs, 'Let the duumvir or the prefect' do this or that. These prefects had the regular authority of the duumvir delegated to them, and come into existence in two different ways, either because the duumvir was absent, or because at the time there was no duumvir. If one of the duumvirs absented himself he was represented by his colleague, but if the second duumvir also absented himself he had to appoint a prefect to represent them both[3]. More important was the arrangement by which the emperor was elected first magistrate of a municipium, and then appointed a prefect to take his place. 'In case the municipium elected Domitian to be their duumvir, and Domitian accepted the honour, and appointed a prefect to represent him, that prefect was to have in every respect the full authority of a duly-elected duumvir;'—so runs the twenty-fourth clause of the law of Salpensa. Hadrian used this system largely, and his biographer mentions him as having been dictator, aedile, duumvir, demarch, quinquennalis, archon, at all sorts of different towns both in Italy and in the provinces[4]. Juba, the literary

---

[1] Cf. Orelli, 3885, 3985. Perrot, *Mer Noire*, pp. 25, 26, may be referred to, though his remarks relate only to non-Roman towns.

[2] Orelli, 3789, 4025; Finazzi, *Antiche Lapide di Bergamo*, p. 83; Zumpt, Comm. Epig. i. 150. The praefectus of Forojulium has been already mentioned. [3] Cf. Lex Urson. § 93; Lex Salp. § 25.

[4] Spartian, Hadrian, 19; Zumpt, i. 56; Marquardt, i. 493, note 3; cf. Orelli, 3817.

king of Numidia, was quinquennalis and patron of Carthagena [1], and a Ptolemy of Egypt was duumvir of Gades [2]. But besides prefects of this character, who are important as representing the encroachments of the central government upon the municipia, we also find in cases where the magistracies were vacant a prefect appointed to fill them by the decree of the decuriones. The earlier arrangement had apparently been that in such cases, as at Rome, an interrex [3] should be appointed. But the *Lex Petronia* passed at the end of the Republican period gave the local Senates the power of choosing prefects, and we find prefects of this kind regularly entitled 'praefecti lege Petronia' or 'praefecti ab decurionibus creati [4].'

The quinquennales of a municipium corresponded to the Roman censors. They were charged with the duties connected with the census, looked after the municipal revenues, and contracted for municipal buildings. We find some cases, even under the Empire, for instance Malaga, where the censorial duties were discharged by the ordinary duoviri; but as these duties became more and more important we find the Romans more and more insisting on something like their own censorship everywhere. In years when there were quinquennales there were no ordinary duoviri; their full title was *duoviri quinquennales;* and they appear to have been chosen instead of the ordinary magistrates. They were called quinquennales not because they held office for five years—their tenure, like that of the other magistrates, was simply annual—but because there was always a five years' interval from one census to another [5].

The quinquennales.

---

[1] C. I. L. ii. 465; Eckhel, iv. 158.   [2] Masdeu, viii. 41.

[3] Cf. the Lex Urson. § 130. This title looks as if much in the municipal arrangement was borrowed straight from old Rome. It is in any case certain that much was borrowed from old *Italy:* it is only necessary to point to the assembly by curies.

[4] Marquardt, i. 494; cf. Orelli, 3679, 3818. At Narbo and Nice the praefectus pro duumviro seems to have been a permanent official; Orelli, 4023, 4024; cf. 4025, 4027.

[5] Marquardt, i. 487; Henzen, p. 423. A few of the inscriptions referring to quinquennales are—Orelli, 3821, 3822, 3823, 3852, 3853. If the emperor

The Augustales and Seviri.

The *Augustales* so frequent in the inscriptions were originally connected with the worship of Augustus, and imitated from the sodales Augustales at Rome. The *Seviri Augustales* are to be distinguished from the regular Augustales; they appear to have been one year members of the same college of which the regular Augustales were life members; and the latter apparently stood in a relation of subordination to them[1]. The Augustales were chosen *decreto decurionum*, and in rank stood next to the decuriones. Their duties were purely religious. Before very long the office, like that of decurio, came to be a burden, and became hereditary. An instance occurs of a man's bequeathing money to Barcino (Barcelona) on condition that his freedmen and their children, if elected seviri, should be 'excused all the burdens of the sevirate[2].'

The decuriones.

The municipal Senate was composed of a definite number of life members, generally 100—we sometimes find the term centumviri used instead of decuriones. It would have been an impertinence for these municipal assemblies to call themselves 'Senate,' and if we do occasionally find the terms 'patres' or 'senators' used of the decuriones, the case was at all events a very exceptional one[3]. We do not know how these municipal Senates were first set going; perhaps its members were chosen by the founder of the colony, or the man who constituted the municipium; but once started, the arrangement was that every five years the quinquennales should hold a lectio senatus, and make up the list of decuriones[4]. In this

---

was elected quinquennalis, there was a praefectus quinquennalitatis; Orelli, 3876.

[1] This is concluded by Henzen, 7165, from an inscription of an unknown colony in which the phrase 'eorum (sc. Augustalium) Seviri' occurs; cf. Orelli, 3706, where the Seviri rank first. The Seviri were divided into Seniores and Juniores; Orelli, 3941, 3944, 3945. General inscriptions relating to the Seviri are—Orelli, 3914, 3920, 3923, 3929 (mostly freedmen).

[2] C. I. L. ii. 4514.

[3] Cf. Orelli, 3750, 4031, 3736, 3892, 3905, for real or apparent exceptions.

[4] Marquardt, i. 50, note.

were put down first the old senators, then the magistrates whose office gave them a claim to a seat, then those citizens who without having held office were qualified by their property to be decurions. Taking an actual album—of Canusium—still existing, we find the following list: thirty-one patrons of senatorial rank; eight patrons of equestrian rank; seven quinquenalicii (men who had been quinquennales); four allecti inter quinquennales; twenty-nine duumviralicii; nineteen aedilicii; nine quaestoricii; thirty-two pedani; twenty-five pretextati. These patrons were influential Romans (elected by the decuriones), from whom a certain protection and assistance at Rome was expected, and who were put first by way of compliment. Two-thirds of the decurions had to vote for a patronus for the vote to have validity; and if any one offered the patrocinium to any Roman except in accordance with such a vote, he was to be fined 10,000 sesterces, and the offer was to be null and void[1]. That they were not really acting members of the Senate is proved by the fact that if we cut them and the pretextati off the list, we have the normal number of 100 left[2]. But if they were not acting members of the municipium they were often considerable benefactors of it, and an immense number of inscriptions record the gratitude of the citizens to some rich and powerful patron[3]. By the *allecti inter quinquennales* must be understood men elected in an extraordinary manner, and not possessing the usual qualifications[4]. They were generally men who had done special services, and who, with the emperor's leave, by decision of the Senate were made decurions. *Pedani*

---

[1] Lex Malac. § 61; cf. Lex Urson. § 97.

[2] Marquardt, i. 508; Cic. de Leg. Agr. ii. 35 for 100 as the normal number.

[3] Orelli, 3771. It is curious to find several instances of women as patrons of municipia; cf. a remarkable inscription, Orelli, 4036, and see Orelli, 5773, 3774. Perhaps such women were friends of the empress, or in other ways possessed exceptional influence.

[4] For the way the verb *adlego* is used cf. Suet. Claud. 24, 'Appium Caecum censorem . . . libertinorum filios in senatum adlegisse docuit;' Marquardt, i. 508; cf. Orelli, 3725, 3745, 3816.

is explained by Aulus Gellius (iii. 18) to mean those who had the right to a place in the Senate, but who were not yet called senators because they had come in after the last lectio Senatus, and so had not yet been formally chosen by the quinquennales [1]. By *praetextati* are meant sons of decuriones, included in the album for some special reason, but not capable of voting [2]. All decuriones, to whichever of these classes they might belong, had to possess a certain amount of property to be eligible [3], and had to pay into the municipal treasury a certain sum of money as honorarium [4].

Authority of the decuriones.
The decuriones were in theory, like the Senate at Rome, the standing executive body, from which the magistrates received their orders, and with whom they consulted on all important matters. Appeal could be made to them from a fine imposed by a duumvir; and all magistrates who had the handling of public moneys were obliged to send in their accounts either to the decuriones or to some inspector appointed by the decuriones [5]. It was to the decuriones that rescripts of the emperor touching the affairs of the municipium were directed [6], and on all public occasions they represented the municipium; for instance, they had the first seats at the games [7]. No valid decree could be passed without a quorum, which was often made a large one, being present [8]. A number of such decrees

---

[1] Zumpt, Stud. Rom. p. 297, discusses the *Pedani*.

[2] Marquardt, i. 509; cf. Orelli, 3745: 'Hunc decuriones, cum esset annorum sexs, ob liberalitatem ordini suo gratis adlegerunt.' Apparently the father wanted the boy made a decurio at the age of six, one cannot tell why, and so restored a temple in the boy's name; cf. 3747.

[3] Pliny, Ep. i. 19, shows that it was 100,000 sest. at Como.

[4] Cf. Plin. Ep. x. 48, 113. See the Decretum Tergestium *supra*, and Marquardt, i. 501. For a use of this pecunia honoraria see Kandler, 43.

[5] Lex Malac. § 67.

[6] So the curious letter of Vespasian to Sabora is addressed to the quattuorviri indecuriones, C. I. L. ii. 195; as also another letter of Vespasian 'to the magistrates and senators of the Vanacini' (N. Corsica), Bruns, p. 173.   [7] Lex Urson. § 125.

[8] Orelli, 4034, 'In Decurionibus fuerunt xxvi;' Lex Urson. § 130. Two-thirds necessary to elect a patron; cf. §§ 96 and 97 of the same law.

have been preserved to us in the form of inscriptions. Most often they refer to statues or some such honour, which is offered in return for some benefaction received. A curious one is the decree of *biselliatus*, or of the right of sitting by yourself in a seat large enough for two,—an honour that appears to have been highly coveted[1]. The most important among such decrees is that of Tergeste, which I have already given in full, but hardly any of them are without antiquarian or historical interest of some kind.

<small>Decrees of the decuriones.</small>

With the constitution, in which though not perfect there seems to have been on the whole a fair balance of power, the municipal towns seem to have flourished at all events during the first century of the Empire. But about the reign of Trajan we see signs of a decay in the vigour and resources of the municipia, one clear evidence of which is the establishment of the new officials known as curators[2].

The curators in the long run superseded the quinquennales, but their functions do not seem to have been identical with those of those officials. The principal function of the quinquennalis was the lectio senatus, whereas with that the curator had nothing whatever to do. The business of the curator was purely financial: he had the charge of the municipal moneys. This is indicated by the Greek name for the office—λογιστής,— by the Latin term—ratiocinatio civitatis[3]—which is applied to it, and by several passages from the Digests[4]. It was probable that it was an annual magistracy, as otherwise it is difficult to

<small>The curators.</small>

---

[1] Cf. Millin, *Pompeii*, p. 78, referred to by Orelli on 4044; cf. Orelli, 4046: 'Liceatque ei omnibus spectaculis municipio nostro bisellio proprio inter Augustales considere.' Cf. 4047, 4048.

[2] The chief modern authorities I have used in this discussion are Zumpt, Comm. Epig. i. 148-158; Renier, *Mélanges d'Epigraphie*, p. 46 foll.; Marquardt, i. 488 foll., to whom I refer for more details.

[3] Dig. xxvii. 1. 15. 7.

[4] Dig. l. 4. 18. 9: 'Sed et curatores qui ad colligendos civitatum publicos reditus eligi solent.' Cf. Ulpian in Dig. l. 8. 3. 1; Paulus in Dig. xxxix. 3. 46; Zumpt, Comm. Epig. In an inscription given by Zumpt, i. 158, we find the same man quinquennalis and curator *of the same place.*

Two classes of curators. account for its being held by such important personages as it is. If we wish to discover how the curators were elected, it is necessary first to distinguish the two different kinds of curators.

Curators for special purposes. 1. Curators for special purposes. 2. Curatores rei publicae. The first class of curators are frequently mentioned in the municipia, and were generally chosen by the assembly [1]. Occasionally we find even these curators appointed by the emperor [2]. Perhaps, as Zumpt conjectures, these towns themselves petitioned the emperor to appoint such officials for them, or that when he had spent money on their buildings he appointed a curator to see that the work was properly performed. Quite

Curatores rei publicae. different from these special curators were the curatores rei publicae, of whom the first example occurs under Nerva or Trajan. If the emperor wanted the accounts of any town to be reorganised he appointed an extraordinary curator, generally a municipal citizen. Thus we have a duumvir quinquennalis of Brixia acting as 'curator rei publicae Bergomatium datus ab imperatore Trajano, curator rei publicae Comensis datus ab imperatore Hadriano [3].' We never find these curators mentioned as appointed in any other way than this. So we gather the origin of these curators. They were always appointed by the emperor. But as long as is added to their title the phrase 'given by such and such an emperor,' they are extraordinary magistrates. Now after Septimius Severus this phrase does not occur, although it is known that there were curators in every municipium. Zumpt's conclusion is that they then ceased to be extraordinary and became ordinary magistrates. The reasons for making this magistracy a permanent one are obvious. Being directly appointed by the emperor the curators had naturally greater powers than the ordinary municipal magis-

---

[1] Orelli, 3882: 'In comitiis facto curatori.' Zumpt says by the decuriones, but he gives no evidence, and appears to think that all magistrates were chosen by the decuriones—an idea which was generally held till the discovery of the laws of Salpensa and Malaga.
[2] Orelli, 4006, 4007, 4011; cf. Suet. Tit. 8.
[3] Orelli, 3898, 3899, 3902.

trates; and as the local finances all over the Empire got more and more into a bad way, the old magistracies got less and less able to deal with them. So either Sept. Severus or Alex. Severus made the curator a regular magistrate. We learn from Ulpian [1] that the curator presided in the municipal senate; and he discusses the office in other respects in a way which shows that it was a regular one in his time, though novel. So the upshot is that originally curatores were appointed by the emperor to meet some special need or distress of a municipality; and then little by little became regular and permanent magistrates. But they still were always appointed directly by the Emperor.

Besides finance, all matters in regard to public buildings, &c. within a municipium were regulated by the curator. Thus we find an inscription of Caere which records that a certain Verbinus wanted to build a phretrium for the municipium at his own expense. So it was determined by the decuriones to write to the curator to ask permission for the work. The curator, who was at Ameria, writes back to give his consent, with a number of complimentary expressions [2]. We find a man curator of several municipia at once [3], or curator of one municipium and decurio of another; and in some cases the duties are discharged by an official of very high rank [4], no doubt in one of the intervals of leisure in Italy which intervened between important provincial commands. *Matters regulated by the curator.*

This system of substituting imperial for municipal officials was probably begun with the best intentions, but it marked an evil change. The brightest feature in the whole Roman system fades before us, as we see this government official taking the duties and the responsibilities out of the hands of the municipal magistrates. With the decrease in power came an increase in the burdens laid upon the magistrates and decuriones. Already in the decree of Tergeste we find the inhabitants eager for the incorporation of new citizens, that they might share the duties of the decurionate, 'which are burdensome to a few.' The *Decay of the municipia.*

---

[1] Dig. l. 9. 4.   [2] Orelli, 3787.   [3] Ib. 3898.   [4] Ib. 3851.

local magistrates were now appointed from the Senate, and the Senate was compulsorily filled up from landholders possessing the needful amount of property. Even before this change came about, and while the elections were still in the hands of the assemblies, we find in an inscription of Aquileia the record of a vote of thanks on a statue being offered to a man because he had of his own accord given in his name to the quattuorvir for municipal office [1]. The tendency in the inscriptions is either to substitute the word *onus* for *honor* when the municipal offices are mentioned, or at all events to put the two words side by side [2]. The office of decurio became hereditary, and in the fourth century it was a regular punishment to make a man decurio [3]. A man could not avoid his responsibilities to the State even by enlisting in the army. The reason of this was that the decuriones were held responsible for the quota of taxation which the town was called upon to furnish; and as the concentration of wealth in a few hands, the dislocation of commerce and industry caused by the barbarian inroads, and the increasing demands of the central administration for the payment of its countless officials and the maintenance of its troops all went together, the weight of the taxation both upon the middle and lower classes, and upon the decuriones who had to make good a deficit, became more than human nature could endure [4].

---

[1] Orelli, 4041.
[2] Ib. 3940 : ' Omnibus oneribus honoribusque functo.'
[3] Marquardt, i. 512.
[4] For the municipia in the Constantine period, see Finlay, i. 110.

CONCLUSION.

How far did this great mass of the Roman Empire form a unity? Along with the many causes which tended to bring about a certain uniformity between all its parts, there were at least two centrifugal causes at work. The essential difference between East and West was never got over, and the rise of a new religion divided for some time the Roman world into the two great classes of Pagans and Christians. It is only with Constantine that Christianity ceases to divide and becomes rather a bond of union. It was as introducing disunion and division that it was so fiercely attacked; and persecutors would have justified themselves by similar reasons to those which have been urged in modern times. But the universal peace, the active trade, the community of feeling caused by the possession of like privileges and like interests, the diffusion of the Romans over the provinces and the way the different races of the Empire penetrated into the parts most removed from their own homes, the one language, and the one administration,—all these tended to make of Europe a single brilliant whole. Nor were the frontiers a strict and impassable line, and we should err if we looked upon the Roman world as a space of light and civilisation surrounded by a black night of barbarism. On every side the light radiated out beyond the frontier, and it is only by slow degrees that it faded into the dim Northern world. The races just beyond the frontier were in many cases in a condition of more or less real subjection. They were visited by Roman traders, and now and then had even the pleasure of listening to a company of Greek or Roman players. If the barbarians had been wholly barbarians they would hardly have shattered the power of Rome. Mere savages never have held their own and never will against civilised troops. Even the typically German hero Arminius had served in the Roman legions and could apparently talk Latin, while his brother Flavus remained faithful to the service which he forsook. Tacfarinas had served as an auxiliary in the Roman camp in Africa, and Boiocalus, chief of the Ampsivarii, had served under Tiberius and Germanicus. When Classicus rebelled he assumed the insignia of a Roman general and Civilis had himself saluted Caesar. Among the Parthians there were the Roman prisoners who had survived Carrhae, and the Germans also had often spared and taken back their captives with them across the Rhine. As the burden of the taxes and the conscription grew heavier, it became a common practice for Roman subjects to settle beyond the frontier, and so secure themselves from the recruiting officer and the tax-gatherer. In this way the barbarians themselves were half Romanised, and it was not till the brutal Huns, lying far outside the radius of Roman influence, had fought their way southwards, that the Southern world felt the full bitterness of conquest. The rapidity with which the invaders of the fourth century adapted themselves to their new position, and the almost timid conservatism which their leaders in some points showed, attest the impression made both on their intellects and their imaginations by the colossal and majestic system which Rome had reared.

BEDFORD STREET, STRAND, LONDON, W.C.
March, 1879.

MACMILLAN & CO.'S CATALOGUE of Works in the Departments of History, Biography, Travels, Critical and Literary Essays, Politics, Political and Social Economy, Law, etc.; and Works connected with Language.

HISTORY, BIOGRAPHY, TRAVELS, &c.

Albemarle.—FIFTY YEARS OF MY LIFE. By GEORGE THOMAS, Earl of Albemarle. With Steel Portrait of the first Earl of Albemarle, engraved by JEENS. Third and Cheaper Edition. Crown 8vo. 7s. 6d.

"*The book is one of the most amusing of its class. . . . These reminiscences have the charm and flavour of personal experience, and they bring us into direct contact with the persons they describe.*"—EDINBURGH REVIEW.

Anderson.—MANDALAY TO MOMIEN; a Narrative of the Two Expeditions to Western China, of 1868 and 1875, under Colonel E. B. Sladen and Colonel Horace Browne. By Dr. ANDERSON, F.R.S.E., Medical and Scientific Officer to the Expeditions. With numerous Maps and Illustrations. 8vo. 21s.

"*A handsome, well-timed, entertaining, and instructive volume.*"—ACADEMY.
"*A pleasant, useful, carefully-written, and important work.*"—ATHENÆUM.

Appleton.—Works by T. G. APPLETON :—
A NILE JOURNAL. Illustrated by EUGENE BENSON. Crown 8vo. 6s.
SYRIAN SUNSHINE. Crown 8vo. 6s.

Arnold.—ESSAYS IN CRITICISM. By MATTHEW ARNOLD. New Edition, Revised and Enlarged. Crown 8vo. 9s.

Atkinson.—AN ART TOUR TO NORTHERN CAPITALS OF EUROPE, including Descriptions of the Towns, the Museums, and other Art Treasures of Copenhagen, Christiania, Stockholm,

Abo, Helsingfors, Wiborg, St. Petersburg, Moscow, and Kief. By J. BEAVINGTON ATKINSON. 8vo. 12s.

"*Although the main purpose of the book is strictly kept in view, and we never forget for long that we are travelling with a student and connoisseur, Mr. Atkinson gives variety to his narrative by glimpses of scenery and brief allusions to history and manners which are always welcome when they occur, and are never wordy or overdone. We have seldom met with a book in which what is principal and what is accessory have been kept in better proportion to each other.*"—SATURDAY REVIEW.

Awdry.—THE STORY OF A FELLOW SOLDIER. By FRANCES AWDRY. With Six Illustrations. Second Edition. Extra fcap. 8vo. 3s. 6d.

"*This is a life of that brave, single-minded, and untiring Christian Soldier, Bishop Patteson, written for the young. It is simply and pleasantly written, and presents a lively picture of the labours, hardships, troubles, and pleasures of earnest Missionary work among the Polynesian Islands.*"—STANDARD.

Baker (Sir Samuel W.)—Works by Sir SAMUEL BAKER, Pacha, M.A., F.R.G.S. :—

ISMAILIA: A Narrative of the Expedition to Central Africa for the Suppression of the Slave Trade, organised by Ismail, Khedive of Egypt. With Portraits, Map, and fifty full-page Illustrations by ZWECKER and DURAND. New and Cheaper Edition. With New Preface. Crown 8vo. 6s.

"*A book which will be read with very great interest.*"—TIMES. "*Well written and full of remarkable adventures.*"—PALL MALL GAZETTE. "*Adds another thrilling chapter to the history of African adventure.*"—DAILY NEWS. "*Reads more like a romance.... incomparably more entertaining than books of African travel usually are.*"—MORNING POST.

THE ALBERT N'YANZA Great Basin of the Nile, and Exploration of the Nile Sources. Fifth Edition. Maps and Illustrations. Crown 8vo. 6s.

"*Charmingly written;*" says the SPECTATOR, "*full, as might be expected, of incident, and free from that wearisome reiteration of useless facts which is the drawback to almost all books of African travel.*"

THE NILE TRIBUTARIES OF ABYSSINIA, and the Sword Hunters of the Hamran Arabs. With Maps and Illustrations. Sixth Edition. Crown 8vo. 6s.

The TIMES *says:* "*It adds much to our information respecting Egyptian Abyssinia and the different races that spread over it. It contains, moreover, some notable instances of English daring and enterprising skill; it abounds in animated tales of exploits dear to the heart of the British sportsman; and it will attract even the least studious reader, as the author tells a story well, and can describe nature with uncommon power.*"

Bancroft.—THE HISTORY OF THE UNITED STATES OF AMERICA, FROM THE DISCOVERY OF THE CONTINENT. By GEORGE BANCROFT. New and thoroughly Revised Edition. Six Vols. Crown 8vo. 54s.

Barker (Lady).—Works by LADY BARKER:—
A YEAR'S HOUSEKEEPING IN SOUTH AFRICA. With Illustrations. New and Cheaper Edition. Crown 8vo. 6s.
"*We have to thank Lady Barker for a very amusing book, over which we have spent many a delightful hour, and of which we will not take leave without alluding to the ineffably droll illustrations which add so very much to the enjoyment of her clear and sparkling descriptions.*"—MORNING POST.

Beesly.—STORIES FROM THE HISTORY OF ROME. By Mrs. BEESLY. Extra fcap. 8vo. 2s. 6d.
"*A little book for which every cultivated and intelligent mother will be grateful for.*"—EXAMINER.

Bismarck—IN THE FRANCO-GERMAN WAR. An Authorized Translation from the German of Dr. MORITZ BUSCH. Two Vols. Crown 8vo. 18s.
The TIMES *says:*—"*The publication of Bismarck's after-dinner talk, whether discreet or not, will be of priceless biographical value, and Englishmen, at least, will not be disposed to quarrel with Dr. Busch for giving a picture as true to life as Boswell's 'Johnson' of the foremost practical genius that Germany has produced since Frederick the Great.*"

Blackburne.—BIOGRAPHY OF THE RIGHT HON. FRANCIS BLACKBURNE, Late Lord Chancellor of Ireland. Chiefly in connexion with his Public and Political Career. By his Son, EDWARD BLACKBURNE, Q.C. With Portrait Engraved by JEENS. 8vo. 12s.

Blanford (W. T.)—GEOLOGY AND ZOOLOGY OF ABYSSINIA. By W. T. BLANFORD. 8vo. 21s.

Brimley.—ESSAYS BY THE LATE GEORGE BRIMLEY, M.A. Edited by the Rev. W. G. CLARK, M.A. With Portrait. Cheaper Edition. Fcap. 8vo. 2s. 6d.

Brontë.—CHARLOTTE BRONTË. A Monograph. By T. WEMYSS REID. With Illustrations. Third Edition. Crown 8vo. 6s.
Mr. Reid's little volume, which is based largely on letters, hitherto unpublished, from Charlotte Brontë to her school-fellow and life-long friend, Miss Ellen Nussey, is meant to be a companion, and not a rival, to Mrs. Gaskell's well-known "Life." To speak of the advantage of making biography autobiographical by the liberal use of correspondence has

she was by nature (as Mr. Reid puts it) "*a happy and high-spirited girl, and that even to the very last she had the faculty of overcoming her sorrows by means of that steadfast courage which was her most precious possession, and to which she was indebted for her successive victories over trials and disappointments of no ordinary character.*"

The book is illustrated by a Portrait of the Rev. Patrick Brontë, several Views of Haworth and its neighbourhood, and a facsimile of one of the most characteristic of Charlotte's letters.

Brooke.—THE RAJA OF SARAWAK: an Account of Sir James Brooke, K.C.B., LL.D. Given chiefly through Letters or Journals. By GERTRUDE L. JACOB. With Portrait and Maps. Two Vols. 8vo. 25s.

"*They who read Miss Jacob's book—and all should read it: all who are under the delusion that in our time there is no scope for heroism, and no place for romantic adventure, and no place for enterprise and ambition—will see how incident is crowded upon incident, and struggle upon struggle, till in the very abundance of materials that come to her hand the authoress can scarcely stop to give sufficient distinctness to her wonderful narrative.*"—ACADEMY.

Brooke.—RECOLLECTIONS OF THE IRISH CHURCH. By RICHARD S. BROOKE, D.D., late Rector of Wyton, Hunts. Crown 8vo. 4s. 6d.

Bryce.—Works by JAMES BRYCE, D.C.L., Regius Professor of Civil Law, Oxford:—

THE HOLY ROMAN EMPIRE. Sixth Edition, Revised and Enlarged. Crown 8vo. 7s. 6d.

"*It exactly supplies a want: it affords a key to much which men read of in their books as isolated facts, but of which they have hitherto had no connected exposition set before them.*"—SATURDAY REVIEW.

TRANSCAUCASIA AND ARARAT: being Notes of a Vacation Tour in the Autumn of 1876. With an Illustration and Map. Third Edition. Crown 8vo. 9s.

"*Mr. Bryce has written a lively and at the same time an instructive description of the tour he made last year in and about the Caucasus. When well-informed a jurist travels into regions seldom visited, and even walks up a mountain so rarely scaled as Ararat, he is justified in thinking that the impressions he brings home are worthy of being communicated to the world at large, especially when a terrible war is casting a lurid glow over the countries he has lately surveyed.*"—ATHENÆUM.

Burgoyne.—POLITICAL AND MILITARY EPISODES DURING THE FIRST HALF OF THE REIGN OF GEORGE III. Derived from the Life and Correspondence of the Right Hon. J. Burgoyne, Lieut.-General in his Majesty's Army, and M.P. for Preston. By E. B. DE FONBLANQUE. With Portrait, Heliotype Plate, and Maps. 8vo. 16s.

Burke.—EDMUND BURKE, a Historical Study. By JOHN MORLEY, B.A., Oxon. Crown 8vo. 7s. 6d.

"*The style is terse and incisive, and brilliant with epigram and point. Its sustained power of reasoning, its wide sweep of observation and reflection, its elevated ethical and social tone, stamp it as a work of high excellence.*"—SATURDAY REVIEW.

Burrows.—WORTHIES OF ALL SOULS: Four Centuries of English History. Illustrated from the College Archives. By MONTAGU BURROWS, Chichele Professor of Modern History at Oxford, Fellow of All Souls. 8vo. 14s.

"*A most amusing as well as a most instructive book.*—GUARDIAN.

Campbell.—LOG-LETTERS FROM THE "CHALLENGER." By LORD GEORGE CAMPBELL. With Map. Fifth and cheaper Edition. Crown 8vo. 6s.

"*A delightful book, which we heartily commend to the general reader.*"—SATURDAY REVIEW.

"*We do not hesitate to say that anything so fresh, so picturesque, so generally delightful, as these log-letters has not appeared among books of travel for a long time.*"—EXAMINER.

"*A more lively and amusing record of travel we have not had the fortune to read for some time. The whole book is pervaded by a spirit of life, animation, and fun.*"—STANDARD.

Campbell.—MY CIRCULAR NOTES: Extracts from Journals; Letters sent Home; Geological and other Notes, written while Travelling Westwards round the World, from July 6th, 1874, to July 6th, 1875. By J. F. CAMPBELL, Author of "Frost and Fire." Cheaper Issue. Crown 8vo. 6s.

"*We have read numbers of books of travel, but we can call to mind few that have given us more genuine pleasure than this. A more agreeable style of narrative than his it is hardly possible to conceive. We seem to be accompanying him in his trip round the world, so life-like is his description of the countries he visited.*"—LAND AND WATER.

Campbell.—TURKS AND GREEKS. Notes of a recent Excursion. By the Hon. DUDLEY CAMPBELL, M.A. With Coloured Map. Crown 8vo. 3s. 6d.

Carstares.—WILLIAM CARSTARES: a Character and Career of the Revolutionary Epoch (1649—1715). By ROBERT STORY, Minister of Rosneath. 8vo. 12s.

Chatterton: A BIOGRAPHICAL STUDY. By DANIEL WILSON, LL.D., Professor of History and English Literature in University College, Toronto. Crown 8vo. 6s. 6d.

Chatterton: A STORY OF THE YEAR 1770. By Professor MASSON, LL.D. Crown 8vo. 5s.

Clark.—MEMORIALS FROM JOURNALS AND LETTERS OF SAMUEL CLARK, M.A., formerly Principal of the National Society's Training College, Battersea. Edited with Introduction by his WIFE. With Portrait. Crown 8vo. 7s. 6d.

Combe.—THE LIFE OF GEORGE COMBE, Author of "The Constitution of Man." By CHARLES GIBBON. With Three Portraits engraved by JEENS. Two Vols. 8vo. 32s.

"*A graphic and interesting account of the long life and indefatigable labours of a very remarkable man.*"—SCOTSMAN.

Cooper.—ATHENÆ CANTABRIGIENSES. By CHARLES HENRY COOPER, F.S.A., and THOMPSON COOPER, F.S.A. Vol. I. 8vo., 1500—85, 18s.; Vol. II., 1586—1609, 18s.

Correggio.—ANTONIO ALLEGRI DA CORREGGIO. From the German of Dr. JULIUS MEYER, Director of the Royal Gallery, Berlin. Edited, with an Introduction, by Mrs. HEATON. Containing Twenty Woodbury-type Illustrations. Royal 8vo. Cloth elegant. 31s. 6d.

"*The best and most readable biography of the master at present to be found in the English language.*"—ACADEMY. "*By its pictures alone the book forms a worthy tribute to the painter's genius.*"—PALL MALL GAZETTE.

Cox (G. V.)—RECOLLECTIONS OF OXFORD. By G. V. Cox, M.A., New College, late Esquire Bedel and Coroner in the University of Oxford. *Cheaper Edition.* Crown 8vo. 6s.

Cunynghame (Sir A. T.)—MY COMMAND IN SOUTH AFRICA, 1874—78. Comprising Experiences of Travel in the Colonies of South Africa and the Independent States. By Sir ARTHUR THURLOW CUNYNGHAME, G.C.B., then Lieutenant-Governor and Commander of the Forces in South Africa. Third Edition. 8vo. 12s. 6d.

The TIMES says:—"*It is a volume of great interest, ... full of incidents which vividly illustrate the condition of the Colonies and the character and habits of the natives. .... It contains valuable illustrations of Cape warfare, and at the present moment it cannot fail to command wide-spread attention.*"

"Daily News."—THE DAILY NEWS' CORRESPONDENCE of the War between Germany and France, 1870—1. Edited with Notes and Comments. New Edition. Complete in One Volume. With Maps and Plans. Crown 8vo. 6s.

THE DAILY NEWS' CORRESPONDENCE of the War between Russia and Turkey, to the fall of Kars. Including the letters of Mr. Archibald Forbes, Mr. J. E. McGahan, and other Special Correspondents in Europe and Asia. Second Edition, enlarged. Cheaper Edition. Crown 8vo. 6s.

FROM THE FALL OF KARS TO THE CONCLUSION OF PEACE. Cheaper Edition. Crown 8vo. 6s.

Davidson.—THE LIFE OF A SCOTTISH PROBATIONER; being a Memoir of Thomas Davidson, with his Poems and Letters. By JAMES BROWN, Minister of St. James's Street Church, Paisley. Second Edition, revised and enlarged, with Portrait. Crown 8vo. 7s. 6d.

Deas.—THE RIVER CLYDE. An Historical Description of the Rise and Progress of the Harbour of Glasgow, and of the Improvement of the River from Glasgow to Port Glasgow. By J. DEAS, M. Inst. C.E. 8vo. 10s. 6d.

Denison.—A HISTORY OF CAVALRY FROM THE EARLIEST TIMES. With Lessons for the Future. By Lieut.-Col. GEORGE DENISON, Commanding the Governor-General's Body Guard, Canada, Author of "Modern Cavalry." With Maps and Plans. 8vo. 18s.

Dilke.—GREATER BRITAIN. A Record of Travel in English-speaking Countries during 1866-7. (America, Australia, India.) By Sir CHARLES WENTWORTH DILKE, M.P. Sixth Edition. Crown 8vo. 6s.

"*Many of the subjects discussed in these pages,*" says the DAILY NEWS, "*are of the widest interest, and such as no man who cares for the future of his race and of the world can afford to treat with indifference.*"

Doyle.—HISTORY OF AMERICA. By J. A. DOYLE. With Maps. 18mo. 4s. 6d.

"*Mr. Doyle's style is clear and simple, his facts are accurately stated, and his book is meritoriously free from prejudice on questions where partisanship runs high amongst us.*"—SATURDAY REVIEW.

Drummond of Hawthornden: THE STORY OF HIS LIFE AND WRITINGS. By PROFESSOR MASSON. With Portrait and Vignette engraved by C. H. JEENS. Crown 8vo. 10s. 6d.

"*Around his hero, Professor Masson groups national and individual episodes and sketches of character, which are of the greatest interest, and which add to the value of a biographical work which we warmly recommend to the lovers of thoroughly healthy books.*"—NOTES AND QUERIES.

Duff.—Works by M. E. GRANT-DUFF, M.P., late Under Secretary of State for India:—
NOTES OF AN INDIAN JOURNEY. With Map. 8vo. 10s. 6d.
"*These notes are full of pleasant remarks and illustrations, borrowed from every kind of source.*"—SATURDAY REVIEW.

MISCELLANIES POLITICAL AND LITERARY. 8vo. 10s. 6d.

Eadie.—LIFE OF JOHN EADIE, D.D., LL.D. By JAMES BROWN, D.D., Author of "The Life of a Scottish Probationer." With Portrait. Second Edition. Crown 8vo. 7s. 6d.
"*An ably written and characteristic biography.*"—TIMES.

Elliott.—LIFE OF HENRY VENN ELLIOTT, of Brighton. By JOSIAH BATEMAN, M.A. With Portrait, engraved by JEENS. Extra fcap. 8vo. Third and Cheaper Edition. 6s.

Elze.—ESSAYS ON SHAKESPEARE. By Dr. KARL ELZE. Translated with the Author's sanction by L. DORA SCHMITZ. 8vo. 12s.

"*A more desirable contribution to criticism has not recently been made.*"—ATHENÆUM.

English Men of Letters. Edited by JOHN MORLEY. A Series of Short Books to tell people what is best worth knowing as to the Life, Character, and Works of some of the great English Writers. In crown 8vo. Price 2s. 6d. each.

I. DR. JOHNSON. By LESLIE STEPHEN. [*Sixth Thousand.*
"*The new series opens will with Mr. Leslie Stephen's sketch of Dr. Johnson. It could hardly have been done better; and it will convey to the readers for whom it is intended a juster estimate of Johnson than either of the two essays of Lord Macaulay*"—PALL MALL GAZETTE.

II. SIR WALTER SCOTT. By R. H. HUTTON. [*Fifth Thousand.*
"*The tone of the volume is excellent throughout.*"—ATHENÆUM.
"*We could not wish for a more suggestive introduction to Scott and his poems and novels.*"—EXAMINER.

III. GIBBON. By J. C. MORISON. [*Fifth Thousand.*
"*As a clear, thoughtful, and attractive record of the life and works of the greatest among the world's historians, it deserves the highest praise.*"—EXAMINER.

IV. SHELLEY. By J. A. SYMONDS. [*Fifth Thousand.*
"*The lovers of this great poet are to be congratulated on having at their command so fresh, clear, and intelligent a presentment of the subject, written by a man of adequate and wide culture.*"—ATHENÆUM.

V. HUME. By Professor HUXLEY. [*Fifth Thousand.*
"*It may fairly be said that no one now living could have expounded Hume with more sympathy or with equal perspicuity.*"—ATHENÆUM.

VI. GOLDSMITH. By WILLIAM BLACK. [*Fifth Thousand.*
"*Mr. Black brings a fine sympathy and taste to bear in his criticism of Goldsmith's writings as well as in his sketch of the incidents of his life.*" ATHENÆUM.

VII. DEFOE. By W. MINTO.
BURNS. By Principal SHAIRP.
SPENCER. By R. W. CHURCH, Dean of St. Paul's.
HAWTHORNE. By HENRY JAMES, Jun.
THACKERAY. By ANTHONY TROLLOPE.
} [*In the press.*
Others in preparation.

Eton College, History of. By H. C. MAXWELL LYTE, M.A. With numerous Illustrations by Professor DELAMOTTE, Coloured Plates, and a Steel Portrait of the Founder, engraved

HISTORY, BIOGRAPHY, TRAVELS, ETC.

by C. H. JEENS. New and cheaper Issue, with Corrections. Medium 8vo. Cloth elegant. 21s.

"*Hitherto no account of the College, with all its associations, has appeared which can compare either in completeness or in interest with this. . . . It is indeed a book worthy of the ancient renown of King Henry's College.*"—DAILY NEWS.

"*We are at length presented with a work on England's greatest public school, worthy of the subject of which it treats. . . . A really valuable and authentic history of Eton College.*"—GUARDIAN.

European History, Narrated in a Series of Historical Selections from the best Authorities. Edited and arranged by E. M. SEWELL and C. M. YONGE. First Series, crown 8vo. 6s.; Second Series, 1088-1228, crown 8vo. 6s. Third Edition.

"*We know of scarcely anything,*" says the GUARDIAN, *of this volume,* "*which is so likely to raise to a higher level the average standard of English education.*"

Faraday.—MICHAEL FARADAY. By J. H. GLADSTONE, Ph.D., F.R.S. Second Edition, with Portrait engraved by JEENS from a photograph by J. WATKINS. Crown 8vo. 4s. 6d.
PORTRAIT. Artist's Proof. 5s.
CONTENTS:—*I. The Story of his Life. II. Study of his Character. III. Fruits of his Experience. IV. His Method of Writing. V. The Value of his Discoveries.*—*Supplementary Portraits. Appendices:—List of Honorary Fellowships, etc.*

Forbes.—LIFE AND LETTERS OF JAMES DAVID FORBES, F.R.S., late Principal of the United College in the University of St. Andrews. By J. C. SHAIRP, LL.D., Principal of the United College in the University of St. Andrews; P. G. TAIT, M.A., Professor of Natural Philosophy in the University of Edinburgh; and A. ADAMS-REILLY, F.R.G.S. 8vo. with Portraits, Map, and Illustrations, 16s.

"*Not only a biography that all should read, but a scientific treatise, without which the shelves of no physicist's library can be deemed complete.*"—STANDARD.

Freeman.—Works by EDWARD A. FREEMAN, D.C.L., LL.D.:—
HISTORICAL ESSAYS. Third Edition. 8vo. 10s. 6d.
CONTENTS:—*I.* "*The Mythical and Romantic Elements in Early English History;*" *II.* "*The Continuity of English History;*" *III.* "*The Relations between the Crowns of England and Scotland;*" *IV.* "*St. Thomas of Canterbury and his Biographers;*" *V.* "*The Reign of Edward the Third;*" *VI.* "*The Holy Roman Empire;*" *VII.* "*The Franks and the Gauls;*" *VIII.* "*The Early Sieges of Paris;*" *IX.* "*Frederick the First, King of Italy;*" *X.* "*The Emperor Frederick the Second;*" *XI.* "*Charles the Bold;*" *XII.* "*Presidential Government.*"

A SECOND SERIES OF HISTORICAL ESSAYS. 8vo. 10s. 6d.

Freeman—*continued.*

The principal Essays are:—"Ancient Greece and Mediæval Italy;" "Mr. Gladstone's Homer and the Homeric Ages;" "The Historians of Athens;" ".The Athenian Democracy;" "Alexander the Great;" "Greece during the Macedonian Period;" "Mommsen's History of Rome;" "Lucius Cornelius Sulla;" "The Flavian Cæsars."

COMPARATIVE POLITICS.—Lectures at the Royal Institution. To which is added the "Unity of History," the Rede Lecture at Cambridge, 1872. 8vo. 14s.

THE HISTORY AND CONQUESTS OF THE SARACENS. Six Lectures. Third Edition, with New Preface. Crown 8vo. 3s. 6d.

"Mr. Freeman opportunely reprints his erudite and valuable lectures."—DAILY TELEGRAPH.

HISTORICAL AND ARCHITECTURAL SKETCHES: chiefly Italian. With Illustrations by the Author. Crown 8vo. 10s. 6d.

"Mr. Freeman may here be said to give us a series of 'notes on the spot' in illustration of the intimate relations of History and Architecture, and this is done in so masterly a manner—there is so much freshness, so much knowledge so admirably condensed, that we are almost tempted to say that we prefer these sketches to his more elaborate studies."—NONCONFORMIST.

HISTORY OF FEDERAL GOVERNMENT, from the Foundation of the Achaian League to the Disruption of the United States. Vol. I. General Introduction. History of the Greek Federations. 8vo. 21s.

OLD ENGLISH HISTORY. With *Five Coloured Maps.* Fourth Edition. Extra fcap. 8vo., half-bound. 6s.

"The book indeed is full of instruction and interest to students of all ages, and he must be a well-informed man indeed who will not rise from its perusal with clearer and more accurate ideas of a too much neglected portion of English history."—SPECTATOR.

HISTORY OF THE CATHEDRAL CHURCH OF WELLS, as illustrating the History of the Cathedral Churches of the Old Foundation. Crown 8vo. 3s. 6d.

"The history assumes in Mr. Freeman's hands a significance, and, we may add, a practical value as suggestive of what a cathedral ought to be, which make it well worthy of mention."—SPECTATOR.

THE GROWTH OF THE ENGLISH CONSTITUTION FROM THE EARLIEST TIMES. Crown 8vo. 5s. Third Edition, revised.

GENERAL SKETCH OF EUROPEAN HISTORY. Being Vol. I. of a Historical Course for Schools edited by E. A. FREEMAN. New Edition, enlarged with Maps, Chronological Table, Index, &c. 18mo. 3s. 6d.

HISTORY, BIOGRAPHY, TRAVELS, ETC.

Freeman—*continued.*

"*It supplies the great want of a good foundation for historical teaching. The scheme is an excellent one, and this instalment has been accepted in a way that promises much for the volumes that are yet to appear.*"—EDUCATIONAL TIMES.

THE OTTOMAN POWER IN EUROPE : its Nature, its Growth, and its Decline. With Three Coloured Maps. Crown 8vo. 7s. 6d.

Galileo.—THE PRIVATE LIFE OF GALILEO. Compiled principally from his Correspondence and that of his eldest daughter, Sister Maria Celeste, Nun in the Franciscan Convent of S. Matthew in Arcetri. With Portrait. Crown 8vo. 7s. 6d.

Geddes.—THE PROBLEM OF THE HOMERIC POEMS. By W. D. GEDDES, LL.D., Professor of Greek in the University of Aberdeen. 8vo. 14s.

Gladstone—Works by the Right Hon. W. E. GLADSTONE, M.P.:—
JUVENTUS MUNDI. The Gods and Men of the Heroic Age. Crown 8vo. cloth. With Map. 10s. 6d. Second Edition.

"*Seldom,*" says the ATHENÆUM, "*out of the great poems themselves, have these Divinities looked so majestic and respectable. To read these brilliant details is like standing on the Olympian threshold and gazing at the ineffable brightness within.*"

HOMERIC SYNCHRONISM. An inquiry into the Time and Place of Homer. Crown 8vo. 6s.

"*It is impossible not to admire the immense range of thought and inquiry which the author has displayed.*"—BRITISH QUARTERLY REVIEW.

Goethe and Mendelssohn (1821—1831). Translated from the German of Dr. KARL MENDELSSOHN, Son of the Composer, by M. E. VON GLEHN. From the Private Diaries and Home Letters of Mendelssohn, with Poems and Letters of Goethe never before printed. Also with two New and Original Portraits, Facsimiles, and Appendix of Twenty Letters hitherto unpublished. Crown 8vo. 5s. Second Edition, enlarged.

"*. . . Every page is full of interest, not merely to the musician, but to the general reader. The book is a very charming one, on a topic of deep and lasting interest.*"—STANDARD.

Goldsmid.—TELEGRAPH AND TRAVEL. A Narrative of the Formation and Development of Telegraphic Communication between England and India, under the orders of Her Majesty's Government, with incidental Notices of the Countries traversed by the Lines. By Colonel Sir FREDERIC GOLDSMID, C.B., K.C.S.I., late Director of the Government Indo-European Telegraph. With numerous Illustrations and Maps. 8vo. 21s.

"*The merit of the work is a total absence of exaggeration, which does not, however, preclude a vividness and vigour of style not always characteristic of similar narratives.*"—STANDARD.

Gordon.—LAST LETTERS FROM EGYPT, to which are added Letters from the Cape. By LADY DUFF GORDON. With a Memoir by her Daughter, Mrs. Ross, and Portrait engraved by JEENS. Second Edition. Crown 8vo. 9s.

"*The intending tourist who wishes to acquaint himself with the country he is about to visit, stands embarrassed amidst the riches presented for his choice, and in the end probably rests contented with the sober usefulness of Murray. He will not, however, if he is well advised, grudge a place in his portmanteau to this book.*"—TIMES.

Gray.—CHINA. A History of the Laws, Manners, and Customs of the People. By the VENERABLE JOHN HENRY GRAY. LL.D., Archdeacon of Hong Kong, formerly H.B.M. Consular Chaplain at Canton. Edited by W. Gow Gregor. With 150 Full-page Illustrations, being Facsimiles of Drawings by a Chinese Artist. 2 Vols. Demy 8vo. 32s.

"*Its pages contain the most truthful and vivid picture of Chinese life which has ever been published.*"—ATHENÆUM.

"*The only elaborate and valuable book we have had for many years treating generally of the people of the Celestial Empire.*"—ACADEMY.

Green.—Works by JOHN RICHARD GREEN :—

HISTORY OF THE ENGLISH PEOPLE. Vol. I.—Early England—Foreign Kings—The Charter—The Parliament. With 8 Coloured Maps. 8vo. 16s. Vol. II.—The Monarchy, 1461—1540; the Restoration, 1540—1603. 8vo. 16s.

"*Mr. Green has done a work which probably no one but himself could have done. He has read and assimilated the results of all the labours of students during the last half century in the field of English history, and has given them a fresh meaning by his own independent study. He has fused together by the force of sympathetic imagination all that he has so collected, and has given us a vivid and forcible sketch of the march of English history. His book, both in its aims and its accomplishments, rises far beyond any of a similar kind, and it will give the colouring to the popular view to English history for some time to come.*"—EXAMINER.

A SHORT HISTORY OF THE ENGLISH PEOPLE. With Coloured Maps, Genealogical Tables, and Chronological Annals. Crown 8vo. 8s. 6d. Fifty-fifth Thousand.

"*To say that Mr. Green's book is better than those which have preceded it, would be to convey a very inadequate impression of its merits. It stands alone as the one general history of the country, for the sake of which all others, if young and old are wise, will be speedily and surely set aside.*"

STRAY STUDIES FROM ENGLAND AND ITALY. Crown 8vo. 8s. 6d. Containing: Lambeth and the Archbishops—The Florence of Dante—Venice and Rome—Early History of Oxford—The District Visitor—Capri—Hotels in the Clouds—Sketches in Sunshine, &c.

"*One and all of the papers are eminently readable.*"—ATHENÆUM.

Hamerton.—Works by P. G. HAMERTON :—

THE INTELLECTUAL LIFE. With a Portrait of Leonardo da Vinci, etched by LEOPOLD FLAMENG. Second Edition. Crown 10s. 6d. 8vo.

"*We have read the whole book with great pleasure, and we can recommend it strongly to all who can appreciate grave reflections on a very important subject, excellently illustrated from the resources of a mind stored with much reading and much keen observation of real life.*"—SATURDAY REVIEW.

THOUGHTS ABOUT ART. New Edition, revised, with an Introduction. Crown 8vo. 8s. 6d.

"*A manual of sound and thorough criticism on art.*"—STANDARD.
"*The book is full of thought, and worthy of attentive consideration.*"—DAILY NEWS.

Hill.—THE RECORDER OF BIRMINGHAM. A Memoir of Matthew Davenport Hill, with Selections from his Correspondence. By his Daughters ROSAMOND and FLORENCE DAVENPORT-HILL. With Portrait engraved by C. H. JEENS. 8vo. 16s.

Hill.—WHAT WE SAW IN AUSTRALIA. By ROSAMOND and FLORENCE HILL. Crown 8vo. 10s. 6d.

"*May be recommended as an interesting and truthful picture of the condition of those lands which are so distant and yet so much like home.*"—SATURDAY REVIEW.

Hodgson.—MEMOIR OF REV. FRANCIS HODGSON, B.D., Scholar, Poet, and Divine. By his Son, the Rev. JAMES T. HODGSON, M.A. Containing numerous Letters from Lord Byron and others. With Portrait engraved by JEENS. Two Vols. Crown 8vo. 18s.

"*A book that has added so much of a healthy nature to our knowledge of Byron, and that contains so rich a store of delightful correspondence.*"—ATHENÆUM.

Hole.—A GENEALOGICAL STEMMA OF THE KINGS OF ENGLAND AND FRANCE. By the Rev. C. HOLE, M.A., Trinity College, Cambridge. On Sheet, 1s.

A BRIEF BIOGRAPHICAL DICTIONARY. Compiled and Arranged by the Rev. CHARLES HOLE, M.A. Second Edition. 18mo. 4s. 6d.

Hooker and Ball.—MAROCCO AND THE GREAT ATLAS: Journal of a Tour in. By Sir JOSEPH D. HOOKER, K.C.S.I., C.B., F.R.S., &c., and JOHN BALL, F.R.S. With an Appendix, including a Sketch of the Geology of Marocco, by G. MAW, F.L.S., F.G.S. With Illustrations and Map. 8vo. 21s.

Hozier (H. M.)—Works by Captain Henry M. Hozier, late Assistant Military Secretary to Lord Napier of Magdala :—

THE SEVEN WEEKS' WAR ; Its Antecedents and Incidents. *New and Cheaper Edition.* With New Preface, Maps, and Plans. Crown 8vo. 6s.

"*All that Mr. Hozier saw of the great events of the war—and he saw a large share of them—he describes in clear and vivid language.*"—SATURDAY REVIEW.

THE INVASIONS OF ENGLAND : a History of the Past, with Lessons for the Future. Two Vols. 8vo. 28s.

The PALL MALL GAZETTE says :—"*As to all invasions executed, or deliberately projected but not carried out, from the landing of Julius Cæsar to the raising of the Boulogne camp, Captain Hozier furnishes copious and most interesting particulars.*"

Hübner.—A RAMBLE ROUND THE WORLD IN 1871. By M. LE BARON HÜBNER, formerly Ambassador and Minister. Translated by LADY HERBERT. New and Cheaper Edition. With numerous Illustrations. Crown 8vo. 6s.

"*It is difficult to do ample justice to this pleasant narrative of travel . . . . it does not contain a single dull paragraph.*"—MORNING POST.

Hughes.—Works by THOMAS HUGHES, Q.C., Author of "Tom Brown's School Days."

MEMOIR OF A BROTHER. With Portrait of GEORGE HUGHES, after WATTS. Engraved by JEENS. Crown 8vo. 5s. Sixth Edition.

"*The boy who can read this book without deriving from it some additional impulse towards honourable, manly, and independent conduct, has no good stuff in him.*"—DAILY NEWS.

ALFRED THE GREAT. New Edition. Crown 8vo. 6s.

Hunt.—HISTORY OF ITALY. By the Rev. W. HUNT, M.A. Being the Fourth Volume of the Historical Course for Schools. Edited by EDWARD A. FREEMAN, D.C.L. 18mo. 3s.

"*Mr. Hunt gives us a most compact but very readable little book, containing in small compass a very complete outline of a complicated and perplexing subject. It is a book which may be safely recommended to others besides schoolboys.*"—JOHN BULL.

Irving.—THE ANNALS OF OUR TIME. A Diurnal of Events, Social and Political, Home and Foreign, from the Accession of Queen Victoria to the Peace of Versailles. By JOSEPH IRVING. *Fourth Edition.* 8vo. half-bound. 16s.

ANNALS OF OUR TIME. Supplement. From Feb. 28, 1871, to March 19, 1874. 8vo. 4s. 6d.

ANNALS OF OUR TIME. Second Supplement. From March, 1874, to the Occupation of Cyprus. 8vo. [*Nearly ready.*

HISTORY, BIOGRAPHY, TRAVELS, ETC. 15

"*We have before us a trusty and ready guide to the events of the past thirty years, available equally for the statesman, the politician, the public writer, and the general reader.*"—TIMES.

James.—Works by HENRY JAMES, Jun. FRENCH POETS AND NOVELISTS. Crown 8vo. 8s. 6d.

CONTENTS :—*Alfred de Musset ; Théophile Gautier ; Baudelaire ; Honoré de Balzac ; George Sand ; The Two Ampères ; Turgenieff, &c.*

THE EUROPEANS. A Novel. Two Vols. Crown 8vo. 21s.

Johnson's Lives of the Poets.—The Six Chief Lives—Milton, Dryden, Swift, Addison, Pope, Gray. With Macaulay's "Life of Johnson." Edited, with Preface, by MATTHEW ARNOLD. Crown 8vo. 6s.

Killen.—ECCLESIASTICAL HISTORY OF IRELAND, from the Earliest Date to the Present Time. By W. D. KILLEN, D.D., President of Assembly's College, Belfast, and Professor of Ecclesiastical History. Two Vols. 8vo. 25s.

"*Those who have the leisure will do well to read these two volumes. They are full of interest, and are the result of great research. . . . We have no hesitation in recommending the work to all who wish to improve their acquaintance with Irish history.*"—SPECTATOR.

Kingsley (Charles).—Works by the Rev. CHARLES KINGSLEY, M.A., Rector of Eversley and Canon of Westminster. (For other Works by the same Author, *see* THEOLOGICAL and BELLES LETTRES Catalogues.)

ON THE ANCIEN RÉGIME as it existed on the Continent before the FRENCH REVOLUTION. Three Lectures delivered at the Royal Institution. Crown 8vo. 6s.

AT LAST : A CHRISTMAS in the WEST INDIES. With nearly Fifty Illustrations. Fifth Edition. Crown 8vo. 6s.

Mr. Kingsley's dream of forty years was at last fulfilled, when he started on a Christmas expedition to the West Indies, for the purpose of becoming personally acquainted with the scenes which he has so vividly described in " Westward Ho !" These two volumes are the journal of his voyage. Records of natural history, sketches of tropical landscape, chapters on education, views of society, all find their place. "*We can only say that Mr. Kingsley's account of a 'Christmas in the West Indies' is in every way worthy to be classed among his happiest productions.*"—STANDARD.

THE ROMAN AND THE TEUTON. A Series of Lectures delivered before the University of Cambridge. New and Cheaper Edition, with Preface by Professor MAX MÜLLER. Crown 8vo. 6s.

PLAYS AND PURITANS, and other Historical Essays. With Portrait of Sir WALTER RALEIGH. New Edition. Crown 8vo. 6s.

In addition to the Essay mentioned in the title, this volume contains other two—one on " Sir Walter Raleigh and his Time," and one on Froude's " History of England."

Kingsley (Henry).—TALES OF OLD TRAVEL. Re-narrated by HENRY KINGSLEY, F.R.G.S. With *Eight Illustrations* by HUARD. Fifth Edition. Crown 8vo. 5*s*.

"We know no better book for those who want knowledge or seek to refresh it. As for the 'sensational,' most novels are tame compared with these narratives."—ATHENÆUM.

Lang.—CYPRUS: Its History, its Present Resources and Future Prospects. By R. HAMILTON LANG, late H.M. Consul for the Island of Cyprus. With Two Illustrations and Four Maps. 8vo. 14*s*.

"The fair and impartial account of her past and present to be found in these pages has an undoubted claim on the attention of all intelligent readers."—MORNING POST.

Laocoon.—Translated from the Text of Lessing, with Preface and Notes by the Right Hon. SIR ROBERT J. PHILLIMORE, D.C.L. With Photographs. 8vo. 12*s*.

Leonardo da Vinci and his Works.—Consisting of a Life of Leonardo Da Vinci, by MRS. CHARLES W. HEATON, Author of "Albrecht Dürer of Nürnberg," &c., an Essay on his Scientific and Literary Works by CHARLES CHRISTOPHER BLACK, M.A., and an account of his more important Paintings and Drawings. Illustrated with Permanent Photographs. Royal 8vo. cloth, extra gilt. 31*s*. 6*d*.

"A beautiful volume, both without and within. Messrs. Macmillan are conspicuous among publishers for the choice binding and printing of their books, and this is got up in their best style. . . . No English publication that we know of has so thoroughly and attractively collected together all that is known of Leonardo."—TIMES.

Liechtenstein.—HOLLAND HOUSE. By Princess MARIE LIECHTENSTEIN. With Five Steel Engravings by C. H. JEENS, after Paintings by WATTS and other celebrated Artists, and numerous Illustrations drawn by Professor P. H. DELAMOTTE, and engraved on Wood by J. D. COOPER, W. PALMER, and JEWITT & Co. Third and Cheaper Edition. Medium 8vo. cloth elegant. 16*s*.

Also, an Edition containing, in addition to the above, about 40 Illustrations by the Woodbury-type process, and India Proofs of the Steel Engravings. Two vols. medium 4to. half morocco elegant. 4*l*. 4*s*.

"When every strictly just exception shall have been taken, she may be conscientiously congratulated by the most scrupulous critic on the production of a useful, agreeable, beautifully-illustrated, and attractive book."—TIMES. "It would take up more room than we can spare to enumerate all the interesting suggestions and notes which are to be found in these volumes. . . . The woodcuts are admirable, and some of the autographs are very interesting."—PALL MALL GAZETTE.

HISTORY, BIOGRAPHY, TRAVELS, ETC.

Lloyd.—THE AGE OF PERICLES. A History of the Arts and Politics of Greece from the Persian to the Peloponnesian War. By W. WATKISS LLOYD. Two Vols. 8vo. 21s.

"*No such account of Greek art of the best period has yet been brought together in an English work. . . . . Mr. Lloyd has produced a book of unusual excellence and interest.*"—PALL MALL GAZETTE.

Macarthur.—HISTORY OF SCOTLAND, By MARGARET MACARTHUR. Being the Third Volume of the Historical Course for Schools, Edited by EDWARD A. FREEMAN, D.C.L. Second Edition. 18mo. 2s.

"*It is an excellent summary, unimpeachable as to facts, and putting them in the clearest and most impartial light attainable.*"—GUARDIAN.
"*No previous History of Scotland of the same bulk is anything like so trustworthy, or deserves to be so extensively used as a text-book.*"—GLOBE.

Macmillan (Rev. Hugh).—For other Works by same Author, see THEOLOGICAL and SCIENTIFIC CATALOGUES.

HOLIDAYS ON HIGH LANDS; or, Rambles and Incidents in search of Alpine Plants. Second Edition, revised and enlarged. Globe 8vo. cloth. 6s.

"*Botanical knowledge is blended with a love of nature, a pious enthusiasm, and a rich felicity of diction not to be met with in any works of kindred character, if we except those of Hugh Miller.*"—TELEGRAPH.
"*Mr. Macmillan's glowing pictures of Scandinavian scenery.*"—SATURDAY REVIEW.

Macready.—MACREADY'S REMINISCENCES AND SELECTIONS FROM HIS DIARIES AND LETTERS. Edited by Sir F. POLLOCK, Bart., one of his Executors. With Four Portraits engraved by JEENS. New and Cheaper Edition. Crown 8vo. 7s. 6d.

"*As a careful and for the most part just estimate of the stage during a very brilliant period, the attraction of these volumes can scarcely be surpassed. . . . . Readers who have no special interest in theatrical matters, but enjoy miscellaneous gossip, will be allured from page to page, attracted by familiar names and by observations upon popular actors and authors.*"—SPECTATOR.

Mahaffy.—Works by the Rev. J. P. MAHAFFY, M.A., Fellow of Trinity College, Dublin:—

SOCIAL LIFE IN GREECE FROM HOMER TO MENANDER. Third Edition, revised and enlarged, with a new chapter on Greek Art. Crown 8vo. 9s.

"*It should be in the hands of all who desire thoroughly to understand and to enjoy Greek literature, and to get an intelligent idea of the old Greek life, political, social, and religious.*"—GUARDIAN.

RAMBLES AND STUDIES IN GREECE. With Illustrations. Crown 8vo. 10s. 6d. New and enlarged Edition, with Map and Illustrations

"*A singularly instructive and agreeable volume.*"—ATHENÆUM.

B

"**Maori.**"—SPORT AND WORK ON THE NEPAUL FRONTIER; or, Twelve Years' Sporting Reminiscences of an Indigo Planter. By "MAORI." With Illustrations. 8vo. 14s.

Margary.—THE JOURNEY OF AUGUSTUS RAYMOND MARGARY FROM SHANGHAE TO BHAMO AND BACK TO MANWYNE. From his Journals and Letters, with a brief Biographical Preface, a concluding chapter by Sir RUTHERFORD ALCOCK, K.C.B., and a Steel Portrait engraved by JEENS, and Map. 8vo. 10s. 6d.

"*There is a manliness, a cheerful spirit, an inherent vigour which was never overcome by sickness or debility, a tact which conquered the prejudices of a strange and suspicious population, a quiet self-reliance, always combined with deep religious feeling, unalloyed by either priggishness, cant, or superstition, that ought to commend this volume to readers sitting quietly at home who feel any pride in the high estimation accorded to men of their race at Yarkand or at Khiva, in the heart of Africa, or on the shores of Lake Seri-kul.*"—SATURDAY REVIEW.

Martin.—THE HISTORY OF LLOYD'S, AND OF MARINE INSURANCE IN GREAT BRITAIN. With an Appendix containing Statistics relating to Marine Insurance. By FREDERICK MARTIN, Author of "The Statesman's Year Book." 8vo. 14s.

"*We have in the editor of the 'Statesman's Year Book' an industrious and conscientious guide, and we can certify that in his 'History of Lloyd's' he has produced a work of more than passing interest.*"—TIMES.

Martineau.—BIOGRAPHICAL SKETCHES, 1852—1875. By HARRIET MARTINEAU. With Additional Sketches, and Autobiographical Sketch. Fifth Edition. Crown 8vo. 6s.

"*Miss Martineau's large literary powers and her fine intellectual training make these little sketches more instructive, and constitute them more genuinely works of art, than many more ambitious and diffuse biographies.*"—FORTNIGHTLY REVIEW.

Masson (David).—For other Works by same Author, see PHILOSOPHICAL and BELLES LETTRES CATALOGUES.

CHATTERTON: A Story of the Year 1770. By DAVID MASSON, LL.D., Professor of Rhetoric and English Literature in the University of Edinburgh. Crown 8vo. 5s.

"*One of this popular writer's best essays on the English poets.*"—STANDARD.

THE THREE DEVILS: Luther's, Goethe's, and Milton's; and other Essays. Crown 8vo. 5s.

WORDSWORTH, SHELLEY, AND KEATS; and other Essays. Crown 8vo. 5s.

HISTORY, BIOGRAPHY, TRAVELS, ETC.

Maurice.—THE FRIENDSHIP OF BOOKS; AND OTHER LECTURES. By the Rev. F. D. Maurice. Edited with Preface, by Thomas Hughes, Q.C. Crown 8vo. 10s. 6d.

"*The high, pure, sympathetic, and truly charitable nature of Mr. Maurice is delightfully visible throughout these lectures, which are excellently adapted to spread a love of literature amongst the people.*"—Daily News.

Mayor (J. E. B.)—WORKS edited by John E. B. Mayor, M.A., Kennedy Professor of Latin at Cambridge :—

CAMBRIDGE IN THE SEVENTEENTH CENTURY. Part II. Autobiography of Matthew Robinson. Fcap. 8vo. 5s. 6d.

LIFE OF BISHOP BEDELL. By his Son. Fcap. 8vo. 3s. 6d.

Melbourne.—MEMOIRS OF THE RT. HON WILLIAM, SECOND VISCOUNT MELBOURNE. By W. M. Torrens, M.P. With Portrait after Sir. T. Lawrence. Second Edition. 2 Vols. 8vo. 32s.

"*As might be expected, he has produced a book which will command and reward attention. It contains a great deal of valuable matter and a great deal of animated, elegant writing.*"—Quarterly Review.

Mendelssohn.—LETTERS AND RECOLLECTIONS. By Ferdinand Hiller. Translated by M. E. Von Glehn. With Portrait from a Drawing by Karl Müller, never before published. Second Edition. Crown 8vo. 7s. 6d.

"*This is a very interesting addition to our knowledge of the great German composer. It reveals him to us under a new light, as the warm-hearted comrade, the musician whose soul was in his work, and the home-loving, domestic man.*"—Standard.

Merewether.—BY SEA AND BY LAND. Being a Trip through Egypt, India, Ceylon, Australia, New Zealand, and America—all Round the World. By Henry Alworth Merewether, one of Her Majesty's Counsel. Crown 8vo. 8s. 6d.

Michael Angelo Buonarotti; Sculptor, Painter, Architect. The Story of his Life and Labours. By C. C. Black, M.A. Illustrated by 20 Permanent Photographs. Royal 8vo. cloth elegant, 31s. 6d.

"*The story of Michael Angelo's life remains interesting whatever be the manner of telling it, and supported as it is by this beautiful series of photographs, the volume must take rank among the most splendid of Christmas books, fitted to serve and to outlive the season.*"—Pall Mall Gazette.

Michelet.—A SUMMARY OF MODERN HISTORY. Translated from the French of M. Michelet, and continued to the present time by M. C. M. Simpson. Globe 8vo. 4s. 6d.

"*We are glad to see one of the ablest and most useful summaries of European history put into the hands of English readers. The translation is excellent.*"—Standard.

Milton.—LIFE OF JOHN MILTON. Narrated in connection with the Political, Ecclesiastical, and Literary History of his Time. By DAVID MASSON, M.A., LL.D., Professor of Rhetoric and English Literature in the University of Edinburgh. With Portraits. Vol. I. 18s. Vol. II., 1638—1643. 8vo. 16s. Vol. III. 1643—1649. 8vo. 18s. Vols. IV. and V. 1649—1660. 32s. Vol. VI. in preparation.

This work is not only a Biography, but also a continuous Political, Ecclesiastical, and Literary History of England through Milton's whole time.

Mitford (A. B.)—TALES OF OLD JAPAN. By A. B. MITFORD, Second Secretary to the British Legation in Japan. With upwards of 30 Illustrations, drawn and cut on Wood by Japanese Artists. New and Cheaper Edition. Crown 8vo. 6s.

"*These very original volumes will always be interesting as memorials of a most exceptional society, while regarded simply as tales, they are sparkling, sensational, and dramatic, and the originality of their idea and the quaintness of their language give them a most captivating piquancy. The illustrations are extremely interesting, and for the curious in such matters have a special and particular value.*"—PALL MALL GAZETTE.

Monteiro.—ANGOLA AND THE RIVER CONGO. By JOACHIM MONTEIRO. With numerous Illustrations from Sketches taken on the spot, and a Map. Two Vols. crown 8vo. 21s.

"*Gives the first detailed account of a part of tropical Africa which is little known to Englishmen. . . . . The remarks on the geography and zoology of the country and the manners and customs of the various races inhabiting it, are extremely curious and interesting.*"—SATURDAY REVIEW. "*Full of valuable information and much picturesque description.*" PALL MALL GAZETTE.

Morison.—THE LIFE AND TIMES OF SAINT BERNARD, Abbot of Clairvaux. By JAMES COTTER MORISON, M.A. New Edition. Crown 8vo. 6s.

The PALL MALL GAZETTE *calls this* "*A delightful and instructive volume, and one of the best products of the modern historic spirit.*"

Moseley.—NOTES BY A NATURALIST ON THE *CHALLENGER*: being an Account of various Observations made during the Voyage of H.M.S. *Challenger*, Round the World, in 1872-76. By H. N. MOSELEY, F.R.S., Member of the Scientific Staff of the *Challenger*. 8vo. with Maps, Coloured Plates, and Woodcuts. 21s.

Murray.—ROUND ABOUT FRANCE. By E. C. GRENVILLE MURRAY. Crown 8vo. 7s. 6d.

"*These short essays are a perfect mine of information as to the present condition and future prospects of political parties in France. . . . It is at once extremely interesting and exceptionally instructive on a subject on which few English people are well informed.*"—SCOTSMAN.

HISTORY, BIOGRAPHY, TRAVELS, ETC.

Napoleon.—THE HISTORY OF NAPOLEON I. By P. LANFREY. A Translation with the sanction of the Author. Vols. I. II. and III. 8vo. price 12s. each.

The PALL MALL GAZETTE *says it is "one of the most striking pieces of historical composition of which France has to boast," and the* SATURDAY REVIEW *calls it "an excellent translation of a work on every ground deserving to be translated. It is unquestionably and immeasurably the best that has been produced. It is in fact the only work to which we can turn for an accurate and trustworthy narrative of that extraordinary career.... The book is the best and indeed the only trustworthy history of Napoleon which has been written."*

Nash.—OREGON; There and Back in 1877. By WALLIS NASH. With Map and Illustrations. Crown 8vo. 7s. 6d.

"This unpretentious little volume is a bright and very clever record of a journey which the author made to Oregon . . . which will tell any one who reads it a very great deal worth knowing about Oregon. . . . Altogether, he has written an interesting and amusing book."—SPECTATOR.

Nichol.—TABLES OF EUROPEAN LITERATURE AND HISTORY, A.D. 200—1876. By J. NICHOL, LL.D., Professor of English Language and Literature, Glasgow. 4to. 6s. 6d.

TABLES OF ANCIENT LITERATURE AND HISTORY, B.C. 1500—A.D. 200. By the same Author. 4to. 4s. 6d.

Oliphant (Mrs.).—THE MAKERS OF FLORENCE: Dante Giotto, Savonarola, and their City. By Mrs. OLIPHANT. With numerous Illustrations from drawings by Professor DELAMOTTE, and portrait of Savonarola, engraved by JEENS. Second Edition. Medium 8vo. Cloth extra. 21s.

"Mrs. Oliphant has made a beautiful addition to the mass of literature already piled round the records of the Tuscan capital."—TIMES.

"We are grateful to Mrs. Oliphant for her eloquent and beautiful sketches of Dante, Fra Angelico, and Savonarola. They are picturesque, full of life, and rich in detail, and they are charmingly illustrated by the art of the engraver."—SPECTATOR.

Oliphant.—THE DUKE AND THE SCHOLAR; and other Essays. By T. L. KINGTON OLIPHANT. 8vo. 7s. 6d.

"This volume contains one of the most beautiful biographical essays we have seen since Macaulay's days."—STANDARD.

Otte.—SCANDINAVIAN HISTORY. By E. C. OTTE. With Maps. Extra fcap. 8vo. 6s.

"We have peculiar pleasure in recommending this intelligent résumé of Northern history as a book essential to every Englishman who interests himself in Scandinavia."—SPECTATOR.

Owens College Essays and Addresses.—By PROFESSORS AND LECTURERS OF OWENS COLLEGE, MANCHESTER. Published in Commemoration of the Opening of the New College Buildings, October 7th, 1873. 8vo. 14s.

Palgrave (R. F. D.)—THE HOUSE OF COMMONS; Illustrations of its History and Practice. By REGINALD F. D. PALGRAVE, Clerk Assistant of the House of Commons. New and Revised Edition. Crown 8vo. 2s. 6d.

Palgrave (Sir F.)—HISTORY OF NORMANDY AND OF ENGLAND. By Sir FRANCIS PALGRAVE, Deputy Keeper of Her Majesty's Public Records. Completing the History to the Death of William Rufus. 4 Vols. 8vo. 4l. 4s.

Palgrave (W. G.)—A NARRATIVE OF A YEAR'S JOURNEY THROUGH CENTRAL AND EASTERN ARABIA, 1862-3. By WILLIAM GIFFORD PALGRAVE, late of the Eighth Regiment Bombay N. I. Sixth Edition. With Maps, Plans, and Portrait of Author, engraved on steel by Jeens. Crown 8vo. 6s.

"*He has not only written one of the best books on the Arabs and one of the best books on Arabia, but he has done so in a manner that must command the respect no less than the admiration of his fellow-countrymen.*"—FORTNIGHTLY REVIEW.

ESSAYS ON EASTERN QUESTIONS. By W. GIFFORD PALGRAVE. 8vo. 10s. 6d.

"*These essays are full of anecdote and interest. The book is decidedly a valuable addition to the stock of literature on which men must base their opinion of the difficult social and political problems suggested by the designs of Russia, the capacity of Mahometans for sovereignty, and the good government and retention of India.*"—SATURDAY REVIEW.

DUTCH GUIANA. With Maps and Plans. 8vo. 9s.

"*His pages are nearly exhaustive as far as facts and statistics go, while they are lightened by graphic social sketches as well as sparkling descriptions of scenery.*"—SATURDAY REVIEW.

Patteson.—LIFE AND LETTERS OF JOHN COLERIDGE PATTESON, D.D., Missionary Bishop of the Melanesian Islands. By CHARLOTTE M. YONGE, Author of "The Heir of Redclyffe." With Portraits after RICHMOND and from Photograph, engraved by JEENS. With Map. Fifth Edition. Two Vols. Crown 8vo. 12s.

"*Miss Yonge's work is in one respect a model biography. It is made up almost entirely of Patteson's own letters. Aware that he had left his home once and for all, his correspondence took the form of a diary, and as we read on we come to know the man, and to love him almost as if we had seen him.*"—ATHENÆUM. "*Such a life, with its grand lessons of unselfishness, is a blessing and an honour to the age in which it is lived; the biography cannot be studied without pleasure and profit, and indeed we should think little of the man who did not rise from the study of it better and wiser. Neither the Church nor the nation which produces such sons need ever despair of its future.*"—SATURDAY REVIEW.

HISTORY, BIOGRAPHY, TRAVELS, ETC. 23

Pauli.—PICTURES OF OLD ENGLAND. By Dr. REINHOLD PAULI. Translated, with the approval of the Author, by E. C. OTTÉ. Cheaper Edition. Crown 8vo. 6s.

Payne.—A HISTORY OF EUROPEAN COLONIES. By E. J. PAYNE, M.A. With Maps. 18mo. 4s. 6d.

The TIMES *says:*—"*We have seldom met with a historian capable of forming a more comprehensive, far-seeing, and unprejudiced estimate of events and peoples, and we can commend this little work as one certain to prove of the highest interest to all thoughtful readers.*"

Persia.—EASTERN PERSIA. An Account of the Journeys of the Persian Boundary Commission, 1870-1-2.—Vol. I. The Geography, with Narratives by Majors ST. JOHN, LOVETT, and EUAN SMITH, and an Introduction by Major-General Sir FREDERIC GOLDSMID, C.B., K.C.S.I., British Commissioner and Arbitrator. With Maps and Illustrations.—Vol. II. The Zoology and Geology. By W. T. BLANFORD, A.R.S.M., F.R.S. With Coloured Illustrations. Two Vols. 8vo. 42s.

"*The volumes largely increase our store of information about countries with which Englishmen ought to be familiar.* . . . . *They throw into the shade all that hitherto has appeared in our tongue respecting the local features of Persia, its scenery, its resources, even its social condition. They contain also abundant evidence of English endurance, daring, and spirit.*"—TIMES.

Prichard.—THE ADMINISTRATION OF INDIA. From 1859 to 1868. The First Ten Years of Administration under the Crown. By I. T. PRICHARD, Barrister-at-Law. Two Vols. Demy 8vo. With Map. 21s.

Raphael.—RAPHAEL OF URBINO AND HIS FATHER GIOVANNI SANTI. By J. D. PASSAVANT, formerly Director of the Museum at Frankfort. With Twenty Permanent Photographs. Royal 8vo. Handsomely bound. 31s. 6d.

The SATURDAY REVIEW *says of them,* "*We have seen not a few elegant specimens of Mr. Woodbury's new process, but we have seen none that equal these.*"

Reynolds.—SIR JOSHUA REYNOLDS AS A PORTRAIT PAINTER. AN ESSAY. By J. CHURTON COLLINS, B.A. Balliol College, Oxford. Illustrated by a Series of Portraits of distinguished Beauties of the Court of George III.; reproduced in Autotype from Proof Impressions of the celebrated Engravings, by VALENTINE GREEN, THOMAS WATSON, F. R. SMITH, E. FISHER, and others. Folio half-morocco. £5 5s.

Rogers (James E. Thorold).—HISTORICAL GLEANINGS: A Series of Sketches. Montague, Walpole, Adam Smith, Cobbett. By Prof. ROGERS. Crown 8vo. 4s. 6d. Second Series. Wiklif, Laud, Wilkes, and Horne Tooke. Crown 8vo. 6s.

Routledge.—CHAPTERS IN THE HISTORY OF POPULAR PROGRESS IN ENGLAND, chiefly in Relation to the Freedom of the Press and Trial by Jury, 1660—1820. With application to later years. By J. ROUTLEDGE. 8vo. 16s.

"*The volume abounds in facts and information, almost always useful and often curious.*"—TIMES.

Rumford.—COUNT RUMFORD'S COMPLETE WORKS, with Memoir, and Notices of his Daughter. By GEORGE ELLIS. Five Vols. 8vo. 4l. 14s. 6d.

Seeley (Professor).—LECTURES AND ESSAYS. By J. R. SEELEY, M.A. Professor of Modern History in the University of Cambridge. 8vo. 10s. 6d.

CONTENTS:—*Roman Imperialism:* 1. *The Great Roman Revolution;* 2. *The Proximate Cause of the Fall of the Roman Empire; The Later Empire.* — *Milton's Political Opinions* — *Milton's Poetry* — *Elementary Principles in Art* — *Liberal Education in Universities* — *English in Schools* — *The Church as a Teacher of Morality* — *The Teaching of Politics: an Inaugural Lecture delivered at Cambridge.*

Shelburne.—LIFE OF WILLIAM, EARL OF SHELBURNE, AFTERWARDS FIRST MARQUIS OF LANSDOWNE. With Extracts from his Papers and Correspondence. By Lord EDMOND FITZMAURICE. In Three Vols. 8vo. Vol. I. 1737—1766, 12s.; Vol. II. 1766—1776, 12s.; Vol. III. 1776—1805. 16s.

"*Lord Edmond Fitzmaurice has succeeded in placing before us a wealth of new matter, which, while casting valuable and much-needed light on several obscure passages in the political history of a hundred years ago, has enabled us for the first time to form a clear and consistent idea of his ancestor.*"—SPECTATOR.

Sime.—HISTORY OF GERMANY. By JAMES SIME, M.A. 18mo. 3s. Being Vol. V. of the Historical Course for Schools Edited by EDWARD A. FREEMAN, D.C.L.

"*This is a remarkably clear and impressive History of Germany. Its great events are wisely kept as central figures, and the smaller events are carefully kept not only subordinate and subservient, but most skilfully woven into the texture of the historical tapestry presented to the eye.*"—STANDARD.

Squier.—PERU: INCIDENTS OF TRAVEL AND EXPLORATION IN THE LAND OF THE INCAS. By E. G. SQUIER, M.A., F.S.A., late U.S. Commissioner to Peru. With 300 Illustrations. Second Edition. 8vo. 21s.

The TIMES says:—"*No more solid and trustworthy contribution has been made to an accurate knowledge of what are among the most wonderful ruins in the world. . . . . The work is really what its title implies.*

While of the greatest importance as a contribution to Peruvian archæology, it is also a thoroughly entertaining and instructive narrative of travel. . . . . Not the least important feature must be considered the numerous well executed illustrations."

Strangford.—EGYPTIAN SHRINES AND SYRIAN SEPULCHRES, including a Visit to Palmyra. By EMILY A. BEAUFORT (Viscountess Strangford), Author of "The Eastern Shores of the Adriatic." New Edition. Crown 8vo. 7s. 6d.

Tait.—AN ANALYSIS OF ENGLISH HISTORY, based upon Green's "Short History of the English People." By C. W. A. TAIT, M.A., Assistant Master, Clifton College. Crown 8vo. 3s. 6d.

Thomas.—THE LIFE OF JOHN THOMAS, Surgeon of the "Earl of Oxford" East Indiaman, and First Baptist Missionary to Bengal. By C. B. LEWIS, Baptist Missionary. 8vo. 10s. 6d.

Thompson.—HISTORY OF ENGLAND. By EDITH THOMPSON. Being Vol. II. of the Historical Course for Schools, Edited by EDWARD A. FREEMAN, D.C.L. New Edition, revised and enlarged, with Maps. 18mo. 2s. 6d.
"*Freedom from prejudice, simplicity of style, and accuracy of statement, are the characteristics of this volume. It is a trustworthy text-book, and likely to be generally serviceable in schools.*"—PALL MALL GAZETTE. "*In its great accuracy and correctness of detail it stands far ahead of the general run of school manuals. Its arrangement, too, is clear, and its style simple and straightforward.*"—SATURDAY REVIEW.

Todhunter.—THE CONFLICT OF STUDIES; AND OTHER ESSAYS ON SUBJECTS CONNECTED WITH EDUCATION. By ISAAC TODHUNTER, M.A., F.R.S., late Fellow and Principal Mathematical Lecturer of St. John's College, Cambridge. 8vo. 10s. 6d.
CONTENTS:—*I. The Conflict of Studies. II. Competitive Examinations. III. Private Study of Mathematics. IV. Academical Reform. V. Elementary Geometry. VI. The Mathematical Tripos.*

Trench (Archbishop).—For other Works by the same Author, see THEOLOGICAL and BELLES LETTRES CATALOGUES, and page 30 of this Catalogue.
GUSTAVUS ADOLPHUS IN GERMANY, and other Lectures on the Thirty Years' War. Second Edition, revised and enlarged. Fcap. 8vo. 4s.
PLUTARCH, HIS LIFE, HIS LIVES, AND HIS MORALS. Five Lectures. Second Edition, enlarged. Fcap. 8vo. 3s. 6d.
LECTURES ON MEDIEVAL CHURCH HISTORY. Being the substance of Lectures delivered in Queen's College, London. Second Edition, revised. 8vo. 12s.

Trench (Maria).—THE LIFE OF ST. TERESA. By MARIA TRENCH. With Portrait engraved by JEENS. Crown 8vo. cloth extra. 8s. 6d.
"*A book of rare interest.*"—JOHN BULL.

Trench (Mrs. R.)—REMAINS OF THE LATE MRS. RICHARD TRENCH. Being Selections from her Journals, Letters, and other Papers. Edited by ARCHBISHOP TRENCH. New and Cheaper Issue, with Portrait. 8vo. 6s.

Trollope.—A HISTORY OF THE COMMONWEALTH OF FLORENCE FROM THE EARLIEST INDEPENDENCE OF THE COMMUNE TO THE FALL OF THE REPUBLIC IN 1831. By T. ADOLPHUS TROLLOPE. 4 Vols. 8vo. Half morocco. 21s.

Uppingham by the Sea.—A NARRATIVE OF THE YEAR AT BORTH. By J. H. S. Crown 8vo. 3s. 6d.

Wallace.—THE MALAY ARCHIPELAGO: the Land of the Orang Utan and the Bird of Paradise. By ALFRED RUSSEL WALLACE. A Narrative of Travel with Studies of Man and Nature. With Maps and numerous Illustrations. Sixth Edition. Crown 8vo. 7s. 6d.
"*The result is a vivid picture of tropical life, which may be read with unflagging interest, and a sufficient account of his scientific conclusions to stimulate our appetite without wearying us by detail. In short, we may safely say that we have never read a more agreeable book of its kind.*"—SATURDAY REVIEW.

Ward.—A HISTORY OF ENGLISH DRAMATIC LITERATURE TO THE DEATH OF QUEEN ANNE. By A. W. WARD, M.A., Professor of History and English Literature in Owens College, Manchester. Two Vols. 8vo. 32s.
"*As full of interest as of information. To students of aramatic literature invaluable, and may be equally recommended to readers for mere pastime.*"—PALL MALL GAZETTE.

Ward (J.)—EXPERIENCES OF A DIPLOMATIST. Being recollections of Germany founded on Diaries kept during the years 1840—1870. By JOHN WARD, C.B., late H.M. Minister-Resident to the Hanse Towns. 8vo. 10s. 6d.

Waterton (C.)—WANDERINGS IN SOUTH AMERICA, THE NORTH-WEST OF THE UNITED STATES, AND THE ANTILLES IN 1812, 1816, 1820, and 1824. With Original Instructions for the perfect Preservation of Birds, etc., for Cabinets of Natural History. By CHARLES WATERTON. New Edition, edited with Biographical Introduction and Explanatory Index by the Rev. J. G. WOOD, M.A. With 100 Illustrations. 8vo. Cloth elegant. 21s.

HISTORY, BIOGRAPHY, TRAVELS, ETC.

Wedgwood.—JOHN WESLEY AND THE EVANGELICAL REACTION of the Eighteenth Century. By JULIA WEDGWOOD. Crown 8vo. 8s. 6d.

"*In style and intellectual power, in breadth of view and clearness of insight, Miss Wedgwood's book far surpasses all rivals.*"—ATHENÆUM.

Whewell.—WILLIAM WHEWELL, D.D., late Master of Trinity College, Cambridge. An Account of his Writings, with Selections from his Literary and Scientific Correspondence. By I. TODHUNTER, M.A., F.R.S. Two Vols. 8vo. 25s.

White.—THE NATURAL HISTORY AND ANTIQUITIES OF SELBORNE. By GILBERT WHITE. Edited, with Memoir and Notes, by FRANK BUCKLAND, A Chapter on Antiquities by LORD SELBORNE, Map, &c., and numerous Illustrations by P. H. DELAMOTTE. Royal 8vo. Cloth, extra gilt. Cheaper Issue. 21s.

Also a Large Paper Edition, containing, in addition to the above, upwards of Thirty Woodburytype Illustrations from Drawings by Prof. DELAMOTTE. Two Vols. 4to. Half morocco, elegant. 4l. 4s.

"*Mr. Delamotte's charming illustrations are a worthy decoration of so dainty a book. They bring Selborne before us, and really help us to understand why White's love for his native place never grew cold.*"—TIMES.

Wilson.—A MEMOIR OF GEORGE WILSON, M.D., F.R.S.E., Regius Professor of Technology in the University of Edinburgh. By his SISTER. New Edition. Crown 8vo. 6s.

"*An exquisite and touching portrait of a rare and beautiful spirit.*"—GUARDIAN.

Wilson (Daniel, LL.D.)—Works by DANIEL WILSON, LL.D., Professor of History and English Literature in University College, Toronto:—

PREHISTORIC ANNALS OF SCOTLAND. New Edition, with numerous Illustrations. Two Vols. demy 8vo. 36s.

"*One of the most interesting, learned, and elegant works we have seen for a long time.*"—WESTMINSTER REVIEW.

PREHISTORIC MAN: Researches into the Origin of Civilization in the Old and New World. New Edition, revised and enlarged throughout, with numerous Illustrations and two Coloured Plates. Two Vols. 8vo. 36s.

"*A valuable work pleasantly written and well worthy of attention both by students and general readers.*"—ACADEMY.

CHATTERTON: A Biographical Study. By DANIEL WILSON, LL.D., Professor of History and English Literature in University College, Toronto. Crown 8vo. 6s. 6d.

Wyatt (Sir M. Digby).—FINE ART: a Sketch of its History, Theory, Practice, and application to Industry. A Course of Lectures delivered before the University of Cambridge. By Sir M. DIGBY WYATT, M.A. Slade Professor of Fine Art. Cheaper Issue. 8vo. 5s.

"*An excellent handbook for the student of art.*"—GRAPHIC. "*The book abounds in valuable matter, and will therefore be read with pleasure and profit by lovers of art.*"—DAILY NEWS.

Yonge (Charlotte M.)—Works by CHARLOTTE M. YONGE, Author of "The Heir of Redclyffe," &c. &c. :—

A PARALLEL HISTORY OF FRANCE AND ENGLAND: consisting of Outlines and Dates. Oblong 4to. 3s. 6d.

CAMEOS FROM ENGLISH HISTORY. From Rollo to Edward II. Extra fcap. 8vo. Third Edition. 5s.

A SECOND SERIES, THE WARS IN FRANCE. Extra fcap. 8vo. Third Edition. 5s.

A THIRD SERIES, THE WARS OF THE ROSES. Extra fcap. 8vo. 5s.

"*Instead of dry details,*" says the NONCONFORMIST, "*we have living pictures, faithful, vivid, and striking.*"

POLITICS, POLITICAL AND SOCIAL ECONOMY, LAW, AND KINDRED SUBJECTS.

Anglo-Saxon Law.—ESSAYS IN. Contents: Law Courts—Land and Family Laws and Legal Procedure generally. With Select cases. Medium 8vo. 18s.

Ball.—THE STUDENT'S GUIDE TO THE BAR. By WALTER W. BALL, M.A., of the Inner Temple, Barrister-at-Law. Crown 8vo. 2s. 6d.

"*The student will here find a clear statement of the several steps by which the degree of barrister is obtained, and also useful advice about the advantages of a prolonged course of 'reading in Chambers.'*"—ACADEMY.

Bernard.—FOUR LECTURES ON SUBJECTS CONNECTED WITH DIPLOMACY. By MONTAGUE BERNARD, M.A., Chichele Professor of International Law and Diplomacy, Oxford. 8vo. 9s.

"*Singularly interesting lectures, so able, clear, and attractive.*"—SPECTATOR.

Bright (John, M.P.)—SPEECHES ON QUESTIONS OF PUBLIC POLICY. By the Right Hon. JOHN BRIGHT, M.P. Edited by Professor THOROLD ROGERS. Author's Popular Edition. Globe 8vo. 3s. 6d.

"*Mr. Bright's speeches will always deserve to be studied, as an apprenticeship to popular and parliamentary oratory; they will form materials for the history of our time, and many brilliant passages, perhaps some entire speeches, will really become a part of the living literature of England.*"—DAILY NEWS.

LIBRARY EDITION. Two Vols. 8vo. With Portrait. 25s.

Bucknill.—HABITUAL DRUNKENNESS AND INSANE DRUNKARDS. By J. C. BUCKNILL, M.D., F.R.S., late Lord Chancellor's Visitor of Lunatics. Crown 8vo. 2s. 6d.

Cairnes.—Works by J. E. CAIRNES, M.A., Emeritus Professor of Political Economy in University College, London.

ESSAYS IN POLITICAL ECONOMY, THEORETICAL and APPLIED. By J. E. CAIRNES, M.A., Professor of Political Economy in University College, London. 8vo. 10s. 6d.

"*The production of one of the ablest of living economists.*"—ATHENÆUM.

Cairnes.—*continued.*

POLITICAL ESSAYS. 8vo. 10s. 6d.

The SATURDAY REVIEW *says:*—"*We recently expressed our high admiration of the former volume; and the present one is no less remarkable for the qualities of clear statement, sound logic, and candid treatment of opponents which were conspicuous in its predecessor. . . . We may safely say that none of Mr. Mill's many disciples is a worthier representative of the best qualities of their master than Professor Cairnes.*"

SOME LEADING PRINCIPLES OF POLITICAL ECONOMY NEWLY EXPOUNDED. 8vo. 14s.

CONTENTS:—*Part I. Value. Part II. Labour and Capital. Part III. International Trade.*

"*A work which is perhaps the most valuable contribution to the science made since the publication, a quarter of a century since, of Mr. Mill's 'Principles of Political Economy.'*"—DAILY NEWS.

THE CHARACTER AND LOGICAL METHOD OF POLITICAL ECONOMY. New Edition, enlarged. 8vo. 7s. 6d.

"*These lectures are admirably fitted to correct the slipshod generalizations which pass current as the science of Political Economy.*"—TIMES.

Clarke.—EARLY ROMAN LAW. THE REGAL PERIOD By E. C. CLARKE, M.A., of Lincoln's Inn, Barrister-at-Law Lecturer in Law and Regius Professor of Civil Law at Cambridge. Crown 8vo. 5s.

"*Mr. Clarke has brought together a great mass of valuable matter in an accessible form.*"—SATURDAY REVIEW.

Cobden (Richard).—SPEECHES ON QUESTIONS OF PUBLIC POLICY. By RICHARD COBDEN. Edited by the Right Hon. John Bright, M.P., and J. E. Thorold Rogers. Popular Edition. 8vo. 3s. 6d.

Fawcett.—Works by HENRY FAWCETT, M.A., M.P., Fellow of Trinity Hall, and Professor of Political Economy in the University of Cambridge:—

THE ECONOMIC POSITION OF THE BRITISH LABOURER. Extra fcap. 8vo. 5s.

MANUAL OF POLITICAL ECONOMY. Fifth Edition, with New Chapters on the Depreciation of Silver, etc. Crown 8vo. 12s.

The DAILY NEWS *says:* "*It forms one of the best introductions to the principles of the science, and to its practical applications in the problems of modern, and especially of English, government and society.*"

PAUPERISM: ITS CAUSES AND REMEDIES. Crown 8vo. 5s. 6d.

The ATHENÆUM *calls the work* "*a repertory of interesting and well digested information.*"

Fawcett.—*continued.*

SPEECHES ON SOME CURRENT POLITICAL QUESTIONS. 8vo. 10s. 6d.

"*They will help to educate, not perhaps, parties, but the educators of parties.*"—DAILY NEWS.

ESSAYS ON POLITICAL AND SOCIAL SUBJECTS. By PROFESSOR FAWCETT, M.P., and MILLICENT GARRETT FAWCETT. 8vo. 10s. 6d.

"*They will all repay the perusal of the thinking reader.*"—DAILY NEWS.

FREE TRADE AND PROTECTION: an Inquiry into the Causes which have retarded the general adoption of Free Trade since its introduction into England. Second Edition. 8vo. 7s. 6d.

"*No greater service can be rendered to the cause of Free Trade than a clear explanation of the principles on which Free Trade rests. Professor Fawcett has done this in the volume before us with all his habitual clearness of thought and expression.*"—ECONOMIST.

Fawcett (Mrs.)—Works by MILLICENT GARRETT FAWCETT.

POLITICAL ECONOMY FOR BEGINNERS. WITH QUESTIONS. New Edition. 18mo. 2s. 6d.

The DAILY NEWS *calls it "clear, compact, and comprehensive;" and the* SPECTATOR *says, "Mrs. Fawcett's treatise is perfectly suited to its purpose."*

TALES IN POLITICAL ECONOMY. Crown 8vo. 3s.

"*The idea is a good one, and it is quite wonderful what a mass of economic teaching the author manages to compress into a small space... The true doctrines of International Trade, Currency, and the ratio between Production and Population, are set before us and illustrated in a masterly manner.*"—ATHENÆUM.

Freeman (E. A.), M.A., D.C.L.—COMPARATIVE POLITICS. Lectures at the Royal Institution, to which is added "The Unity of History," being the Rede Lecture delivered at Cambridge in 1872. 8vo. 14s.

"*We find in Mr. Freeman's new volume the same sound, careful, comprehensive qualities which have long ago raised him to so high a place amongst historical writers. For historical discipline, then, as well as historical information, Mr. Freeman's book is full of value.*"—PALL MALL GAZETTE.

Goschen.—REPORTS AND SPEECHES ON LOCAL TAXATION. By GEORGE J. GOSCHEN, M.P. Royal 8vo. 5s.

"*The volume contains a vast mass of information of the highest value.*"—ATHENÆUM.

Guide to the Unprotected, in Every Day Matters Relating to Property and Income. By a BANKER'S DAUGHTER. Fourth Edition, Revised. Extra fcap. 8vo. 3s. 6d.

"*Many an unprotected female will bless the head which planned and the hand which compiled this admirable little manual. . . . This book was very much wanted, and it could not have been better done.*"—MORNING STAR.

Hamilton.—MONEY AND VALUE: an Inquiry into the Means and Ends of Economic Production, with an Appendix on the Depreciation of Silver and Indian Currency. By ROWLAND HAMILTON. 8vo. 12s.

"*The subject is here dealt with in a luminous style, and by presenting it from a new point of view in connection with the nature and functions of money, a genuine service has been rendered to commercial science.*"—BRITISH QUARTERLY REVIEW.

Harwood.—DISESTABLISHMENT: a Defence of the Principle of a National Church. By GEORGE HARWOOD, M.A. 8vo. 12s.

Hill.—Works by OCTAVIA HILL:—

HOMES OF THE LONDON POOR. Extra fcap. 8vo. 3s. 6d.
"*She is clear, practical, and definite.*"—GLOBE.

OUR COMMON LAND; and other Short Essays. Extra fcap. 8vo. 3s. 6d.

CONTENTS:—*Our Common Land. District Visiting. A More Excellent Way of Charity. A Word on Good Citizenship. Open Spaces. Effectual Charity. The Future of our Commons.*

Historicus.—LETTERS ON SOME QUESTIONS OF INTERNATIONAL LAW. Reprinted from the *Times*, with considerable Additions. 8vo. 7s. 6d. Also, ADDITIONAL LETTERS. 8vo. 2s. 6d.

Holland.—THE TREATY RELATIONS OF RUSSIA AND TURKEY FROM 1774 TO 1853. A Lecture delivered at Oxford, April 1877. By T. E. HOLLAND, D.C.L., Professor of International Law and Diplomacy, Oxford. Crown 8vo. 2s.

Hughes (Thos.)—THE OLD CHURCH: WHAT SHALL WE DO WITH IT? By THOMAS HUGHES, Q.C. Crown 8vo. 6s.

Jevons.—Works by W. STANLEY JEVONS, M.A., Professor of Political Economy in University College, London. (For other Works by the same Author, *see* EDUCATIONAL and PHILOSOPHICAL CATALOGUES.)

WORKS IN POLITICS, ETC.

Jevons.—*continued.*

THE COAL QUESTION: An Inquiry Concerning the Progress of the Nation, and the Probable Exhaustion of our Coal Mines. Second Edition, revised. 8vo. 10s. 6d.

THE THEORY OF POLITICAL ECONOMY. 8vo. 9s.

"*Professor Jevons has done invaluable service by courageously claiming political economy to be strictly a branch of Applied Mathematics.*"—WESTMINSTER REVIEW.

PRIMER OF POLITICAL ECONOMY. 18mo. 1s.

Laveleye.—PRIMITIVE PROPERTY. By EMILE DE LAVELEYE. Translated by G. R. L. MARRIOTT, LL.B., with an Introduction by T. E. CLIFFE LESLIE, LL.B. 8vo. 12s.

"*It is almost impossible to over-estimate the value of the well-digested knowledge which it contains; it is one of the most learned books that have been contributed to the historical department of the literature of economic science.*"—ATHENÆUM.

Leading Cases done into English. By an APPRENTICE OF LINCOLN'S INN. Third Edition. Crown 8vo. 2s. 6d.

"*Here is a rare treat for the lovers of quaint conceits, who in reading this charming little book will find enjoyment in the varied metre and graphic language in which the several tales are told, no less than in the accurate and pithy rendering of some of our most familiar 'Leading Cases.'*"—SATURDAY REVIEW.

Macdonell.—THE LAND QUESTION, WITH SPECIAL REFERENCE TO ENGLAND AND SCOTLAND. By JOHN MACDONELL, Barrister-at-Law. 8vo. 10s. 6d.

Martin.—THE STATESMAN'S YEAR-BOOK: A Statistical and Historical Annual of the States of the Civilized World, for the year 1879. By FREDERICK MARTIN. Sixteenth Annual Publication. Revised after Official Returns. Crown 8vo. 10s. 6d.

The Statesman's Year-Book is the only work in the English language which furnishes a clear and concise account of the actual condition of all the States of Europe, the civilized countries of America, Asia, and Africa, and the British Colonies and Dependencies in all parts of the world. The new issue of the work has been revised and corrected, on the basis of official reports received direct from the heads of the leading Governments of the world, in reply to letters sent to them by the Editor. Through the valuable assistance thus given, it has been possible to collect an amount of information, political, statistical, and commercial, of the latest date, and of unimpeachable trustworthiness, such as no publication of the same kind has ever been able to furnish. "As indispensable as Bradshaw."—TIMES.

Monahan.—THE METHOD OF LAW: an Essay on the Statement and Arrangement of the Legal Standard of Conduct. By J. H. MONAHAN, Q.C. Crown 8vo. 6s.

"*Will be found valuable by careful law students who have felt the importance of gaining clear ideas regarding the relations between the parts of the complex organism they have to study.*"—BRITISH QUARTERLY REVIEW.

Paterson.—THE LIBERTY OF THE SUBJECT AND THE LAWS OF ENGLAND RELATING TO THE SECURITY OF THE PERSON. Commentaries on. By JAMES PATERSON, M.A., Barrister at Law, sometime Commissioner for English and Irish Fisheries, etc. Cheaper issue. Two Vols. Crown 8vo. 21s.

"*Two or three hours' dipping into these volumes, not to say reading them through, will give legislators and stump orators a knowledge of the liberty of a citizen of their country, in its principles, its fulness, and its modification, such as they probably in nine cases out of ten never had before.*"—SCOTSMAN.

Phillimore.—PRIVATE LAW AMONG THE ROMANS, from the Pandects. By JOHN GEORGE PHILLIMORE, Q.C. 8vo. 16s.

Rogers.—COBDEN AND POLITICAL OPINION. By J. E. THOROLD ROGERS. 8vo. 10s. 6d.

"*Will be found most useful by politicians of every school, as it forms a sort of handbook to Cobden's teaching.*"—ATHENÆUM.

Stephen (C. E.)—THE SERVICE OF THE POOR; Being an Inquiry into the Reasons for and against the Establishment of Religious Sisterhoods for Charitable Purposes. By CAROLINE EMILIA STEPHEN. Crown 8vo. 6s. 6d.

"*The ablest advocate of a better line of work in this direction that we have ever seen.*"—EXAMINER.

Stephen.—Works by Sir JAMES F. STEPHEN, K.C.S.I., Q.C. A DIGEST OF THE LAW OF EVIDENCE. Third Edition with New Preface. Crown 8vo. 6s.

A DIGEST OF THE CRIMINAL LAW. (Crimes and Punishments.) 8vo. 16s.

"*We feel sure that any person of ordinary intelligence who had never looked into a law-book in his life might, by a few days' careful study of this volume, obtain a more accurate understanding of the criminal law, a more perfect conception of its different bearings a more thorough and intelligent insight into its snares and pitfalls, than an ordinary practitioner can boast of after years of study of the ordinary text-books and practical experience of the Courts unassisted by any competent guide.*"—SATURDAY REVIEW.

A GENERAL VIEW OF THE CRIMINAL LAW OF ENGLAND. Two Vols. Crown 8vo. [*New edition in the press.*

Stubbs.—VILLAGE POLITICS. Addresses and Sermons on the Labour Question. By C. W. STUBBS, M.A., Vicar of Granborough, Bucks. Extra fcap. 8vo. 3*s*. 6*d*.

Thornton.—Works by W. T. THORNTON, C.B., Secretary for Public Works in the India Office :—

ON LABOUR: Its Wrongful Claims and Rightful Dues; Its Actual Present and Possible Future. Second Edition, revised, 8vo. 14*s*.

A PLEA FOR PEASANT PROPRIETORS: With the Outlines of a Plan for their Establishment in Ireland. New Edition, revised. Crown 8vo. 7*s*. 6*d*.

INDIAN PUBLIC WORKS AND COGNATE INDIAN TOPICS. With Map of Indian Railways. Crown 8vo. 8*s*. 6*d*.

Walker.—Works by F. A. WALKER, M.A., Ph.D., Professor of Political Economy and History, Yale College :—

THE WAGES QUESTION. A Treatise on Wages and the Wages Class. 8vo. 14*s*.

MONEY. 8vo. 16*s*.

"*It is painstaking, laborious, and states the question in a clear and very intelligible form. . . . The volume possesses a great value as a sort of encyclopædia of knowledge on the subject.*"—ECONOMIST.

Work about the Five Dials. With an Introductory Note by THOMAS CARLYLE. Crown 8vo. 6*s*.

"*A book which abounds with wise and practical suggestions.*"—PALL MALL GAZETTE.

WORKS CONNECTED WITH THE SCIENCE OR THE HISTORY OF LANGUAGE.

Abbott.—A SHAKESPERIAN GRAMMAR: An Attempt to illustrate some of the Differences between Elizabethan and Modern English. By the Rev. E. A. ABBOTT, D.D., Head Master of the City of London School. New and Enlarged Edition. Extra fcap. 8vo. 6*s*.

"*Valuable not only as an aid to the critical study of Shakespeare, but as tending to familiarize the reader with Elizabethan English in general.*"—ATHENÆUM.

Besant.—STUDIES IN EARLY FRENCH POETRY. By WALTER BESANT, M.A. Crown 8vo. 8*s*. 6*d*.

Breymann.—A FRENCH GRAMMAR BASED ON PHILO-LOGICAL PRINCIPLES. By HERMANN BREYMANN, Ph.D., Professor of Philology in the University of Munich late Lecturer on French Language and Literature at Owens College, Manchester. Extra fcap. 8vo. 4s. 6d.

"*We dismiss the work with every feeling of satisfaction. It cannot fail to be taken into use by all schools which endeavour to make the study of French a means towards the higher culture.*"—EDUCATIONAL TIMES.

Ellis.—PRACTICAL HINTS ON THE QUANTITATIVE PRONUNCIATION OF LATIN, FOR THE USE OF CLASSICAL TEACHERS AND LINGUISTS. By A. J. ELLIS, B.A., F.R.S., &c. Extra fcap. 8vo. 4s. 6d.

Fleay.—A SHAKESPEARE MANUAL. By the Rev. F. G. FLEAY, M.A., Head Master of Skipton Grammar School. Extra fcap. 8vo. 4s. 6d.

Goodwin.—SYNTAX OF THE GREEK MOODS AND TENSES. By W. W. GOODWIN, Professor of Greek Literature in Harvard University. New Edition. Crown 8vo. 6s. 6d.

Hadley.—ESSAYS PHILOLOGICAL AND CRITICAL. Selected from the Papers of JAMES HADLEY, LL.D., Professor of Greek in Yale College, &c. 8vo. 16s.

Hales.—LONGER ENGLISH POEMS. With Notes, Philological and Explanatory, and an Introduction on the Teaching of English. Chiefly for use in Schools. Edited by J. W. HALES, M.A., Professor of English Literature at King's College, London, &c. &c. Fifth Edition. Extra fcap. 8vo. 4s. 6d.

Helfenstein (James).—A COMPARATIVE GRAMMAR OF THE TEUTONIC LANGUAGES: Being at the same time a Historical Grammar of the English Language, and comprising Gothic, Anglo-Saxon, Early English, Modern English, Icelandic (Old Norse), Danish, Swedish, Old High German, Middle High German, Modern German, Old Saxon, Old Frisian, and Dutch. By JAMES HELFENSTEIN, Ph.D. 8vo. 18s.

Masson (Gustave).—A COMPENDIOUS DICTIONARY OF THE FRENCH LANGUAGE (French-English and English-French). Followed by a List of the Principal Diverging Derivations, and preceded by Chronological and Historical Tables. By GUSTAVE MASSON, Assistant-Master and Librarian, Harrow School. Fourth Edition. Crown 8vo. Half-bound. 6s.

"*A book which any student, whatever may be the degree of his advancement in the language, would do well to have on the table close at hand while he is reading.*"—SATURDAY REVIEW.

Mayor.—A BIBLIOGRAPHICAL CLUE TO LATIN LITERATURE. Edited after Dr. E. HUBNER. With large Additions by JOHN E. B. MAYOR, M.A., Professor of Latin in the University of Cambridge. Crown 8vo. 6s. 6d.

"*An extremely useful volume that should be in the hands of all scholars.*"—ATHENÆUM.

Morris.—Works by the Rev. RICHARD MORRIS, LL.D., Member of the Council of the Philol. Soc., Lecturer on English Language and Literature in King's College School, Editor of "Specimens of Early English," etc., etc. :—

HISTORICAL OUTLINES OF ENGLISH ACCIDENCE, comprising Chapters on the History and Development of the Language, and on Word-formation. Sixth Edition. Fcap. 8vo. 6s.

ELEMENTARY LESSONS IN HISTORICAL ENGLISH GRAMMAR, containing Accidence and Word-formation. Third Edition. 18mo. 2s. 6d.

Oliphant.—THE OLD AND MIDDLE ENGLISH. By T. L. KINGTON OLIPHANT, M.A., of Balliol College, Oxford. A New Edition, revised and greatly enlarged, of "The Sources of Standard English. Extra fcap. 8vo. 9s.

"*Mr. Oliphant's book is, to our mind, one of the ablest and most scholarly contributions to our standard English we have seen for many years.*"—SCHOOL BOARD CHRONICLE. "*The book comes nearer to a history of the English language than anything we have seen since such a history could be written, without confusion and contradictions.*"—SATURDAY REVIEW.

Peile (John, M.A.)—AN INTRODUCTION TO GREEK AND LATIN ETYMOLOGY. By JOHN PEILE, M.A., Fellow and Tutor of Christ's College, Cambridge. Third and revised Edition. Crown 8vo. 10s. 6d.

"*The book may be accepted as a very valuable contribution to the science of language.*"—SATURDAY REVIEW.

Philology.—THE JOURNAL OF SACRED AND CLASSICAL PHILOLOGY. Four Vols. 8vo. 12s. 6d. each.

THE JOURNAL OF PHILOLOGY. New Series. Edited by JOHN E. B. MAYOR, M.A., and W. ALDIS WRIGHT, M.A. 4s. 6d. (Half-yearly.)

Roby (H. J.)—A GRAMMAR OF THE LATIN LANGUAGE, FROM PLAUTUS TO SUETONIUS. By HENRY JOHN ROBY, M.A., late Fellow of St. John's College, Cambridge. In Two Parts. Second Edition. Part I. containing :—Book I. Sounds. Book II. Inflexions. Book III. Word Formation. Appendices. Crown 8vo. 8s. 6d. Part II.—Syntax, Prepositions, &c. Crown 8vo. 10s. 6d.

"*The book is marked by the clear and practical insight of a master in his art. It is a book which would do honour to any country.*"— ATHENÆUM. "*Brings before the student in a methodical form the best results of modern philology bearing on the Latin language.*"—SCOTSMAN.

Schmidt.—THE RYTHMIC AND METRIC OF THE CLASSICAL LANGUAGES. To which are added, the Lyric Parts of the "Medea" of Euripides and the "Antigone" of Sophocles; with Rhythmical Scheme and Commentary. By Dr. J. H. SCHMIDT. Translated from the German by J. W. WHITE, D.D. 8vo. 10s. 6d.

Taylor.—Works by the Rev. ISAAC TAYLOR, M.A.:—

ETRUSCAN RESEARCHES. With Woodcuts. 8vo. 14s.

The TIMES *says :*—"*The learning and industry displayed in this volume deserve the most cordial recognition. The ultimate verdict of science we shall not attempt to anticipate; but we can safely say this, that it is a learned book which the unlearned can enjoy, and that in the descriptions of the tomb-builders, as well as in the marvellous coincidences and unexpected analogies brought together by the author, readers of every grade may take delight as well as philosophers and scholars.*"

WORDS AND PLACES ; or, Etymological Illustrations of History, Ethnology, and Geography. By the Rev. ISAAC TAYLOR. Third Edition, revised and compressed. With Maps. Globe 8vo. 6s.

Trench.—Works by R. CHENEVIX TRENCH, D.D., Archbishop of Dublin. (For other Works by the same Author, *see* THEOLOGICAL CATALOGUE.)

SYNONYMS OF THE NEW TESTAMENT. Eighth Edition, enlarged. 8vo. cloth. 12s.

"*He is,*" *the* ATHENÆUM *says,* "*a guide in this department of knowledge to whom his readers may entrust themselves with confidence.*"

ON THE STUDY OF WORDS. Lectures Addressed (originally) to the Pupils at the Diocesan Training School, Winchester. Seventeenth Edition, enlarged. Fcap. 8vo. 5s.

ENGLISH PAST AND PRESENT. Tenth Edition, revised and improved. Fcap. 8vo. 5s.

Trench—*continued.*

A SELECT GLOSSARY OF ENGLISH WORDS USED FORMERLY IN SENSES DIFFERENT FROM THEIR PRESENT. Fourth Edition, enlarged. Fcap. 8vo. 4*s.*

Whitney.—A COMPENDIOUS GERMAN GRAMMAR. By W. D. WHITNEY, Professor of Sanskrit and Instructor in Modern Languages in Yale College. Crown 8vo. 6*s.*

"*After careful examination we are inclined to pronounce it the best grammar of modern language we have ever seen.*"—SCOTSMAN.

Whitney and Edgren.—A COMPENDIOUS GERMAN AND ENGLISH DICTIONARY, with Notation of Correspondences and Brief Etymologies. By Professor W. D. WHITNEY, assisted by A. H. EDGREN. Crown 8vo. 7*s.* 6*d.*

The GERMAN-ENGLISH Part may be had separately. Price 5*s.*

Yonge.—HISTORY OF CHRISTIAN NAMES. By CHARLOTTE M. YONGE, Author of "The Heir of Redclyffe." Cheaper Edition. Two Vols. Crown 8vo. 12*s.*

www.ingramcontent.com/pod-product-compliance
Lightning Source LLC
Chambersburg PA
CBHW031342230426
43670CB00006B/420